The Sower's Book

A workbook and planning guide for homilists and preachers for Lectionary Cycle A

Jay Cormier

Sheed & Ward

For Rev. Cryil Schweinberg, C.P.
Forty years a priest and preacher
of the good news
that God loves us always . . .
and *in all ways*.

The author makes grateful acknowledgment of the following:

Excerpt from *Creative Ministry* by Henri J.M. Nouwen. Copyright© 1971 by Henri J.M. Nouwen. Reprinted with permission of Bantam, Doubleday, Dell Publishing Group, Inc.

Excerpts from *Are You Happy?* by Dennis Wholey. Copyright© 1986 by Dennis Wholey. Reprinted by permission of Houghton Mifflin Company.

Excerpt from *A Crucified Christ in Holy Week* by Raymond E. Brown. Copyright© 1986 by The Order of St. Benedict, Inc. Published by The Liturgical Press, Collegeville, Minnesota. Used with permission.

Excerpt from "Seven Stanzas at Easter" by John Updike. Copyright© 1961 by John Updike. Reprinted from *Telephone Polls and Other Poems,* by John Updike, by permission of Random House, Inc.

Excerpt from *When All You've Ever Wanted Isn't Enough* by Harold S. Kushner. Copyright© 1986 by Kushner Enterprises, Inc. Reprinted with permission of Simon & Schuster, Inc.

Excerpt from *Markings* by Dag Hammarskjold. Copyright© 1964 by Alfred A. Knopf, Inc. and Faber and Faber, Ltd. Reprinted by permission of the publishers.

Copyright© 1989
Jay Cormier

Sheed & Ward™ is a service of National Catholic Reporter Publishing Company, Inc.

ISBN: 1-55612-254-3

Published by: Sheed & Ward
                 115 E. Armour Blvd. P.O. Box 419492
                 Kansas City, MO 64141-6492

To order, call: (800) 333-7373

Contents

How Homilists Can Use *The Sower's Book*

Come Thanksgiving, if this book is dogged-eared and torn, with scribblings filling every margin and available white space, and clippings and notes taped, stapled and pasted on pages that are clinging to the binding by little more than faith, good work!

This journal has been designed to be a workbook for you, the homilist. The Scriptural and thematic notes and worksheets have been planned to help you reflect on the Sunday Lectionary themes, to think through and compose your homily and to deliver it concisely and effectively. If you're looking for a volume chockfull of good homily outlines and great sermon texts, this book isn't it; but if you're looking for help in writing and giving good homilies—homilies that are *yours*—this book is your ally.

1. Seeds

On the preceding Sunday night, read the Lectionary selections for the following Sunday and read them again each evening during the week. Let them simmer in your mind and heart during the week. Something you see, something you read, something you remember may give you an idea for the homily. The Scriptural notes, suggested themes and musings included in this book are thoughts and ideas to consider as you reflect on the readings assigned for Sunday's liturgy.

The first journal section, titled *Seeds*, is for your first notes on the homily. You may even want to attach clippings and articles you have come across right onto the page (unlike the "Think-and-Do" books of your grammar school days, neatness does not count here). The *Seeds* section of the journal also asks you to consider important variables that should affect your approach. The most critical is the specific response you seek from your listeners—exactly what do you want your congregation to do or think or feel as a result of listening to your homily? Most of the homilies that are dismissed as meaningless by congregations usually fail here. This should be one of the first *seeds* planted.

2. Planting

Later on in the week, when the homily begins to come together in your mind, start work on the section titled *Planting*. When you can complete that first section in one sentence—"The point I want to make in this homily"—you're ready to begin writing your homily (what the academic types among us would call the "thesis" statement). Exactly what do you want to say to the folks this Sunday? Write it in one sentence. That's probably how most people will remember your homily: in one sentence.

The Homily Outline in the *Planting* section is designed to help you pull it all together:

• Your *opening "story."* "Story" here means not only personal recollections, jokes and anecdotes with all the narrative devices of plot, characterization and punchline, but any image that your listeners can see, hear and feel. Jesus' images of fishing nets and fig trees were stories in this sense. A song, a headline, a movie quote or popular slogan that touches an emotion within all of us can be a "story." The most important work in writing a good homily is developing the "story" you will share.

• The *three main points*—and three are plenty, thank you. These three main points should not be independent "mini-sermons" but should flow from the story and relate both to the story and to each other. Your first point might apply your story to the Scriptural theme you are addressing; your second point might connect that theme to the life experiences of you and your listeners; the third and final point should articulate the response you are seeking from your listeners (which you have already determined under the *Seeds* section).

• Your *closing*. The same care that goes into developing the opening story should also go into the closing. Write it out as completely as you can. It should refer back to the story and reinforce the response you seek from your listeners, thoughtfully tying the whole message together.

3. Harvest

A homily is a very special form of communication. A good homily is not communicated by the words alone but by the *speaker* of those words. The effectiveness of the homily ultimately depends on the homilist's ability to give life and meaning to those words.

The *Harvest* section is designed to help you prepare *yourself* for giving *your* homily by:

• guiding you as you practice your homily *out loud* before Sunday. Not only your words but your voice, facial expressions and body language also communicate your homily's message. So don't wait until Saturday evening to introduce these elements into your homily. You'll discover that some of the words and expressions are easier and more natural to you than others. You may find that there are simpler, clearer ways to express your ideas. And you will realize that just the way you *say* a single word can express a kaleidoscope of meanings. But you'll never realize any of this potential unless you rehearse your homily OUT LOUD; and only by rehearsing your delivery out loud as often as possible will you be able to make this homily your own.

• by keeping your *focus* sharp, clear and on-target. The homilist who rants and raves or who takes his/her listeners through a maze of tangents and unrelated points is a victim of his/her own poor preparation.

• by helping you make the best use of *time*. Realize that your homily is only one of thousands of messages and communications that will assault your listeners' senses each week. So make each word, phrase, sentence and idea count.

Consider each item on the *Harvest* checklist carefully—and honestly (no cheating on the rehearsal time!). The checklist is designed to prepare the most important element in any good homily: *you*, the homilist.

4. Gleanings

After the homily is delivered, make notes about anything that struck you: what worked exceptionally well, what worked only so-so and what didn't work at all; reactions from listeners; and areas you feel you need to work on in your delivery. You might also jot down on this page any ideas you discover later on for approaching this theme.

Other Uses for *The Sower's Book*

The Sower's Book might also be of use to groups as well as to individuals.

Small groups of homilists and preachers might use this book as a basis for forming homily support groups. The notes and reflections could be used to focus a weekly discussion on the Lectionary readings in preparation for writing and delivering their homilies the following Sunday.

This book might also be helpful to Scripture study groups, enabling participants to begin an exploration of the Sunday readings in the contexts of the entire history of salvation, the Church's liturgical cycle and our own experience at the threshold of the 21st century.

. . . and a final meditation before beginning

Homiletics is not just a liturgical function; it is *ministry*. Father Henri Nouwen has observed that

"Every time real preaching occurs, the crucifixion is realized again: for no preacher can bring anyone to the light without having entered the darkness of the cross himself. Perhaps

Anthony Trollope was right when he said that the necessity of listening to sermons is the greatest hardship inflicted on humankind in civilized and free countries.

"If we want countries to become really free and civilized, let us hope that there will always be ministers to endure the hardship of preaching and lead people through their own darkness to the light of God." *

May the seeds of faith you sow in the year ahead take root and flower in the hearts of your community!

*Creative Ministry by Henri Nouwen (Garden City: Doubleday & Company, Inc., 1971).

The Proper of the Seasons

First Sunday of Advent

The Readings:

READING 1: Isaiah 2: 1-5

> *They shall beat their swords into plowshares*
> *and their spears into pruning hooks;*
> *One nation shall not raise the sword against another*
> *nor shall they train for war ever again.*

Isaiah is the prophet of the Advent season who proclaims most eloquently and poetically the coming of the "Servant of God," "Emmanuel," who will re-create Israel.

Isaiah preaches to the Jews living in the southern kingdom of Judah eight centuries before Christ. The northern kingdom of Israel had been destroyed by the Assyrians (722 B.C.); the people of Judah are terrified that the same fate will befall them. But Isaiah preaches that God will not abandon them, that a new era of peace, justice and unity—the era of the Messiah—will dawn if only the Israelites reject sinfulness and return to the Lord, the Holy One of Israel.

READING 2: Romans 13: 11-14

> *The night is far spent; the day draws near. Let us cast off deeds of darkness and put on the armor of light.*

Paul's letter to the Romans is similar to Isaiah's call of 800 years earlier: better times are ahead—the Risen Lord will return to claim the people he has called to be his own. Paul reminds us that we are a people not of the darkness but of the light—the Risen Christ is the Light of a new day. Paul warns us (in his straightforward and intense style) that our pursuit of the "good life" can sidetrack us from the genuinely important things of life. Our lives should reflect the light of the Risen One, rather than the dark emptiness of a consumer-oriented lifestyle.

GOSPEL: Matthew 24: 37-44

> *If the owner of the house knew when the thief was coming he would keep a watchful eye and not allow his house to be broken into. You must be prepared in the same way.*

Although Matthew is writing his Gospel for a Christian community who expected Christ's return during their lifetimes, this Gospel can also be read as Jesus teaching us about the reality of our own deaths and being ready at every moment we are given to meet the Lord and claim our share in the new life of the Resurrection.

Themes:

• light and darkness

All three readings contrast the darkness of a world without God with the light of the Lord: "let us walk in the light of the Lord" (Isaiah 2: 5); "the night is far spent, the day draw nears" and "put on the armor of light" (Romans 13:12); "the day the Lord is coming" (Matthew 24: 42).

Light is central to our Christmas observance. The celebration of Christmas, itself, was a "Christianizing" of the ancient Roman feast of "Sol Invinctus"—the Birthday of the New Sun. Sometime in the third century after Christ, the Church adopted the Birthday of the *Sun* to celebrate the Birthday of the *Son* of God.

Our Christmas lights illuminate the darkest days of the year: the sun sets in the late afternoon and rises later in the morning; the days of winter are shorter and colder. We already yearn for the warmth of the spring that we know will come.

The lights of our Christmas trees and window candles and Yule logs are not only pretty decorations—the lights of Christmas proclaim the dawning of the Christ, the Light of the Father, who illuminates the darkness of injustice and alienation.

• waiting for the Lord

Today's three readings all speak to hurting, broken people who are clinging to the hopes of generations before them—hope for the promised justice and freedom from oppression, hope for the promised Messiah, hope for the promised coming of the Lord's kingdom at last. Our season of Advent is about waiting, but not for Santa Claus as a kind of surrogate Messiah nor for Christmas as an event to enjoy and then put away for another year. Our identity as Christians is that of an Advent people rather than a Christmas people—we live our lives waiting in patient faith for the Lord's return at the end of time.

For Reflection:

• How can the busy days ahead of Christmas shopping, decorating, cooking and cleaning, Christmas-card addressing and mailing help us understand the faith dimensions of Advent?

• What stories, remembrances and experiences do you have of *light*? Have you ever experienced a prolonged period of darkness (such as being trapped in an elevator or being without electrical power for a long time) that made you especially grateful for light?

• Do you have any special memories of Christmas lights? How will your church use lights this holiday season?

• How is Christmas an "adult" feast?

Second Sunday of Advent

The Readings:

READING 1: Isaiah 11: 1-10

A shoot shall sprout from the stump of Jesse
and from his roots a bud shall blossom.
He shall judge the poor with justice
and decide aright for the land's afflicted.
Then the wolf shall be the guest of the lamb,
and the leopard shall lie down with the kid;
The calf and the young lion shall browse together,
with a little child to guide them.

Isaiah continues to preach to the people of devastated Judah during the Assyrian crisis. God will raise up a new king, like David, to lead his people, Isaiah proclaims; but this "shoot from Jesse's stump" will not be the great warrior-king that Israel longs for. In Isaiah's vision, the Messiah, instead, will be "armed" with wisdom and understanding. The Messiah comes not to rebuild the nation but to re-create individual hearts and minds. Rather than bring political and imperial power to Israel, Isaiah's Messiah will bring a new era of peace and justice, not just to Israel, but to all of the world.

READING 2: Romans 15: 4-9

May God, the source of all patience and encouragement, enable you to live in perfect harmony
with one another according to the Spirit of Christ Jesus, so that with one heart and voice you
may glorify God, the Father of our Lord Jesus Christ.

Paul's letter to the Romans, his longest epistle, is a systematic treatise on God's plan of salvation and its fulfillment in Jesus Christ. Paul writes that the era of the Messiah's peace, prophesied by Isaiah, has dawned upon the world. We have been given a new spirit that should enable us to break down the barriers that separate us from one another. If we are faithful to our call as Christians, we will work ceaselessly to build "perfect harmony" among all God's people.

GOSPEL: Matthew 3: 1-12

John the Baptizer made his appearance in the desert of Judea:
"I baptize you in water for the sake of reform, but the one who will follow me is more powerful
than I. He it is will baptize you in the Holy Spirit and fire."

John the Baptizer makes his appearance this Advent season, preaching a baptism of repentance and conversion of life.

Matthew's details about John's appearance is intended to recall the austere dress of the great prophet Elijah (2 Kings1: 8). The Jews believed that Elijah would return from heaven to announce the long-awaited restoration of Israel as God's kingdom. For Matthew, this expectation is fulfilled in the Baptizer's ministry. Through the figure of John, the evangelist makes the Old Testament touch the New.

Matthew reports that John strikes a responsive chord in the people who have come from throughout the region to hear him at the River Jordan. He has tough words for the Pharisees and Sadducees who step up for his baptism but have no intention of embracing the spirit of conversion and renewal to make their own lives ready for the Messiah who comes.

Themes:

• to be prophets of the Lord

Each one of us is called to be a prophet of Christ. The word "prophet" comes from the Greek word meaning "one who proclaims." Not all prophets wear camel skins and eat locusts—there are prophets among us right now who proclaim in their ministries, in their compassion and their kindness, in their courageous commitment to what is right that Jesus the Messiah has come.

• living our baptism

Our baptisms (which, for some of us, took place *so* long ago!) should be a living, thriving reality in our lives. John excoriates those who come to the Jordan to be baptized but have no intention of re-creating their lives in the life of God.

In the same way, our baptism was more than just a "naming ceremony," more than just a symbolic ritual of water poured over our heads. In baptism, we were given new eyes, new minds and new hearts to approach the world. We *live* our baptism as we grow in the "knowledge of the Lord" (Isaiah 11:9) and as living "wheat" rather than lifeless straw (Matthew 3:12).

• toleration and acceptance

On Christmas we will sing the song of the angels over Bethlehem: "Glory to God in the highest. Peace on earth to those on whom his favor rests." But we have a great deal of difficulty in being at peace with one another—progressive against traditionalist, liberal against conservative, social activist against contemplative, rich against poor, labor against management, black against white, social revolution against status quo, Jew against Gentile. Advent is the season for setting the stage for the angels' song, for seeking common ground, for recognizing and building upon interests and values shared by all men and women. The Messiah, Jesus, comes to reveal to the world that God is Father of all of us, a revelation that should make the distinctions and labels we create to separate one person from another disappear.

For Reflection:

• Prophets of the here and now:

In his writings and lectures Nobel Peace Prize laureate Dr. Elie Wiesel keeps alive the memory of the millions of Jews—including his own parents and sisters—who perished during the Holocaust...

From a rundown tenement in New York City, the sisters of Mother Teresa's community, the Missionaries of Charity, quietly go about their work of caring for the homeless and hungry, the abandoned and the abused . . .

Despite the demands of their studies and jobs, a group of college students make the time to spend a couple of hours each week as Big Brothers and Big Sisters to youngsters who have lost a parent.

Do you know any other "prophets" who proclaim the Messiah in our community and our world today?

• What stories in this week's news reflect the sin of intolerance, racism, elitism and discrimination? In what ways has the light of Christ appeared in these situations—or might the light of Christ be brought to illuminate such darkness—to break down the walls of hate existing here?

• Have you seen or witnessed in your own experience the fulfillment of Isaiah's prophecy: the wolf being the guest of the lamb, the leopard resting with the kid, the calf and young lion browsing together, all under the "guidance" of the "child"?

Date: _____

HOMILY WORKSHEET for the Second Sunday of Advent

1. SEEDS

What today's readings say *to me*: _____

_____

_____

PARABLES, STORIES and EXPERIENCES that speak to the themes of today's readings: _____

_____

_____

SPECIAL CONSIDERATIONS this week: Audience? Events in the community? Unique dimensions to this celebration?

_____

_____

_____

What RESPONSE do I seek from my listeners?
❑ to affirm/enlighten them in their faith?
❑ to teach/inform them about _____

_____

❑ to have them take a specific action _____

_____

2. PLANTING

The point I want to make in this homily (*ONE sentence*): _____

_____

_____

HOMILY OUTLINE

OPENING (*introductory STORY*): _____

_____

_____

_____

_____

_____

Point 1. APPLICATION of STORY to Scripture themes: _____

_____

_____

_____

_____

_____

Point 2. CONNECTION between Scriptural themes and the listeners' life experience: _____

_____

_____

_____

_____

_____

_____

Point 3. RESPONSE/CONSIDERATION sought from listeners: _____

_____

_____

_____

_____

_____

_____

CLOSING STATEMENT (*refers back to STORY*): _____

_____

_____

_____

_____

_____

3. HARVEST—A Checklist:

❑ Does my completed homily make the point I articulated above (*under PLANTING*)?

❑ Am I excited about this homily. Am I readily able to convey my own enthusiasm, my sincere conviction of what I am going to say?

❑ Am I ready to preach this homily? Have I rehearsed this homily out loud until:

    ❑ I am comfortable with the *flow* of this homily: I can make the *transitions* from point to point, from idea to idea, smoothly and clearly;

    ❑ I am using *words* and *expressions* that my listeners can understand and appreciate: I am not speaking in theological jargon or "holy card" talk;

    ❑ my *delivery* (voice, gestures, speaking rate, pronunciation and enunciation, pauses, etc.) and

    ❑ my *inflection* and *emphasis* of key words and phrases are natural and effective?

❑ My homily lasts _____ minutes.   Is it ❑ too long? ❑ too short? ❑ just about right?

4. GLEANINGS—Thoughts and notes AFTER the Homily

What worked, what didn't work in this homily; response and reactions from the community; ideas for next time; etc.

_____

_____

_____

_____

_____

_____

_____

_____

_____

_____

_____

_____

Third Sunday of Advent

The Readings:

READING 1: Isaiah 35: 1-6, 10

The desert and the parched land will exalt;
the steppe will rejoice and bloom.
Then will the eyes of the blind be opened,
the ears of the deaf be cleared.

Today Isaiah prophesies that the Messiah will come as a *healer*. From our New Testament perspective, our first thoughts are of the miraculous works and healings of Jesus; but Isaiah's prophecy speaks of the Messiah as a *reconciler* who heals the divisions among peoples, who restores the justice and peace of God and who brings men and women back to the Lord.

READING 2: James 5: 7-10

See how the farmer awaits the precious yield of the soil. He looks forward to it patiently while the soil receives the winter and spring rains. You, too, must be patient. Steady your hearts, because the coming of the Lord is at hand.

This is one of the few "official" Lectionary appearances of this obscure letter assigned to the authorship of James, "the brother of the Lord." This parable on patience might assure the "little people" in the community that their long wait for Christmas will soon be rewarded; but for the "big people" in the congregation, the image of the farmer waiting for the return of spring broadens our view of Advent from the festive anticipation of Jesus' birth to the deeper and sobering anticipation of our imminent re-birth in the Resurrection. James' parable also echoes the Advent theme of waiting, acknowledging the frustration and doubt of "hanging in there," of waiting so long and in such turmoil for the promised return of Christ (remember that James is speaking to the same small, persecuted minority of Christians as does Paul).

GOSPEL: Matthew 11: 2-11

Go back and report to John what you hear and see: the blind recover their sight, cripples walk, lepers are cured, the deaf hear, the dead are raised to life, and the poor have the good news preached to them.

The picture of John the Baptizer in today Gospel's is quite different from last Sunday's thundering, charismatic figure preaching to the crowds along the Jordan. John has been thrown into prison by Herod for publicly denouncing the king's incestuous marriage to Herodias. Left to waste away in prison, John knew that his end was near.

This must have been an anxious time of doubt and despair for John—he had staked his life on proclaiming the coming of the Messiah, and his witness will soon cost him his life. Like any human being, John had to wonder if he had been deluding himself. And so, he sends friends to ask Jesus if he is the Messiah.

Jesus sends the messengers back to John to report all they have seen Jesus do, fulfilling the prophecies of Isaiah and the prophets of old. While praising John for his faithful witness to the Messiah, Jesus tells his followers that great things will come to all who become prophets of the kingdom of God.

Themes:

• Advent: the season of hope

In Charles Dickens' timeless tale, Bob Cratchit returns from church with his young crippled son, Tiny Tim. Mother Cratchit asks if Tim behaved himself during the service. His father reports:

> "Little Tim was as good as gold. And better. Somehow, he gets thoughtful sitting by himself so much, and thinks the strangest thoughts you ever heard. Little Tim told me that he hoped people saw him in the church, because he was a cripple, and it might be pleasant for them to remember upon Christmas Day who it was who made the lame beggars walk and blind men see."

Tiny Tim serves as a kind of Isaiah and John the Baptizer, serving to remind his neighbors that Christ has come. Sometimes our troubles and doubts overwhelm us. We feel abandoned by God, that he is far, far away from us. But Advent/Christmas is the season of hope: God has not abandoned us but continues to call us back. God gives us the gift of himself in Christ Jesus in order to constantly re-create and renew our lives.

• Advent: a time for healing

All three readings today begin with lifeless, depressing images that are transformed into life-giving and enriching images: the parched desert (Isaiah 35), the farmer's soil in the dead of winter (James 5) and the tragic figure of John in prison (Matthew 11). In each of these situations, the Messiah brings healing—not a physical healing as much as a psychological healing, a reconciliation.

Christmas is the time when families and friends gather together to celebrate; it is, therefore, the ideal time for healing the divisions among us, for not only renewing old friendships but for re-creating broken relationships. We are called to bring healing to our world through the same love and selflessness taught and lived by Jesus.

For Reflection:

• Are there "parched deserts" around us that cry out for life?

• Who are the healers of our age—those who, like Christ, bring sight to the blind, breathe life into the dead and give voice to the silent?

• Have you ever faced a hopeless situation in your life that, somehow, was transformed into joyful promise?

• How can some of our many Christmas traditions be opportunities for healing, for reconciliation?

Date: _____

HOMILY WORKSHEET for the Third Sunday of Advent

1. SEEDS

What today's readings say *to me*: _____

_____

_____

PARABLES, STORIES and EXPERIENCES that speak to the themes of today's readings: _____

_____

_____

SPECIAL CONSIDERATIONS this week: Audience? Events in the community? Unique dimensions to this celebration?

_____

_____

_____

What RESPONSE do I seek from my listeners?
❑ to affirm/enlighten them in their faith?
❑ to teach/inform them about _____

_____

❑ to have them take a specific action _____

_____

2. PLANTING

The point I want to make in this homily (*ONE sentence*): _____

_____

_____

HOMILY OUTLINE

OPENING (*introductory STORY*): _____

_____

_____

_____

_____

_____

Point 1. APPLICATION of STORY to Scripture themes: _____

_____

_____

_____

_____

_____

Point 2. CONNECTION between Scriptural themes and the listeners' life experience: _____

_____
_____
_____
_____
_____

Point 3. RESPONSE/CONSIDERATION sought from listeners: _____

_____
_____
_____
_____
_____

CLOSING STATEMENT (*refers back to STORY*): _____

_____
_____
_____
_____
_____

3. HARVEST—A Checklist:

❏ Does my completed homily make the point I articulated above (*under PLANTING*)?

❏ Am I excited about this homily. Am I readily able to convey my own enthusiasm, my sincere conviction of what I am going to say?

❏ Am I ready to preach this homily? Have I rehearsed this homily out loud until:

❏ I am comfortable with the *flow* of this homily: I can make the *transitions* from point to point, from idea to idea, smoothly and clearly;

❏ I am using *words* and *expressions* that my listeners can understand and appreciate: I am not speaking in theological jargon or "holy card" talk;

❏ my *delivery* (voice, gestures, speaking rate, pronunciation and enunciation, pauses, etc.) and

❏ my *inflection* and *emphasis* of key words and phrases are natural and effective?

❏ My homily lasts _____ minutes. Is it ❏ too long? ❏ too short? ❏ just about right?

4. GLEANINGS—Thoughts and notes AFTER the Homily

What worked, what didn't work in this homily; response and reactions from the community; ideas for next time; etc.

_____
_____
_____
_____
_____
_____
_____
_____
_____
_____
_____

Fourth Sunday of Advent

The Readings:

READING 1: Isaiah 7: 10-14

The Lord himself will give you this sign:
the virgin shall be with child,
and bear a son,
and shall name him Emmanuel.

Ahaz was king of Judah from 735-715 B.C. Politically naive, the headstrong young leader forged an alliance with Assyria against Israel and Syria. The alliance had disastrous consequences for Judah, costing the nation its independence. Isaiah counsels the foolish king to return to the ways of God which he has abandoned. The prophet challenges Ahaz to ask God for some sign from the Lord that God will once again return and save Judah. Ahaz responds ("I will not tempt the Lord!") with sarcasm. Isaiah then speaks the most famous prophecy regarding the Messiah. Many interpreted this oracle as referring to Hezekiah, Judah's next king, but Matthew and the New Testament writers see Isaiah's words as fulfilled ultimately in Jesus Christ.

READING 2: Romans 1: 1-7

Greetings from Paul, called to be an apostle and set apart to proclaim the Gospel of God which he promised long ago through his prophets, as the holy Scriptures record—the Gospel concerning his Son, who was descended from David according to the flesh but made the Son of God in power, according to the spirit of holiness, by his resurrection from the dead.

Paul has completed his three journeys through the eastern world, and now looks westward beyond Jerusalem to Rome and even all the way to Spain to preach the Gospel. The letter to the Romans was written to introduce himself to the Christian community at Rome in anticipation of his journey there—a journey that Paul eventually made, but as a prisoner. Writing from Greece (most probably Corinth), Paul introduces himself to the Roman community as an apostle of "Jesus Christ, descended from David . . . but made the Son of God according to the spirit of holiness." Jesus as the perfect fulfillment of the Mosaic covenant will be a major theme throughout Paul's letter to the Christians of Rome.

GOSPEL: Matthew 1: 18-24

"Joseph, son of David, have no fear about taking Mary as your wife. It is by the Holy Spirit that she has conceived this child. She is to have a son and you are to name him Jesus because he will save his people from their sins."

Today's Gospel is Matthew's version of Jesus' birth. It is not Luke's familiar story of a child born in a Bethlehem stable, but that of a young unmarried woman suddenly finding herself pregnant and her very hurt and confused husband not knowing what to do. Matthew's point here, as throughout his Gospel, is that Jesus is the Emmanuel promised of old—Isaiah's prophecy has finally been fulfilled in Jesus: the virgin has given birth to a son, one who is a descendent of David's house (through Joseph). Jesus is truly Emmanuel—God is with us.

Themes:

• Christ: the fulfillment of God's promise

The Spirit of God is the principal albeit unseen player in the events of Christmas. Matthew's concern is not historical but theological: Jesus' birth is the work of the Holy Spirit—God has directly intervened in human history. God's Spirit, who inspired the prophets to preach, who enabled the nation of Israel to enter into the covenant with Yahweh, continues at work in the world in new and creative ways. Jesus Christ is the ultimate and perfect fulfillment of that covenant.

• God's presence in our times

The classic movie, *Miracle on 34th Street,* is the story of an old man named Kris Kringle (Edmund Gwenn), a department store Santa Claus, who is convinced that he actually is St. Nick himself. Befriended by a woman and her daughter, the old man attempts to bring the joy of Christmas into the struggle of their lives. At one point, Kris tells the mother (Maureen O'Hara) of the skeptical little girl (Natalie Wood): "Oh, Christmas isn't just a day. It's a frame of mind. And that's why I'm glad I'm here. Maybe I can do something about it. And I'm glad I met you and your daughter. You two are a test case for me."

The Christmas event has sanctified all time: God and humankind meet in the Child of Bethlehem. In the birth of Jesus, God has directly touched human history. Christmas, then, is more than "just a day. . . but a frame of mind," a constant awareness of God's presence in every moment of the time we are given.

For Reflection:

• Share stories of "Emmanuel"—stories of "God with us" in the ordinary and the every day, stories of God's Spirit present and working in our world as it was in the events of the Incarnation.

• How do our Christmas customs and traditions express the mystery of "Emmanuel"—"God with us"?

Date: _____

HOMILY WORKSHEET for the Fourth Sunday of Advent

1. SEEDS

What today's readings say *to me*: _____
_____
_____

PARABLES, STORIES and EXPERIENCES that speak to the themes of today's readings: _____
_____
_____

SPECIAL CONSIDERATIONS this week: Audience? Events in the community? Unique dimensions to this celebration?
_____
_____
_____

What RESPONSE do I seek from my listeners?
❑ to affirm/enlighten them in their faith?
❑ to teach/inform them about _____
_____

❑ to have them take a specific action _____
_____

2. PLANTING

The point I want to make in this homily (*ONE sentence*): _____
_____
_____

HOMILY OUTLINE

OPENING (*introductory STORY*): _____
_____
_____
_____
_____
_____

Point 1. APPLICATION of STORY to Scripture themes: _____
_____
_____
_____
_____
_____

Point 2. CONNECTION between Scriptural themes and the listeners' life experience: _____

_____
_____
_____
_____
_____

Point 3. RESPONSE/CONSIDERATION sought from listeners: _____

_____
_____
_____
_____
_____

CLOSING STATEMENT (*refers back to STORY*): _____

_____
_____
_____
_____
_____

3. HARVEST—A Checklist:

❑ Does my completed homily make the point I articulated above (*under PLANTING*)?

❑ Am I excited about this homily. Am I readily able to convey my own enthusiasm, my sincere conviction of what I am going to say?

❑ Am I ready to preach this homily? Have I rehearsed this homily out loud until:

    ❑ I am comfortable with the *flow* of this homily: I can make the *transitions* from point to point, from idea to idea, smoothly and clearly;

    ❑ I am using *words* and *expressions* that my listeners can understand and appreciate: I am not speaking in theological jargon or "holy card" talk;

    ❑ my *delivery* (voice, gestures, speaking rate, pronunciation and enunciation, pauses, etc.) and

    ❑ my *inflection* and *emphasis* of key words and phrases are natural and effective?

❑ My homily lasts _____ minutes. Is it ❑ too long? ❑ too short? ❑ just about right?

4. GLEANINGS—Thoughts and notes AFTER the Homily

What worked, what didn't work in this homily; response and reactions from the community; ideas for next time; etc.

_____
_____
_____
_____
_____
_____
_____
_____
_____
_____
_____
_____

Christmas

The Readings:

(NOTE: The following are the Lectionary readings for The Mass at Midnight, which may be read at any Mass on Christmas and its vigil.)

READING 1: Isaiah 9: 1-6

The people who walked in darkness
*   have seen a great light:*
Upon those who dwelt in the land of gloom
*   a light has shone.*
For a child is born to us, a son is given us;
*   upon his shoulder dominion rests.*
They name him Wonder-Counselor, God-Hero,
*   Father-Forever, Prince of Peace.*

In this passage from Isaiah's "Book of Emmanuel" (Chapters 6-12), the prophet describes Emmanuel as the new David, the ideal king who will free his enslaved people. The "day of Midian" refers to Gideon's decisive defeat of the Midianites, a nomadic nation of outlaws who ransacked the Israelites' farms and villages (Judges 6-8).

READING 2: Titus 2: 11-14

The grace of God has appeared, offering salvation to all.

These verses from one of Paul's three pastoral letters to his co-workers Timothy and Titus articulate the heart of the mystery of the Incarnation: the grace of God himself has come to us in the person of Jesus Christ.

GOSPEL: Luke 2: 1-14 (or 2: 1-20)

This day is David's city a savior has been born to you, the Messiah and Lord.

Centuries of hope in God's promise have come to fulfillment. The Messiah is born!

Luke's account of Jesus' birth begins by placing the Christmas event during the reign of Caesar Augustus. Augustus, who ruled from 27 B.C.-14 A.D.), was honored as "savior" and "god" in ancient Greek inscriptions. His long reign was hailed as the *pax Romana*—a period of peace throughout the vast Roman world. Luke, then, very deliberately points out that it is during the rule of Augustus, the savior, god and peace-maker, that Jesus the Christ, the long-awaited Savior and Messiah, the Son of God and Prince of Peace, enters human history.

Throughout his Gospel, Luke shows how it is the poor, the lowly, the outcast and the sinner who immediately hear and embrace the preaching of Jesus. The announcement of the Messiah's birth to shepherds—who were among the most isolated and despised in the Jewish community—is in keeping with Luke's theme that the poor are especially blessed of God.

Themes:

• Christmas: feast for all humanity

From the Christmas story in Luke's Gospel, we have a romantic image of shepherds as gentle, peaceful figures. But that manger scene image is a far cry from reality: in fact, the shepherds of Biblical times were tough, earthy characters who fearlessly used their clubs to defend their flocks from wolves and other wild animals. They had even less patience for the pompous scribes and Pharisees who treated them as second and third-class citizens, barring these ill-bred rustics from the synagogue and courts.

And yet it was to shepherds that God first revealed the birth of the Messiah. The shepherds' vision on the Bethlehem hillside proclaims to all people of all times and all lands that Christ comes for the sake of all of humankind.

• Christmas: the beginning of the Christ event

A favorite story of Martin Buber, the great Jewish philosopher, concerned a rabbi in Jerusalem to whom it was excitedly announced that the Messiah had come. The rabbi calmly looked out of the window, surveyed the scene carefully, and announced that to him nothing seemed to have changed, and then calmly returned to his study.

The Messiah *has* come—but what difference does that make in our lives? If the rabbi were to look out his window tonight, he would certainly see many different things: he would see the lights and decorations and illuminated trees and wreathes; he would see carolers and hear their songs about "joy to the world" and "peace on earth," he would see the smiles and joy of people extending greetings to one another.

But what would the rabbi see out of his window tomorrow? or next week? or a day in February? or April? or July? But the Messiah *has* come! What happened one Palestinian night when a son was born to a carpenter and his young bride was a watershed in the power of sin over humanity. In Christ, we can live in love. Has it made a difference? Has our world become a better place since the Son of God became incarnate here? Has anything changed? May this Christmas be the beginning of a difference in our world, a difference described by Martin Buber this way: "Men (and women) become what they are, sons (and daughters) of God, by *becoming* what they are, brothers of their brothers (sisters of their sisters)."

For Reflection:

• It has been a busy time, getting to this day. Was it all worth it?

• "We need a little Christmas . . ." so the song goes. Why do we need Christmas *this* year?

• How is the first Christmas as described by Luke at odds with our Christmas celebration? How can we reconcile the difference in the simplicity of the first Christmas and the extravangance of our celebration?

• Luke's Gospel has been called the "Gospel of the poor." How can we make "shepherds," outcasts, the poor and imprisoned part of our Christmas?

Date: _____

HOMILY WORKSHEET for Christmas

1. SEEDS

What today's readings say *to me*: _____

_____

_____

PARABLES, STORIES and EXPERIENCES that speak to the themes of today's readings: _____

_____

_____

SPECIAL CONSIDERATIONS this week: Audience? Events in the community? Unique dimensions to this celebration?

_____

_____

_____

What RESPONSE do I seek from my listeners?
❑ to affirm/enlighten them in their faith?
❑ to teach/inform them about _____

_____

❑ to have them take a specific action _____

_____

2. PLANTING

The point I want to make in this homily (*ONE sentence*): _____

_____

_____

HOMILY OUTLINE

OPENING (*introductory STORY*): _____

_____

_____

_____

_____

_____

Point 1. APPLICATION of STORY to Scripture themes: _____

_____

_____

_____

_____

_____

Point 2. CONNECTION between Scriptural themes and the listeners' life experience: _____
_____
_____
_____
_____
_____

Point 3. RESPONSE/CONSIDERATION sought from listeners: _____
_____
_____
_____
_____
_____

CLOSING STATEMENT (*refers back to STORY*): _____
_____
_____
_____
_____
_____

3. HARVEST—A Checklist:

❑ Does my completed homily make the point I articulated above (*under PLANTING*)?

❑ Am I excited about this homily. Am I readily able to convey my own enthusiasm, my sincere conviction of what I am going to say?

❑ Am I ready to preach this homily? Have I rehearsed this homily out loud until:

  ❑ I am comfortable with the *flow* of this homily: I can make the *transitions* from point to point, from idea to idea, smoothly and clearly;

  ❑ I am using *words* and *expressions* that my listeners can understand and appreciate: I am not speaking in theological jargon or "holy card" talk;

  ❑ my *delivery* (voice, gestures, speaking rate, pronunciation and enunciation, pauses, etc.) and

  ❑ my *inflection* and *emphasis* of key words and phrases are natural and effective?

❑ My homily lasts _____ minutes. Is it ❑ too long? ❑ too short? ❑ just about right?

4. GLEANINGS—Thoughts and notes AFTER the Homily

What worked, what didn't work in this homily; response and reactions from the community; ideas for next time; etc.

_____
_____
_____
_____
_____
_____
_____
_____
_____
_____

Feast of the Holy Family

The Readings:

READING 1: Sirach 3: 2-6, 12-14

The Lord sets a father in honor over his children;
a mother's authority he confirms over her sons.
He who honors his father atones for his sins;
he stores up riches who reveres his mother.

The Book of Sirach is a collection of carefully-crafted maxims and commentaries based on the Law. The author ("Jesus, son of Eleazar, son of Sirach"—50: 27), a wise and experienced observer of life, writes on a variety of topics in order to help his contemporaries understand the role of faith in everyday life. He counsels on family, friendship, wealth, learning and worship, as well as offering meditations on the sacred writings and the great heroes of the Covenant. Today's first reading is a beautiful reflection on the fourth commandment. To honor one's parents, Ben Sira writes, is to honor the Lord God himself.

READING 2: Colossians 3: 12-21

Forgive as the Lord has forgiven you. Christ's peace must reign in your hearts. Dedicate yourselves to thankfulness. Whatever you do, whether in speech or in action, do in the name of the Lord Jesus.

This letter is considered one of Paul's "captivity epistles." He wrote the epistle (presumably from prison) at the urging of Epaphras, the leader of the church there. The young church was being torn apart by adherents of Gnosticism ("knowledge"), a philosophy that stressed the superiority of knowledge over faith. Paul writes that such Gnostic teachings are but "shadows"; Christ is "reality," the "image of the invisible God, the first-born of all creation" in whom we are redeemed.

In today's reading from Colossians, Paul presents a picture of real community, formed in the perfect, unconditional love of Christ.

GOSPEL: Matthew 2: 13-15, 19-23

The angel of the Lord appeared in a dream to Joseph:

"Get up and take the child and his mother, and flee to Egypt. Stay there until I tell you otherwise. Herod is searching for the child to destroy him."

Matthew continues his story of Jesus' early years, focusing on his principal theme: that Jesus is the Messiah promised by God long ago.

Matthew portrays the Holy Family as outcasts, refugees in their own country. Bound together by love and trust in God and in one another, they embark on the dangerous journey to Egypt to flee the insane rage of Herod. Jesus relives the Exodus experience of Israel: he will come out of Egypt, the land of slavery, to establish a new covenant of liberation for the new Israel.

Themes:

• the love of family

Today's feast is a celebration of family—that unique nucleus of society that gives us life, nurturing and support throughout one's journey on earth. The Fathers of Vatican II called the family "the first and vital cell of humanity. . .the domestic sanctuary of the Church." Families of faith reflect the love of Christ: love that is totally selfless, limitless and unconditional, both in good times and (especially) in bad times.

• the value of memories

Christmas is the season for making memories. Many of our most cherished memories of family are the memories of Christmases past. But if not for actually making memories, then Christmas is certainly a marker for keeping track of them. We seem to measure the years in terms of Christmases: the Christmas he was in the service, the Christmas she was pregnant with their first child, the first Christmas in the new house, Grandpa's last Christmas, the somber, quieter Christmas during times of war, assassination, imprisonment and death. As we store away the memories of another Christmas, may we always know the love and support, the forgiveness and acceptance that is "family."

For Reflection:

• What "rituals" and "customs" in your own family reflect the spiritual dimension of Christmas?

• What experiences has your family shared that have brought you closer together? Consider both the wonderful and the catastrophic; times of trial, tension and tragedy; times that demanded extraordinary efforts to forgive and reconcile.

• Can your family identify with the plight of Joseph, Mary and the Child in today's Gospel?

Date: _____

HOMILY WORKSHEET for the Feast of the Holy Family

1. SEEDS

What today's readings say *to me*: _____

_____

_____

PARABLES, STORIES and EXPERIENCES that speak to the themes of today's readings: _____

_____

_____

SPECIAL CONSIDERATIONS this week: Audience? Events in the community? Unique dimensions to this celebration?

_____

_____

_____

What RESPONSE do I seek from my listeners?
❑ to affirm/enlighten them in their faith?
❑ to teach/inform them about _____

_____

❑ to have them take a specific action _____

_____

2. PLANTING

The point I want to make in this homily (*ONE sentence*): _____

_____

_____

HOMILY OUTLINE

OPENING (*introductory STORY*): _____

_____

_____

_____

_____

_____

Point 1. APPLICATION of STORY to Scripture themes: _____

_____

_____

_____

_____

_____

Point 2. CONNECTION between Scriptural themes and the listeners' life experience: _____

_____
_____
_____
_____
_____
_____

Point 3. RESPONSE/CONSIDERATION sought from listeners: _____

_____
_____
_____
_____
_____
_____

CLOSING STATEMENT (*refers back to STORY*): _____

_____
_____
_____
_____
_____
_____

3. HARVEST—A Checklist:

❑ Does my completed homily make the point I articulated above (*under PLANTING*)?

❑ Am I excited about this homily. Am I readily able to convey my own enthusiasm, my sincere conviction of what I am going to say?

❑ Am I ready to preach this homily? Have I rehearsed this homily out loud until:

> ❑ I am comfortable with the *flow* of this homily: I can make the *transitions* from point to point, from idea to idea, smoothly and clearly;

> ❑ I am using *words* and *expressions* that my listeners can understand and appreciate: I am not speaking in theological jargon or "holy card" talk;

> ❑ my *delivery* (voice, gestures, speaking rate, pronunciation and enunciation, pauses, etc.) and

> ❑ my *inflection* and *emphasis* of key words and phrases are natural and effective?

❑ My homily lasts _____ minutes. Is it ❑ too long? ❑ too short? ❑ just about right?

4. GLEANINGS—Thoughts and notes AFTER the Homily

What worked, what didn't work in this homily; response and reactions from the community; ideas for next time; etc.

_____
_____
_____
_____
_____
_____
_____
_____
_____
_____
_____

Solemnity of Mary, the Mother of God: New Year's Day

The Readings:

(NOTE: With the permission of the local Ordinary, the Mass for the World Day of Peace may be celebrated on January 1.)

READING 1: Numbers 6: 22-27

This is how you shall bless the Israelites:
The Lord bless you and keep you!
The Lord let his face shine upon you,
    and be gracious to you!
The Lord look upon you kindly
    and kindly give you peace!

From the Book of Numbers, one of the five books of the Law, the Lord gives to Moses and Aaron words of priestly blessing.

READING 2: Galatians 4: 4-7

God sent forth his Son born of a woman, to deliver from the Law those who were subjected to it, so that we might receive our status as adopted sons.

The Church of Galatia is facing defections because of Judaic preachers who insist that pagan converts submit to the Jewish rite of circumcision and the observance of the Law. Paul's letter maintains that salvation is through Christ alone, that Christ's followers are no longer under the yoke of the old Law. In today's second reading, Paul puts the Christmas event in perspective: through Christ, born of Mary, we become sons and daughters of "Abba," Father.

GOSPEL: Luke 2: 16-21

Mary treasured all these things and reflected on them in her heart. The name Jesus was given the child, the name the angel had given him before he was conceived.

Jesus is given the name "Yeshua"—"God saves." The rite of circumcision unites Mary's child with the chosen people and makes him an heir to the promises God made to Abraham—promises to be fulfilled in the child himself.

Themes:

• a year for "newness"

G.K. Chesterton made this observation about New Year's:

"The object of a new year is not that we should have a new year. It is that we should have a new soul and a new nose, new feet, a new backbone, new ears and new eyes."

Today a new year lies before us like a blank page or canvas. So many possibilities—much more than just the simple resolutions we steadfastly keep usually until kick-off time for today's first football game. May this New Year be truly *new* for each one of us—a time for renewal, for re-creation, for making this year a year of peace in our lives and homes, for becoming the people of compassion and integrity we want to be, for re-centering our lives in the things of God.

• Mary: Our mother and sister

Her statues have always radiated sweetness. She is always young and pink-cheeked and slender, with hair cascading down to her waist.

But the Mary of the Gospels is neither a fairy tale princess nor the romanticized "lovely lady dressed in blue." The flesh-and-blood Mary was an altogether human woman:

- the pregnant adolescent who was painfully misunderstood by the man she loved;
- the frantic parent searching for her lost child in Jerusalem;
- the caring woman who was not afraid to speak her mind or voice her questions;
- the anguished mother who stood by courageously while her son was executed.

The figure we venerate in mysterious icons was a woman with her feet firmly planted on earth. Mary of Nazareth knew the pain that only a mother could feel; she knew the joy that only a totally selfless and giving woman of faith could experience.*

Luke's Gospel reveals an uneducated adolescent who, in a dusty village in a small conquered nation, said, "Be it done to me according to your word," stuck by that decision and changed the course of history. If Mary, the young unmarried pregnant girl, can believe in the incredible thing that she is to be a part of, if she can trust herself and believe in her role in the great story, then the most ordinary people can believe in their parts in the drama, too.

Mary is the perfect symbol of our own salvation. She is the promise of what the Church is called to be and will be. She is the hope and the comfort of a pilgrim people walking on the road of faith.

For Reflection:

- In what ways is the Mary of the Gospels a real companion to us on our journey through the New Year?

- What was your "favorite year"? What made it a special time for you? How can you resolve to bring those elements into the New Year before you?

- Share the hopes, the challenges, the promises that the New Year presents. How can we make this new year "anno Domini"—a year of the Lord?

*Adapted from *The Fire in the Thornbush*, pastoral letter by Bishop Matthew H. Clark.

Date: _____

God

HOMILY WORKSHEET for the Solemnity of Mary, Mother of

1. SEEDS

What today's readings say *to me*: _____
_____
_____

PARABLES, STORIES and EXPERIENCES that speak to the themes of today's readings: _____
_____
_____

SPECIAL CONSIDERATIONS this week: Audience? Events in the community? Unique dimensions to this celebration?
_____
_____
_____

What RESPONSE do I seek from my listeners?
❑ to affirm/enlighten them in their faith?
❑ to teach/inform them about _____
_____

❑ to have them take a specific action _____
_____

2. PLANTING

The point I want to make in this homily (*ONE sentence*): _____
_____
_____

HOMILY OUTLINE

OPENING (*introductory STORY*): _____
_____
_____
_____
_____
_____

Point 1. APPLICATION of STORY to Scripture themes: _____
_____
_____
_____
_____
_____

Point 2. CONNECTION between Scriptural themes and the listeners' life experience: _____

_____

_____

_____

_____

_____

Point 3. RESPONSE/CONSIDERATION sought from listeners: _____

_____

_____

_____

_____

_____

CLOSING STATEMENT (*refers back to STORY*): _____

_____

_____

_____

_____

_____

3. HARVEST—A Checklist:

❑ Does my completed homily make the point I articulated above (*under PLANTING*)?

❑ Am I excited about this homily. Am I readily able to convey my own enthusiasm, my sincere conviction of what I am going to say?

❑ Am I ready to preach this homily? Have I rehearsed this homily out loud until:

❑ I am comfortable with the *flow* of this homily: I can make the *transitions* from point to point, from idea to idea, smoothly and clearly;

❑ I am using *words* and *expressions* that my listeners can understand and appreciate: I am not speaking in theological jargon or "holy card" talk;

❑ my *delivery* (voice, gestures, speaking rate, pronunciation and enunciation, pauses, etc.) and

❑ my *inflection* and *emphasis* of key words and phrases are natural and effective?

❑ My homily lasts _____ minutes. Is it ❑ too long? ❑ too short? ❑ just about right?

4. GLEANINGS—Thoughts and notes AFTER the Homily

What worked, what didn't work in this homily; response and reactions from the community; ideas for next time; etc.

_____

_____

_____

_____

_____

_____

_____

_____

_____

_____

_____

Epiphany

The Readings:

READING 1: Isaiah 60: 1-6

> *Rise up in splendor, Jerusalem!*
> *Your light has come;*
> *the glory of the Lord shines upon you.*
> *Nations shall walk by your light,*
> *and kings by your shining radiance.*

This reading from Trito-Isaiah (chapters 56-66) is a song of encouragement to the exiled Jews who are returning to Jerusalem from Babylon to rebuild their nation and their way of life. Jerusalem will be a light for all nations, a gathering place not only for the scattered Jews but for the entire world. God will once again dwell in the midst of his faithful people Israel.

READING 2: Ephesians 3: 2-3, 5-6

> *In Christ Jesus the Gentiles are now co-heirs with the Jews, members of the same body and sharers of the promise through the preaching of the Gospel.*

The letter to the Ephesians is Paul's "synthesis" on the nature of the Church. In this reading, Paul writes that the Church transcends national and cultural identities: in Christ, Jew and Gentile form one body and share equally in the promise of the Resurrection.

GOSPEL: Matthew 2: 1-12

> *"Where is the newborn king of the Jews? We observed his star at its rising and have come to pay him homage."*

Today's Gospel, the story of the astrologers and the star of Bethlehem, is unique to Matthew's Gospel. Note that Matthew does not call them kings or "magi" but "astrologers," nor does he give their names or report where they came from—in fact, Matthew never even specifies the number of astrologers (because three gifts are reported, it has been a tradition since the fifth century to picture "three wise men"). In stripping away the romantic layers that have been added to the story we can perhaps better concentrate on Matthew's point.

A great many Old Testament ideas and images are presented in this story. The star, for example, is reminiscent of Balaam's prophecy that "a star shall advance from Jacob" (Numbers 24: 17). Many of the details in Matthew's story about the child Jesus parallel the story of the child Moses and the Exodus.

Matthew's story also provides a preview of what is to come. First, the reactions of the various parties to the birth of Jesus parallel the effects Jesus' teaching will have on those who hear it. Herod reacts with anger and hostility to the Jesus of the poor who comes to threaten the powerful and rich. The chief priests and scribes greet the news with haughty indifference toward the Jesus who comes to give new life and meaning to the rituals and laws of the scribes. But the astrologers—non-believers in the eyes of Israel—possess the faith and the openness of mind and heart to seek and welcome the Jesus who will institute the Second Covenant between the Father and the New Israel.

Secondly, the gifts of the astrologers indicate the principal dimensions of Jesus' mission:

• *gold* is a gift fitting for a king, a ruler, one with power and authority;

• *frankincense* is a gift fitting for a priest, one who offers sacrifice (frankincense was an aromatic perfume sprinkled on the animals sacrificed in the Temple);

• *myrrh* is a fitting "gift" for someone who is to die (myrrh was used in ancient times for embalming the bodies of the dead before burial).

Themes:

• the universal nature of the Messiah

Epiphany celebrates the manifestation of Christ to all nations, the Messiah who comes to reveal the love of God to all of humankind. Racism, bigotry, narrow-mindedness, sectarianism, elitism and discrimination in all of their ugly forms and shadows are the antithesis of the Gospel. The newborn king of the Jews sought by the astrologers is the Word of love that breaks down the walls of alienation and estrangement between peoples, the Prince of Peace who bridges the boundaries between nations, and the Light of God who illuminates the long night of despair, hatred and selfishness.

• the search for God in our lives

Cardinal Newman said that "to be earnest in seeking the truth is an essential requisite in finding it." The astrologers' following of the star is a journey of faith, a journey that each one of us experiences in the course of our own lives. Unlike Herod and the scribes, may we not fear to seek the way and the truth of Jesus the Christ.

For Reflection:

• Epiphany comes from the Greek word meaning appearance or manifestation. Think about the "epiphanies" around us—the many ways the Lord "appears" or "manifests" his presence among us.

• How is your particular parish called to be "universal"? In what ways does the Gospel challenge your community to abandon the "safety" of itself to reach out to those considered "outside" of it (new immigrants, the poor, etc.)?

• Who are the "wise" men and women in our world who have dedicated themselves to seeking Christ? What are their stories?

Date: _____

HOMILY WORKSHEET for the Epiphany

1. SEEDS

What today's readings say *to me*: _____

_____

_____

PARABLES, STORIES and EXPERIENCES that speak to the themes of today's readings: _____

_____

_____

SPECIAL CONSIDERATIONS this week: Audience? Events in the community? Unique dimensions to this celebration?

_____

_____

_____

What RESPONSE do I seek from my listeners?
❑ to affirm/enlighten them in their faith?
❑ to teach/inform them about _____

_____

❑ to have them take a specific action _____

_____

2. PLANTING

The point I want to make in this homily (*ONE sentence*): _____

_____

_____

HOMILY OUTLINE

OPENING (*introductory STORY*): _____

_____

_____

_____

_____

_____

Point 1. APPLICATION of STORY to Scripture themes: _____

_____

_____

_____

_____

_____

Point 2. CONNECTION between Scriptural themes and the listeners' life experience: _____

_____

_____

_____

_____

_____

Point 3. RESPONSE/CONSIDERATION sought from listeners: _____

_____

_____

_____

_____

_____

CLOSING STATEMENT (*refers back to STORY*): _____

_____

_____

_____

_____

_____

3. HARVEST—A Checklist:

❑ Does my completed homily make the point I articulated above (*under PLANTING*)?

❑ Am I excited about this homily. Am I readily able to convey my own enthusiasm, my sincere conviction of what I am going to say?

❑ Am I ready to preach this homily? Have I rehearsed this homily out loud until:

   ❑ I am comfortable with the *flow* of this homily: I can make the *transitions* from point to point, from idea to idea, smoothly and clearly;

   ❑ I am using *words* and *expressions* that my listeners can understand and appreciate: I am not speaking in theological jargon or "holy card" talk;

   ❑ my *delivery* (voice, gestures, speaking rate, pronunciation and enunciation, pauses, etc.) and

   ❑ my *inflection* and *emphasis* of key words and phrases are natural and effective?

❑ My homily lasts _____ minutes. Is it ❑ too long? ❑ too short? ❑ just about right?

4. GLEANINGS—Thoughts and notes AFTER the Homily

What worked, what didn't work in this homily; response and reactions from the community; ideas for next time; etc.

_____

_____

_____

_____

_____

_____

_____

_____

_____

_____

_____

The Baptism of the Lord

The Readings:

READING 1: Isaiah 42: 1-4, 6-7

Here is my servant whom I uphold,
my chosen one with whom I am pleased,
upon whom I have put my spirit;
I formed you, and set you
as a covenant of the people,
a light for the nations.

This is the first of the "Servant songs" in Deutero-Isaiah in which the prophet tells of the "Servant" of God who will come to redeem Israel. In this first song, Isaiah speaks of the servant as God's "chosen one with whom I am pleased"—words that will be heard at the River Jordan.

READING 2: Acts 10: 34-38

Peter's sermon in Cornelius' house:
"I take it you know what has been reported all over Judea about Jesus of Nazareth, begin-
ning in Galilee with the baptism John preached . . . ."

Cornelius was a Roman centurion, a good and kind man who deeply respected and observed the high moral code and noble style of worship of Judaism. In a dream, Cornelius is told to send for this Peter and listen to what he has to say. Cornelius invites Peter to address his household. Peter's sermon typifies early Christian preaching to the Gentiles: while God revealed his plan to his chosen nation of Israel, the Lord invites all people and nations to enter into the new Covenant of the Risen Christ.

GOSPEL: Matthew 3: 13-17

Jesus appeared before John at the Jordan to be baptized by him. John tried to refuse him.
"Give in for now. We must do this if we would fulfill all of God's demands."

John's refusal at first to baptize Jesus and Jesus' response to his refusal (a dialogue that appears only in Matthew's gospel) speaks to Matthew's continuing theme of Jesus as the fulfillment of the Old Testament prophecies. Jesus clearly did not need to be baptized. But his baptism by John is an affirmation that God was with this man Jesus in a very special way (Isaiah's prophecy is fulfilled: "my favor rests on him.") Jesus has come to identify with sinners, to bring them forgiveness; hence the propriety of Jesus' acceptance of John's baptism.

Baptism was a ritual performed by the Jews, but only for those who entered Judaism from another religion. It was natural that the sin-stained, polluted pagan should be "washed" in baptism, but no Jew could conceive of needing baptism, being born a son of Abraham, one of God's chosen people and therefore assured of God's salvation. But John's baptism—a baptism affirmed by Jesus—was not one of initiation, but one of reformation, a rejection of one's own life. In Christ, baptism becomes a sacrament of rebirth, a reception of new life.

Themes:

• baptism: to become "servants"

We tend to see baptism as a single event in our lives. But baptism is more than just a "naming" ceremony—it is an ongoing process that continues in every moment of our lives. To be baptized is to claim the name of Christian; to claim that name means to live as Christ did: to live for others rather than

33

for ourselves. Our baptisms make each one of us the "servant" of today's readings: to bring forth in our world the justice, reconciliation and enlightenment of Christ, the "beloved Son" and "favor" of God.

• the Spirit of God "hovering" over us

All four evangelists use a similar description in their accounts of John's baptizing Jesus: the Spirit of God descended like a dove and "hovered" over him—in other words, the peace and compassion of God was a constant presence within him. In baptism, we embrace that same Spirit. Pope Paul VI offered this insight into this presence of the Spirit: "Peace demands a mentality and a spirit which, before turning to others, must first *permeate* the person who wishes to bring peace. Peace is first and foremost personal, before it is social. And it is precisely this spirit of peace which is the duty of every true follower of Christ to cultivate." May Christ's spirit of peace "hover like a dove" over us as a constant presence in all of our relationships and decisions.

• the New Year: a time for new beginnings

That big January credit card statement notwithstanding, Christmas is now behind us. We are now totally immersed in the business of the new year. In today's Gospel Jesus begins the "business" of his mission at the Jordan. May we begin this new year in the same way that Jesus began his public ministry: by embracing the Spirit of forgiveness, of compassion, of peace. Although Christmas has been put away for another year, let us resolve to continue the *work* of Christmas: to find the lost, to heal the hurting, to feed the hungry, to free the imprisoned, to rebuild nations, to bring peace to all peoples everywhere.

For Reflection:

• How are names important? What can a name tell us about a person?

• Share stories about people we know in whom the Spirit of God "hovers like a dove."

• What "work" of Christmas remains to be done in your parish community? How have things changed—for the better and for the worse—since we celebrated Christmas?

Date: _____

HOMILY WORKSHEET for the Baptism of the Lord

1. SEEDS

What today's readings say *to me*: _____

_____

_____

PARABLES, STORIES and EXPERIENCES that speak to the themes of today's readings: _____

_____

_____

SPECIAL CONSIDERATIONS this week: Audience? Events in the community? Unique dimensions to this celebration?

_____

_____

_____

What RESPONSE do I seek from my listeners?
❏ to affirm/enlighten them in their faith?
❏ to teach/inform them about _____

_____

❏ to have them take a specific action _____

_____

2. PLANTING

The point I want to make in this homily (*ONE sentence*): _____

_____

_____

HOMILY OUTLINE

OPENING (*introductory STORY*): _____

_____

_____

_____

_____

_____

Point 1. APPLICATION of STORY to Scripture themes: _____

_____

_____

_____

_____

_____

Point 2. CONNECTION between Scriptural themes and the listeners' life experience: _____

_____
_____
_____
_____
_____

Point 3. RESPONSE/CONSIDERATION sought from listeners: _____

_____
_____
_____
_____
_____

CLOSING STATEMENT (*refers back to STORY*): _____

_____
_____
_____
_____
_____

3. HARVEST—A Checklist:

❑ Does my completed homily make the point I articulated above (*under PLANTING*)?

❑ Am I excited about this homily. Am I readily able to convey my own enthusiasm, my sincere conviction of what I am going to say?

❑ Am I ready to preach this homily? Have I rehearsed this homily out loud until:

> ❑ I am comfortable with the *flow* of this homily: I can make the *transitions* from point to point, from idea to idea, smoothly and clearly;

> ❑ I am using *words* and *expressions* that my listeners can understand and appreciate: I am not speaking in theological jargon or "holy card" talk;

> ❑ my *delivery* (voice, gestures, speaking rate, pronunciation and enunciation, pauses, etc.) and

> ❑ my *inflection* and *emphasis* of key words and phrases are natural and effective?

❑ My homily lasts _____ minutes. Is it ❑ too long? ❑ too short? ❑ just about right?

4. GLEANINGS—Thoughts and notes AFTER the Homily

What worked, what didn't work in this homily; response and reactions from the community; ideas for next time; etc.

_____
_____
_____
_____
_____
_____
_____
_____
_____
_____
_____

Ash Wednesday

The Readings:

READING 1: Joel 2: 12-18

Rend your hearts, not your garments,
and return to the Lord, your God.

In the fourth century before Christ, a terrible invasion of locusts ravaged Judah. The prophet Joel visualized this catastrophe as a symbol of the coming "Day of the Lord." The prophet summoned the people to repent, to turn to the Lord with fasting, prayer and works of charity.

READING 2: 2 Corinthians 5: 20 - 6: 2

In Christ, we might become the very holiness of God.

In his second letter to the Corinthians, Paul alternates between anger and compassion, between frustration and affection. He defends his authority and mandate as an apostle in the face of attack by some members of the Corinthian community. In this reading, Paul appeals for reconciliation among the members of the community, a return to one faith shared by the entire Church.

GOSPEL: Matthew 6: 1-6, 16-18

"Your Father who sees what is hidden will repay you."

In his Sermon on the Mount, Jesus instructs his listeners on the Christian attitude and disposition toward prayer, fasting and almsgiving.

Themes:

• Lent: a time for rebirth

During the next few weeks, the world around us is going to change dramatically. The days will grow longer and warmer. The ice and snow will melt away and the first buds of spring will appear. The winter crispness in the air will be replaced by the warmth of summer. The drab and darkness of winter will be transformed into the color and promise of spring. Likewise, the symbols of ashes and purple and somberness that mark today's liturgy will be eclipsed in six weeks by the light and flowers and Alleluias of the Easter celebration.

The change we see *around* us should also be experienced *within* us during these weeks of Lent. The very word "lent" has come down to us from the ancient Anglo-Saxon word, "lencten," meaning "springtime." Unfortunately, we tend to see Lent as something to be *endured* rather than to be observed, a time of "not doing this" and "giving up that," a time to feel lousy now in order to feel all the better on Easter Sunday. Sadly, we often approach Lent as a time for *not* doing, for *avoiding*, instead of as a time for *doing*, for *becoming*; but, like springtime, Lent should be a time for transformation, for change, for becoming the people that God has called us to be. It is a time, as the prophet Joel tells us in the first reading, for "rending our hearts and not our garments."

The ashes we are about to receive should be quiet symbols of something much deeper, much more powerful, much more lasting going on within us. In accepting these ashes we acknowledge the fact that we are sinners—that we are less than faithful to our baptismal name of Christian. But in accepting these ashes we also accept the challenge to become, as Paul wrote to the Corinthians, "the very holiness of God."

• Lent: a desert experience

The season of Lent that we begin today is a time to stop in the "busy-ness" of our everyday lives, to consider the truly important things in our lives, to realize the many blessings we possess in this world and the promised blessings of the next. Unfortunately, we have been conditioned to see Lent as a time for not doing and avoiding, instead of as a time for doing, for becoming. Lent is the season for making our lives all that the Lord intends for them to be.

Lent should be our own "desert experience," a time to peacefully and quietly renew and re-create our relationship with God, that he might become the center of our lives in every season.

• Lent: a time for transformation

In New Orleans and Quebec and many other cities around the world, this has been Mardi Gras or "Carnival" week. Carnival celebrations go back centuries before Christ. Like many customs and celebrations, the early Church "adopted" them and made them celebrations of their young faith. In fact, one of the merriest and funniest parts of Carnival makes a very important and sobering point about Lent.

The end of Carnival and the beginning of Lent are celebrated by putting "death to death." Carnival celebrants depict death as an ugly devil or a grumpy old-man winter or the "king of fools." On the last night of Carnival, this figure of death is tossed into a lake or chased into exile or reduced to ashes during a midnight bonfire. When death "dies," Carnival comes to an immediate halt. Masks are removed, greasepaint is wiped off. The past is left behind in ashes. Everything that is false or deceiving has been destroyed or exiled. The symbols of destruction are, themselves, destroyed.

The most important—and difficult—dimension of Lent is laying aside the masks we wear not only to hide from others but from ourselves as well. Lent demands painful self-honesty: to acknowledge that, yes, we are sinners; but, yes, we want to change, we want to transform our lives into becoming what God has called us to be. As we begin our pilgrimage towards Easter, may we discover the world not through the eyes of Carnival masks, but through the eyes of Easter faith.

For Reflection:

• Can the case be made that we *need* Lent?

• How can Lent be made a time for doing, for becoming?

• What is your parish doing to make this a meaningful Lent for the community?

Date: _____

HOMILY WORKSHEET for Ash Wednesday

1. SEEDS

What today's readings say *to me*: _____

_____

_____

PARABLES, STORIES and EXPERIENCES that speak to the themes of today's readings: _____

_____

_____

SPECIAL CONSIDERATIONS this week: Audience? Events in the community? Unique dimensions to this celebration?

_____

_____

_____

What RESPONSE do I seek from my listeners?
❑ to affirm/enlighten them in their faith?
❑ to teach/inform them about _____

_____

❑ to have them take a specific action _____

_____

2. PLANTING

The point I want to make in this homily (*ONE sentence*): _____

_____

_____

HOMILY OUTLINE

OPENING (*introductory STORY*): _____

_____

_____

_____

_____

_____

Point 1. APPLICATION of STORY to Scripture themes: _____

_____

_____

_____

_____

_____

Point 2. CONNECTION between Scriptural themes and the listeners' life experience: _____

_____
_____
_____
_____
_____
_____

Point 3. RESPONSE/CONSIDERATION sought from listeners: _____

_____
_____
_____
_____
_____
_____

CLOSING STATEMENT (*refers back to STORY*): _____

_____
_____
_____
_____
_____
_____

3. HARVEST—A Checklist:

❏ Does my completed homily make the point I articulated above (*under PLANTING*)?

❏ Am I excited about this homily. Am I readily able to convey my own enthusiasm, my sincere conviction of what I am going to say?

❏ Am I ready to preach this homily? Have I rehearsed this homily out loud until:

> ❏ I am comfortable with the *flow* of this homily: I can make the *transitions* from point to point, from idea to idea, smoothly and clearly;

> ❏ I am using *words* and *expressions* that my listeners can understand and appreciate: I am not speaking in theological jargon or "holy card" talk;

> ❏ my *delivery* (voice, gestures, speaking rate, pronunciation and enunciation, pauses, etc.) and

> ❏ my *inflection* and *emphasis* of key words and phrases are natural and effective?

❏ My homily lasts _____ minutes. Is it ❏ too long? ❏ too short? ❏ just about right?

4. GLEANINGS—Thoughts and notes AFTER the Homily

What worked, what didn't work in this homily; response and reactions from the community; ideas for next time; etc.

_____
_____
_____
_____
_____
_____
_____
_____
_____
_____
_____
_____

First Sunday of Lent

The Readings:

READING 1: Genesis 2: 7-9, 3: 1-7

The Lord God formed man out of clay of the ground and blew into his nostrils the breath of life, and so man became a living being.

Then the Lord God planted a garden in Eden . . . with the tree of life in the middle of the garden and the tree of knowledge of good and evil.

The Sunday Lenten journey this year begins quite literally at the beginning—the creation of humankind and the Genesis account of humankind's "fall" from grace.

There are two powerful images in this reading: First, God creates human life by "breathing life" into his new creation. On Easter night, the Risen Christ will "breathe" the life of the Holy Spirit into his new creation, the Church. The point of Genesis is that we first come to know God as the generous Creator who "breathes" his own life into us.

Consider, secondly, the image of the trees in the center of the garden—the tree of life and the tree of the knowledge of good and evil. The serpent's prophecy comes to pass: "God knows well that the moment you eat of it you will be like gods who know what is good and what is bad." Adam's imprudent apple-munching represents our free will to make choices for both good and evil. The season of Lent— the 40 days leading to the celebration of Easter, humankind's second creation—calls us to look at the values behind the choices we make.

READING 2: Romans 5: 12-19 (or 5: 12, 17-19)

Through Christ's obedience to the Father, all receive acquittal and life.

Paul's commentary in Romans on Christ as the new Adam puts the Genesis story in the new perspective of the Resurrection: God's gift of Jesus reverses the trend of sin and selfishness that humankind has known since the "first Adam," the beginning of time.

GOSPEL: Matthew 4: 1-11

Jesus is led into the desert by the Spirit to be tempted by the devil.

Jesus is confronted with choices in today's Gospel. The devil offers him comfort, wealth and power, but Jesus chooses, instead, the course that the Father has chosen for him.

Now, one has to wonder what the devil the devil is doing here. Does the devil *really* expect Jesus, the Divine Son of Satan's most despised enemy, to switch sides, just like that? Old Beelzebub is wasting some perfectly good temptations here, isn't he?

The point is that "the tempter" is a reality in human existence. God gives each one of us a great many gifts, talents and abilities: the choices we make in how we use these gifts is the mark of faith.

Themes

• Lent: making choices

The season of Lent calls us to recognize the important role that faith should play in the moral and ethical choices we make. Do the values we hold, in fact, reflect the values professed by men and women of faith?

• Lent: a time of re-creation, to make things new

Most of us grew up with the idea of "keeping a good Lent" by penance and acts of self-denial. But more in keeping with the total spirit of Lent is the idea of freeing ourselves from "business as usual" in order to focus more fully on God's presence in our lives. The season of Lent should be a "desert experience" for us—a time to renew our relationship with God, to reset our priorities and values to the things of God.

For Reflection:

• What was the most difficult choice you ever had to make? What values were behind the choice you made?

• How can the same talent or gift be used both for good and for evil, for obtaining both positive and negative results, for the benefit of another and for one's own narrow interests?

• How, in your life or in the life of the community, has a painful, destructive situation become "new" through someone's compassionate determination to "breathe life" into it and thereby transform it?

Date: _____

HOMILY WORKSHEET for the First Sunday of Lent

1. SEEDS

What today's readings say *to me*: _____

_____

_____

PARABLES, STORIES and EXPERIENCES that speak to the themes of today's readings: _____

_____

_____

SPECIAL CONSIDERATIONS this week: Audience? Events in the community? Unique dimensions to this celebration?

_____

_____

_____

What RESPONSE do I seek from my listeners?
❑ to affirm/enlighten them in their faith?
❑ to teach/inform them about _____

_____

❑ to have them take a specific action _____

_____

2. PLANTING

The point I want to make in this homily (*ONE sentence*): _____

_____

_____

HOMILY OUTLINE

OPENING (*introductory STORY*): _____

_____

_____

_____

_____

_____

Point 1. APPLICATION of STORY to Scripture themes: _____

_____

_____

_____

_____

_____

Point 2. CONNECTION between Scriptural themes and the listeners' life experience: _____

_____
_____
_____
_____
_____
_____

Point 3. RESPONSE/CONSIDERATION sought from listeners: _____

_____
_____
_____
_____
_____

CLOSING STATEMENT (*refers back to STORY*): _____

_____
_____
_____
_____
_____

3. HARVEST—A Checklist:

❏ Does my completed homily make the point I articulated above (*under PLANTING*)?

❏ Am I excited about this homily. Am I readily able to convey my own enthusiasm, my sincere conviction of what I am going to say?

❏ Am I ready to preach this homily? Have I rehearsed this homily out loud until:

    ❏ I am comfortable with the *flow* of this homily: I can make the *transitions* from point to point, from idea to idea, smoothly and clearly;

    ❏ I am using *words* and *expressions* that my listeners can understand and appreciate: I am not speaking in theological jargon or "holy card" talk;

    ❏ my *delivery* (voice, gestures, speaking rate, pronunciation and enunciation, pauses, etc.) and

    ❏ my *inflection* and *emphasis* of key words and phrases are natural and effective?

❏ My homily lasts _____ minutes. Is it ❏ too long? ❏ too short? ❏ just about right?

4. GLEANINGS—Thoughts and notes AFTER the Homily

What worked, what didn't work in this homily; response and reactions from the community; ideas for next time; etc.

_____
_____
_____
_____
_____
_____
_____
_____
_____
_____
_____
_____

Second Sunday of Lent

The Readings:

READING 1: Genesis 12: 1-4

The Lord's Covenant with Abraham:
"I will make of you a great nation . . . all communities of the earth shall find blessing in you."

At God's call, Abram (later Abraham) leaves his home for the land God will show him. He forsakes family and friends in Haran, one of the very cultured cities of the time, to create God's new nation.

READING 2: 2 Timothy 1: 8-10

God has saved us and called us to a holy life.

Paul writes to Timothy, his former companion and now administrator of the church at Ephesus. Paul encourages his friend to keep faith in the face of inevitable troubles and conflicts, for the Risen Christ is present in his teaching.

GOSPEL: Matthew 17: 1-9

Jesus is transfigured before Peter, Jesus and John.

The apostles witness the extraordinary transformation of Jesus that we know as the "Transfiguration." Matthew's account is filled with images from the Old Testament: the voice which repeats Isaiah's "Servant" proclamation, the appearances of Moses and Elijah, the dazzling white garments of Jesus. As the disciples will later understand, the Transfiguration is a powerful sign that the events ahead of them in Jerusalem are indeed the Father's will.

Themes:

• Lent: a time for transformation

The use of the Greek word "transfiguration" indicates that what the disciples saw in Jesus on Mount Tabor was a divinity that shone from *within* him. This Lenten season is a time for each of us to experience such a "transfiguration" within ourselves.

In the first reading, God reveals to Abram his plan to transform Abram's clan into the Lord's very own special nation. Our community is called to be God's own as well, to be his special possession, a sign to the world of God's constant presence.

• Lent: the God of joy and suffering

Peter's reaction to the Christ of the Transfiguration contrasts sharply with his reaction to the Christ of Good Friday. When confronted with the Christ of the cross, Peter is afraid to even acknowledge knowing him. It's easy to accept the God of joy, the God of blessing; but when that God becomes the God of suffering, the God of the poor and afflicted, we begin to hide, to rationalize, to cower from our relationship with him. Accepting God's many gifts is not a problem, but responding to the call of God to rebuild the world into his kingdom (as Abraham is called to do in Reading 1) is much more difficult. We continue this Lenten season seeking the courage and the strength to accept not only the glorified Christ but the crucified Christ as well.

For Reflection:

• Consider the many ways in which God calls individuals to do the work of the Gospel.

• Do you know of individuals who have *transformed* their part of the world, who have brought joy and hope into desperate situations by their compassion and sense of human dignity?

• Have you experienced times of great suffering or turmoil that have enriched your life, enabling you to do better things?

• Share examples of how both the Christ of the Transfiguration and the Christ of the cross are present in your community.

Date: _____

HOMILY WORKSHEET for the Second Sunday of Lent

1. SEEDS

What today's readings say *to me*: _____

_____

_____

PARABLES, STORIES and EXPERIENCES that speak to the themes of today's readings: _____

_____

_____

SPECIAL CONSIDERATIONS this week: Audience? Events in the community? Unique dimensions to this celebration?

_____

_____

_____

What RESPONSE do I seek from my listeners?
❑ to affirm/enlighten them in their faith?
❑ to teach/inform them about _____

_____

❑ to have them take a specific action _____

_____

2. PLANTING

The point I want to make in this homily (*ONE sentence*): _____

_____

_____

HOMILY OUTLINE

OPENING (*introductory STORY*): _____

_____

_____

_____

_____

_____

Point 1. APPLICATION of STORY to Scripture themes: _____

_____

_____

_____

_____

_____

Point 2. CONNECTION between Scriptural themes and the listeners' life experience: _____

_____
_____
_____
_____
_____
_____

Point 3. RESPONSE/CONSIDERATION sought from listeners: _____

_____
_____
_____
_____
_____
_____

CLOSING STATEMENT (*refers back to STORY*): _____

_____
_____
_____
_____
_____
_____

3. HARVEST—A Checklist:

❑ Does my completed homily make the point I articulated above (*under PLANTING*)?

❑ Am I excited about this homily. Am I readily able to convey my own enthusiasm, my sincere conviction of what I am going to say?

❑ Am I ready to preach this homily? Have I rehearsed this homily out loud until:

    ❑ I am comfortable with the *flow* of this homily: I can make the *transitions* from point to point, from idea to idea, smoothly and clearly;

    ❑ I am using *words* and *expressions* that my listeners can understand and appreciate: I am not speaking in theological jargon or "holy card" talk;

    ❑ my *delivery* (voice, gestures, speaking rate, pronunciation and enunciation, pauses, etc.) and

    ❑ my *inflection* and *emphasis* of key words and phrases are natural and effective?

❑ My homily lasts _____ minutes. Is it ❑ too long? ❑ too short? ❑ just about right?

4. GLEANINGS—Thoughts and notes AFTER the Homily

What worked, what didn't work in this homily; response and reactions from the community; ideas for next time; etc.

_____
_____
_____
_____
_____
_____
_____
_____
_____
_____
_____

Third Sunday of Lent

The Readings:

READING 1: Exodus 17: 3-7

Moses brings forth water from the rock of Horeb.

The great escape from Egypt doesn't seem so great to the Israelites any more. Lost in the desert and desperate for water, the Israelites are ready to stone Moses for leading them on this foolish adventure. But the Lord instructs Moses to strike the rock in Horeb to bring forth the badly-needed water.

READING 2: Romans 5: 1-2, 5-8

Through Christ we have gained access to the grace of God . . . . While we were still sinners, Christ died for us.

A bumper-sticker making the rounds not too long ago proclaimed: "Christians aren't perfect, just forgiven." Paul expresses that same sentiment in this reading from his letter to the Romans. Acknowledging the darkness of sin, Paul rejoices—"boasts"—in the forgiveness obtained for all humanity through Christ, the Perfect Reconciler.

GOSPEL: John 4: 5-42 (or 4:5-15, 19-26, 39, 40-42)

Jesus meets the Samaritan woman at Jacob's well:

"Whoever drinks the water I give will never be thirsty; the water I give shall become a fountain within (them), leaping up to provide eternal life."

Jesus' meeting of the Samaritan woman at Jacob's well illustrates the principal role of Jesus as the Messiah: to reconcile all men and women with the Father. As a Samaritan, the woman is considered an outcast by the Jews; as a known adulteress, she is an outcast in her own community. With kindness and dignity, Jesus accepts her, separating the person from the sin. This Gospel has long had a special place in baptismal catechesis: in revealing himself as the Messiah to the Samaritan woman, Jesus speaks to her of the fountain of water he will give—the life-giving waters of baptism.

Themes:

• baptism/water

Water is the predominant symbol in today's readings: God saves the desert-bound Israelites by bringing forth water from the rock at Horeb (Reading 1); Paul speaks of loved "poured out in our hearts through the Holy Spirit" (Reading 2); and at Jacob's well, Jesus promises the Samaritan woman a water that will be a "fountain. . . of eternal life" (Gospel).

Water sustains life. It also cleans away the grime and filth that can diminish and destroy life. In the waters of baptism, the sins that alienate us from God are washed away and we are reborn in the Spirit of compassion and community.

• community and reconciliation

Jesus tears down walls and breaks down barriers that divide people from one another and from God. He promises water that removes the sin that separates the woman from her neighbors; he comes to lead all people to "worship in Spirit and truth," thus removing the barrier that separates the woman from the community of Israel.

The Samaritan woman cannot contain her desire to share with her neighbors the Messiah she has met. By telling her neighbors—neighbors who, in all probability, scorned her—she becomes an agent of reconciliation within her own community of Shechem. Like her, we are called not to be a people of judgment or condemnation, but to be a people of reconciliation, reaching out to one another, sinners all; but we cannot communicate Christ to others until we have discovered him in ourselves.

The Paschal mystery begins with a recognition of sin. We confront our sinfulness and, in doing so, we realize our need for God. Think about the Samaritan woman's excited proclamation to her neighbors: "Come and see someone who told me everything I ever did! Could this not be the Messiah?" Jesus makes the woman confront her sin; but instead of feeling embarrassment or anger, she is excited and filled with joy that God accepts her just the same and forgives her. Sin is a reality in the lives of each one of us; but through Christ, forgiveness, reconciliation and rebirth, are also realities.

For Reflection:

• How have you experienced or witnessed rebirth and re-creation through forgiveness and reconciliation?

• How can our Church be a true Church of reconciliation?

• Who is/are the "Messiahs" who reach out and give hope to today's "Samaritan women"?

• Who are the "Samaritans" of our time: those considered different, out of step with the world, outcasts, who can show the rest of us the loving presence and mercy of God?

Date: _____

HOMILY WORKSHEET for the Third Sunday of Lent

1. SEEDS

What today's readings say *to me*: _____

_____

_____

PARABLES, STORIES and EXPERIENCES that speak to the themes of today's readings: _____

_____

_____

SPECIAL CONSIDERATIONS this week: Audience? Events in the community? Unique dimensions to this celebration?

_____

_____

_____

What RESPONSE do I seek from my listeners?
❏ to affirm/enlighten them in their faith?
❏ to teach/inform them about _____

_____

❏ to have them take a specific action _____

_____

2. PLANTING

The point I want to make in this homily (*ONE sentence*): _____

_____

_____

HOMILY OUTLINE

OPENING (*introductory STORY*): _____

_____

_____

_____

_____

_____

Point 1. APPLICATION of STORY to Scripture themes: _____

_____

_____

_____

_____

_____

Point 2. CONNECTION between Scriptural themes and the listeners' life experience: _____

_____
_____
_____
_____
_____

Point 3. RESPONSE/CONSIDERATION sought from listeners: _____

_____
_____
_____
_____
_____

CLOSING STATEMENT (*refers back to STORY*): _____

_____
_____
_____
_____
_____

3. HARVEST—A Checklist:

❑ Does my completed homily make the point I articulated above (*under PLANTING*)?

❑ Am I excited about this homily. Am I readily able to convey my own enthusiasm, my sincere conviction of what I am going to say?

❑ Am I ready to preach this homily? Have I rehearsed this homily out loud until:

❑ I am comfortable with the *flow* of this homily: I can make the *transitions* from point to point, from idea to idea, smoothly and clearly;

❑ I am using *words* and *expressions* that my listeners can understand and appreciate: I am not speaking in theological jargon or "holy card" talk;

❑ my *delivery* (voice, gestures, speaking rate, pronunciation and enunciation, pauses, etc.) and

❑ my *inflection* and *emphasis* of key words and phrases are natural and effective?

❑ My homily lasts _____ minutes. Is it ❑ too long? ❑ too short? ❑ just about right?

4. GLEANINGS—Thoughts and notes AFTER the Homily

What worked, what didn't work in this homily; response and reactions from the community; ideas for next time; etc.

_____
_____
_____
_____
_____
_____
_____
_____
_____
_____
_____

Fourth Sunday of Lent

The Readings:

READING 1: 1 Samuel 16: 1, 6-7, 10-13

"Not as man sees does God see, because man sees the appearance but the Lord looks into the heart."

Then Samuel, with horn of oil in hand, anointed David in the midst of his brothers.

Today's Old Testament reading recounts God's election of David as Saul's successor as king of Israel. The Lord instructs the venerable prophet Samuel to go to the family of Jesse. Samuel assumes that the older and stronger Eliab is to be the king, but God sees in the young shepherd David what people cannot see, for "the Lord looks into the heart."

READING 2: Ephesians 5: 8-14

There was a time when you were in darkness, but now you are light in the Lord.

Paul uses the image of light to describe the Christian's new life in the Risen Christ. The "darkness" of one's old life is contrasted with the illumination of baptism.

GOSPEL: John 9: 1-41 (or 9: 1, 6-9, 13-17, 34-38)

Jesus spat on the ground, made mud with his saliva, and smeared the man's eyes with mud. Then he told him, "Go, wash in the pool of Siloam." So the man went and washed, and came back able to see.

While his synoptic counterparts report on Jesus' miracles as signs of Jesus' great love and compassion, the evangelist John has another agenda. In John's Gospel, miracles emphasize some dimension of the redemptive nature of his mission as the Messiah. John's dramatic account of the healing of the man born blind challenges the spiritual myopia of Israel's leaders.

The healing of the blind beggar heightens the tension between Jesus and the Pharisees. The teaching of this itinerant Rabbi threatens the structured and exalted life of the scribes and Pharisees. They seek to discredit Jesus anyway they can—and this "miracle" gives them the opportunity. In using spittle, kneading clay and rubbing it on the man's eyes, Jesus had broken the strict rules prohibiting any kind of manual labor on the Sabbath. The miracle itself becomes secondary; the issue becomes Jesus' breaking of the Sabbath.

The inquisition of the blind man and his parents and his being cast out of the temple are important parts of the story for the evangelist and his readers—John and his community of Jewish-Christians are experiencing this same rejection by the synagogue leadership, who label them heretics for their continued preaching about Jesus.

At this point in John's Gospel, the Pharisees are so embittered against Jesus that they are prepared to do anything—even manipulate ecclesiastical procedures—to destroy Jesus.

Themes:

• conversion and renewal

The Greek philosopher Plato said: "We can easily forgive a child who is afraid of the dark; the real tragedy of life is when adults are afraid of the light."

Sometimes we have so ordered and arranged our lives that anything that disrupts or challenges that order we immediately consider evil. Change is viewed with suspicion. New ideas challenging the status quo are resisted and discredited. The AIDS epidemic, the nuclear arms race, the impact of the federal deficit on the poor, even the changes we've experienced in the Church since Vatican II incite passionate debate among people. These and other questions demand reconsideration of the deeply rooted attitudes and beliefs on which many people have based their entire lives.

The curing of the blind man demands that kind of reconsideration by the Pharisees; but Jesus has so challenged "the system"—a system that was working very well for them—that they are too afraid to be open to the joy and spirit that Jesus proclaimed. During the Lenten season, may we detach ourselves from anything that causes us to close our minds and hearts to the light and spirit of the Gospel.

• vision of faith

Our faith gives us a special way to "see" life, a special perspective that allows us to order our lives according to a higher set of values. With the eyes of faith, we should be able to see beyond appearances and superficialities and look deeper, into the heart—including our own hearts. To see the world with eyes of faith empowers us to re-create our world, to illuminate the darkness of injustice and hate with the light of justice and compassion.

For Reflection:

• Challenging institutions and traditions can be frightening and costly, but, in the long run, liberating. Share stories of people who, in challenging them, have enabled institutions to do better things.

• Looking beyond the exterior to the inner motivation of someone is a special grace. Consider times when you misunderstood the motives behind someone's action or behavior, or you were unjustly accused of having ulterior motives.

• Considering the context of the images of light and darkness, sight and blindness, in today's readings, think about situations when it is safer and more comfortable to remain in the dark.

Date: _____

HOMILY WORKSHEET for the Fourth Sunday of Lent

1. SEEDS

What today's readings say *to me*: _____

_____

_____

PARABLES, STORIES and EXPERIENCES that speak to the themes of today's readings: _____

_____

_____

SPECIAL CONSIDERATIONS this week: Audience? Events in the community? Unique dimensions to this celebration?

_____

_____

_____

What RESPONSE do I seek from my listeners?
❑ to affirm/enlighten them in their faith?
❑ to teach/inform them about _____

_____

❑ to have them take a specific action _____

_____

2. PLANTING

The point I want to make in this homily (*ONE sentence*): _____

_____

_____

HOMILY OUTLINE

OPENING (*introductory STORY*): _____

_____

_____

_____

_____

_____

Point 1. APPLICATION of STORY to Scripture themes: _____

_____

_____

_____

_____

_____

Point 2. CONNECTION between Scriptural themes and the listeners' life experience: _____

_____
_____
_____
_____
_____
_____

Point 3. RESPONSE/CONSIDERATION sought from listeners: _____

_____
_____
_____
_____
_____
_____

CLOSING STATEMENT (*refers back to STORY*): _____

_____
_____
_____
_____
_____

3. HARVEST—A Checklist:

❑ Does my completed homily make the point I articulated above (*under PLANTING*)?

❑ Am I excited about this homily. Am I readily able to convey my own enthusiasm, my sincere conviction of what I am going to say?

❑ Am I ready to preach this homily? Have I rehearsed this homily out loud until:

  ❑ I am comfortable with the *flow* of this homily: I can make the *transitions* from point to point, from idea to idea, smoothly and clearly;

  ❑ I am using *words* and *expressions* that my listeners can understand and appreciate: I am not speaking in theological jargon or "holy card" talk;

  ❑ my *delivery* (voice, gestures, speaking rate, pronunciation and enunciation, pauses, etc.) and

  ❑ my *inflection* and *emphasis* of key words and phrases are natural and effective?

❑ My homily lasts _____ minutes. Is it ❑ too long? ❑ too short? ❑ just about right?

4. GLEANINGS—Thoughts and notes AFTER the Homily

What worked, what didn't work in this homily; response and reactions from the community; ideas for next time; etc.

_____
_____
_____
_____
_____
_____
_____
_____
_____
_____
_____

Fifth Sunday of Lent

The Readings:

READING 1: Ezekiel 37: 12-14

You shall know that I am the Lord,
when I open your graves
and have you rise from them.

Ezekiel preached in Babylon to the Jews who had been banished from their homeland six centuries before Christ. This oracle is the conclusion of Ezekiel's vision of the dry bones which, at God's prophesy, come to life as an immense army. God promises that he will restore the nation of Israel like the dead rising from their graves.

READING 2: Romans 8: 8-11

If Christ is in you, the body is indeed dead because of sin, while the spirit lives because of justice.

Resurrection is also the theme in this selection from Paul's letter to the Romans. People who live according to the ways of the world are spiritually dead, but those who belong to Christ are alive in the Spirit.

GOSPEL: John 11: 1-45 (or 11: 3-7, 17, 20-27, 33-45)

"Lazarus, come out!" The dead man came out, bound hand and foot with linen strips, his face wrapped in a cloth. "Untie him," Jesus told them, "and let him go free."

As was the case in last Sunday's Gospel of the healing of the blind man, the raising of Lazarus is more than just a sign of Jesus' love and compassion. Each of the seven miracles that John includes in his Gospel ("the book of signs," as this section of John's narrative is titled) is reported by the evangelist to underscore some dimension of the redemptive nature of Jesus' work. Today's reading, the climactic sign in John's Gospel, is clearly intended to demonstrate Jesus' power over life and death. The raising of Lazarus reads like a rehearsal for the events next week's liturgies will celebrate.

Themes:

• resurrection: the Easter promise

On this last Sunday before Holy Week, the readings focus on resurrection. Today's readings are an affirmation of the promise that "the Spirit of him who raised Jesus from the dead dwells in (us)" (Reading 2) and through that Spirit we can rise from death to life. Lazarus' experience prefigures the life that Jesus, the Resurrection and the Life (who will, ironically, be put to death because, in part, of his gift of life to Lazarus), will give to all who believe in him once he has been raised from the dead.

• resurrection: rebirth of spirit

Today's readings speak not only of future resurrection, but resurrection now, in the present.

Rabbi Harold S. Kushner, in his contribution to the book, *Are You Happy?* points out that "a person who does not own his or her own time is a slave today. The person who has an income of six figures but cannot take off a morning to see a son pitch in the Little League or a daughter perform in a dance recital is a slave. That person may be a very well-paid slave, but that person doesn't own his or her own time."*

*ARE YOU HAPPY? Some Answers to the Most Important Question in Your Life, edited by Dennis Wholey (Boston: Houghton Mifflin and Company, 1986), page 13.

Many of us are trapped and held hostage by the obsessive pursuit of wealth, status or power. Jesus calls not only to Lazarus but to all of us: Come out! Go free! As Jesus called out to Lazarus to be untied from the wrappings of the dead and to be free to live once again, so we are called to be free from those things that keep us too busy from loving and being loved. This season of Lent calls us to such freedom: by embracing the Spirit of resurrection, we can bring new life and joy into our homes and communities.

• resurrection: bringing forth life

While very few of us can heal the sick or bring the dead back to life as Jesus did, there are many situations into which we can bring forth healing and resurrection. We can bring forth resurrection by spending some time with a child or an elderly relative or neighbor, by sharing what we have with someone in need, by taking the first step toward reconciliation with someone who has hurt us or by asking forgiveness of someone we have hurt. There are so many people who are awaiting resurrection—to rise from despair, cynicism and alienation to joy, hope and a sense of belonging. Such is the resurrection and healing that we can bring to our world as we await the promise of Christ's resurrection.

For Reflection:

• Do you know any stories of resurrection—people who have been "dead" (as Paul describes death in Reading 2) but have been freed from the "bindings" of death?

• How can we bring "resurrection" to our everyday lives?

• John writes that although the raising of Lazarus caused many of the Jews "to put their faith in him," the raising of Lazarus was cause for alarm among the leaders of the Jewish people. Consider the diverse and contradictory reactions people might have about the raising of Lazarus and what those reactions say about the human condition.

Date: _____

HOMILY WORKSHEET for the Fifth Sunday of Lent

1. SEEDS

What today's readings say *to me*: _____

_____

_____

PARABLES, STORIES and EXPERIENCES that speak to the themes of today's readings: _____

_____

_____

SPECIAL CONSIDERATIONS this week: Audience? Events in the community? Unique dimensions to this celebration?

_____

_____

_____

What RESPONSE do I seek from my listeners?
❑ to affirm/enlighten them in their faith?
❑ to teach/inform them about _____

_____

❑ to have them take a specific action _____

_____

2. PLANTING

The point I want to make in this homily (*ONE sentence*): _____

_____

_____

HOMILY OUTLINE

OPENING (*introductory STORY*): _____

_____

_____

_____

_____

_____

Point 1. APPLICATION of STORY to Scripture themes: _____

_____

_____

_____

_____

Point 2. CONNECTION between Scriptural themes and the listeners' life experience: _____

_____
_____
_____
_____
_____
_____

Point 3. RESPONSE/CONSIDERATION sought from listeners: _____

_____
_____
_____
_____
_____
_____

CLOSING STATEMENT (*refers back to STORY*): _____

_____
_____
_____
_____
_____

3. HARVEST—A Checklist:

❑ Does my completed homily make the point I articulated above (*under PLANTING*)?

❑ Am I excited about this homily. Am I readily able to convey my own enthusiasm, my sincere conviction of what I am going to say?

❑ Am I ready to preach this homily? Have I rehearsed this homily out loud until:

  ❑ I am comfortable with the *flow* of this homily: I can make the *transitions* from point to point, from idea to idea, smoothly and clearly;

  ❑ I am using *words* and *expressions* that my listeners can understand and appreciate: I am not speaking in theological jargon or "holy card" talk;

  ❑ my *delivery* (voice, gestures, speaking rate, pronunciation and enunciation, pauses, etc.) and

  ❑ my *inflection* and *emphasis* of key words and phrases are natural and effective?

❑ My homily lasts _____ minutes.   Is it ❑ too long? ❑ too short? ❑ just about right?

4. GLEANINGS—Thoughts and notes AFTER the Homily

What worked, what didn't work in this homily; response and reactions from the community; ideas for next time; etc.

_____
_____
_____
_____
_____
_____
_____
_____
_____
_____
_____

Passion (Palm) Sunday

The Readings:

GOSPEL during the Blessing of the Palms: Matthew 21: 1-11

The disciples went off and brought back the ass and the colt and laid their cloaks on them, and he mounted. The huge crowd began to cut branches from the trees and laid them along his path.

Matthew's account of Jesus' entry into the city of Jerusalem is framed by the prophecy of Zechariah (9: 9). The Messiah will come, not as a conquering warrior astride a noble steed, but in lowliness and peace, riding on an ass. This king is one with God's just—the poor and lowly of the world.

Jesus' entry into Jerusalem in such a public and deeply symbolic way (which is followed immediately in Matthew's text by the routing of the moneychangers from the temple) sets up the final confrontation between Jesus and the chief priests and scribes.

READING 1: Isaiah 50: 4-7

The Lord God has given me
a well-trained tongue,
That I might know how to speak to the weary
a word that will rouse them.
I gave my back to those who beat me,
my cheek to those who plucked my beard;
My face I did not shield from buffets and spitting.

This reading is taken from Deutero-Isaiah's "Servant songs," the prophet's foretelling of the "servant of God" who will come to redeem Israel. In this third song, Isaiah portrays the servant as a devoted teacher of God's word who is ridiculed and abused by those who are threatened by his teaching.

READING 2: Philippians 2: 6-11

Your attitude must be Christ's: He emptied himself and took the form of a slave, and it was thus that he humbled himself, obediently accepting even death, death on a cross!

In his letter to the Christian community at Philippi (in northeastern Greece), Paul quotes what many scholars believe is an early Christian hymn. As Christ totally and unselfishly "emptied himself" to accept crucifixion for our sakes, so we must "empty" ourselves for others.

GOSPEL: Matthew 26: 14 - 27: 66 (or 27: 11-54)

The Passion of Our Lord Jesus Christ.

As he does throughout his Gospel, Matthew frames his account of the Passion events in the context of the Old Testament prophecies concerning the Messiah. Matthew portrays a Jesus who is totally alone, abandoned by everyone, but who is finally vindicated by God (the portrait of the Messiah depicted in Isaiah and Psalm 22).

Scripture scholars believe that Matthew (and Luke) adapted their material from the evangelist Mark. Many of the details in Matthew are drawn from Mark; Matthew, however, has added a few details not found in Mark's Gospel, including the death of Judas, Pilate's washing his hands, Pilate's wife's dream and the guards placed at the tomb.

Themes:

• the faith we profess and the faith we live

There is a certain incongruity about today's Palm Sunday Liturgy. We begin with a sense of celebration—we carry palm branches and echo the hosannas of the people of Jerusalem as Jesus enters the city. But Matthew's account of the Passion confronts us with that great chasm that often exists between what we say we believe and the beliefs we actually live. We welcome the Christ of victory, the Christ of Palm Sunday; but we turn our backs on the Christ of suffering and of the poor, the Christ of Good Friday.

Rev. Raymond E. Brown writes in *A Crucified Christ in Holy Week*:

"We readers or hearers are meant to participate (in the Passion narratives) by asking ourselves how we would have stood in relation to the trial and crucifixion of Jesus. With which character in the narrative would I identify myself? The distribution of palm in church may too quickly assure me that I would have been among the crowd that hailed Jesus appreciatively. Is it not more likely that I might have been among the crowd the disciples who fled from danger, abandoning him? Or at moments in my life have I not played the role of Peter, denying Jesus, or even of Judas, betraying him? Like the Pilate (in Matthew's account), have I made a bad decision and then washed my hands so that the record could show that I was blameless? Or most likely of all, might I have not stood among the religious leaders who condemned Jesus?"*

These branches of palm serve as symbols of that incongruity that often exists between the faith we profess on our lips and the faith we profess in our lives.

• the "attitude" of Christ, the Suffering Servant

Often lost in today's dramatic liturgy with the procession and blessing of palms and the reading of Matthew's account of the Passion are the words of the second reading—Paul's letter to the Philippians. In this ancient hymn, Paul sets the theme for Holy Week quite clearly and succinctly: "Your attitude must be Christ's."

"Attitude," according to Webster: "a manner of acting, feeling or thinking that shows one's disposition, opinion or mood," as in the phrase "attitude problem": principals and teachers confront students with "attitude problems". . . a million-dollar ballplayer—who wants to become a TWO-million-dollar player—is traded to another team because he has an "attitude problem" . . . otherwise good workers are transferred or laid off because of their "attitude" . . . teenagers are quick to notice anyone who exhibits "an ATTITUDE."

To act, to feel, to think like Christ: not standing on legalisms nor demanding what is rightfully ours; emptying ourselves, becoming nothing, for the sake of others; reaching out to heal the hurt and comfort the despairing around us despite our own betrayal; carrying on, with joy and in hope, despite rejection, humiliation and suffering.

As we begin this Holy Week, let us embrace the *attitude* of Christ's compassion and total selflessness, becoming servants of God by being servants to one another.

For Reflection:

• Consider stories and examples of individuals who possessed the courage to maintain their convictions and beliefs while left abandoned and alone in the face of opposition, ridicule and popular belief.

• In what ways are we confronted with the reality of the cross?

• How is Christ's attitude, as articulated in Paul's hymn in Philippians, the antithesis to the "atitude" of today's world?

*A CRUCIFIED CHRIST IN HOLY WEEK: Essays on the Four Gospel Passion Narratives, by Raymond E. Brown (Collegeville, Minnesota: The Liturgical Press, 1986), page 11.

Date: _____

HOMILY WORKSHEET for Passion (Palm) Sunday

1. SEEDS

What today's readings say *to me*: _____

_____

_____

PARABLES, STORIES and EXPERIENCES that speak to the themes of today's readings: _____

_____

_____

SPECIAL CONSIDERATIONS this week: Audience? Events in the community? Unique dimensions to this celebration?

_____

_____

_____

What RESPONSE do I seek from my listeners?
❏ to affirm/enlighten them in their faith?
❏ to teach/inform them about _____

_____

❏ to have them take a specific action _____

_____

2. PLANTING

The point I want to make in this homily (*ONE sentence*): _____

_____

_____

HOMILY OUTLINE

OPENING (*introductory STORY*): _____

_____

_____

_____

_____

_____

Point 1. APPLICATION of STORY to Scripture themes: _____

_____

_____

_____

_____

_____

Point 2. CONNECTION between Scriptural themes and the listeners' life experience: _____

_____
_____
_____
_____
_____
_____

Point 3. RESPONSE/CONSIDERATION sought from listeners: _____

_____
_____
_____
_____
_____
_____

CLOSING STATEMENT (*refers back to STORY*): _____

_____
_____
_____
_____
_____
_____

3. HARVEST—A Checklist:

❑ Does my completed homily make the point I articulated above (*under PLANTING*)?

❑ Am I excited about this homily. Am I readily able to convey my own enthusiasm, my sincere conviction of what I am going to say?

❑ Am I ready to preach this homily? Have I rehearsed this homily out loud until:

❑ I am comfortable with the *flow* of this homily: I can make the *transitions* from point to point, from idea to idea, smoothly and clearly;

❑ I am using *words* and *expressions* that my listeners can understand and appreciate: I am not speaking in theological jargon or "holy card" talk;

❑ my *delivery* (voice, gestures, speaking rate, pronunciation and enunciation, pauses, etc.) and

❑ my *inflection* and *emphasis* of key words and phrases are natural and effective?

❑ My homily lasts _____ minutes. Is it ❑ too long? ❑ too short? ❑ just about right?

4. GLEANINGS—Thoughts and notes AFTER the Homily

What worked, what didn't work in this homily; response and reactions from the community; ideas for next time; etc.

_____
_____
_____
_____
_____
_____
_____
_____
_____
_____

Holy Thursday

The Readings:

READING 1: Exodus 12: 1-8, 11-14

This day shall be a memorial feast for you, which all your generations shall celebrate with pilgrimage to the Lord, as a perpetual institution.

Tonight's first reading outlines the origin and ritual of the feast of Passover, the Jewish celebration of God's breaking the chains of the Israelites' slavery in Egypt and leading them to their own land, establishing a covenant with them and making of them a people of his own.

READING 2: 1 Corinthians 11: 23-26

Every time you eat this bread and drink this cup, you proclaim the death of the Lord until he comes!

The deep divisions in the Corinthian community have led to abuses and misunderstandings concerning the "breaking of the bread." In addressing these problems and articulating the proper spirit in which to approach the Lord's Supper, Paul provides us with the earliest written account of the institution of the Eucharist, the Passover of the new covenant.

GOSPEL: John 13: 1-15

"If I washed your feet—
I who am Teacher and Lord—
then you must wash each other's feet.
What I have done was to give you an example;
as I have done, so you must do."

The word "Maundy" is derived from the Latin word for "commandment"—"mandatum." At the Last Supper, a Passover seder, Jesus established a new Passover to celebrate God's covenant with the new Israel. The special character of this second covenant is the "mandatum" of the washing of the feet—to love one another as we have been loved by Christ.

Themes:

• Eucharist: becoming the body of Christ

Tonight's liturgy is like a song that is a note or two out of tune or a photograph noticeably out of focus. Things are "out of sync" tonight. Jesus' last Passover seder sinks into betrayal, denial and total abandonment. The holy kiss of peace is turned inside out. While his twelve closest friends carry on a petty squabble over who is the greatest among them, Jesus gives them the gift of perfect unity, the Eucharist. With his ultimate triumph at hand, Jesus humiliates himself by taking on the foot-washing duties of the lowliest of slaves. While his betrayer sets his scheme into motion, Jesus makes the eleven others—who have little or no idea what is happening—the first priests of the new covenant.

True, we remember that this is the night on which the Lord Jesus gave us himself in the Eucharist and instituted the ministerial priesthood. But there are shadows: the joy of the Eucharist is shadowed by Christ's challenge to become Eucharist for one another; the authority and dignity of priesthood is shadowed by the stark command to "wash one another's feet" not as overseers but as servants.

We begin the Easter Triduum tonight "out of sync." As we gather to celebrate the night of the Last Supper, we confront how "out of sync," how shadowed our lives are in relation to the life to which God calls us. Let us partake of the Eucharist tonight vowing to become the body of Christ to our hurting world. Let us proclaim our faith tonight renewing our baptismal promise to become the priestly people of the new Israel, to do for others as our Teacher and Lord has done for us.

• the parable of the "Mandatum"

Tonight, the Rabbi who taught in parables teaches what is perhaps his most touching and dramatic parable.

In the middle of the meal, Jesus—the revered Teacher, the Worker of miracles and wonders, the Rabbi the crowds wanted to make a king just a few days before—suddenly rises from his place as presider, removes his robe, wraps a towel around his waist and—like the lowliest of slaves—begins to wash the feet of the Twelve. We can sense the shock that must have shot through that room. But, quietly, Jesus goes about the task . . . first one, then the next. Jesus on his knees, washing the dirt and dust off the feet of the fisherman, then the tax collector. Despite Peter's embarrassment and inability to comprehend what is happening, Jesus continues the humiliating and degrading task.

When he is finished, Jesus explains his "parable": "What I just did was to give you an example: as I have done, so you must do."

The Teacher, who revealed the wonders of God in stories about mustard seeds, fishing nets and ungrateful children, this last night of his life—as we know life—leaves his small band of disciples his most beautiful parable: As I, your Teacher and Lord, have done for you, so you must do for one another. As I have washed your feet like a slave, so you must wash the feet of each other and serve one another. As I have loved you without limit or condition, so you must love one another without limit or condition. As I am about to suffer and die for you, so you must suffer and, if necessary, die for one another.

Tonight's parable is so simple, but its lesson is so central to what being a real disciple of Christ is all about.

For Reflection:

• How can we be "Eucharist" to one another?

• In what ways can we wash the feet of others?

• Consider the ways our faith is "out of sync" with our human experience.

• Explore the range of emotions that are present both in the scene depicted in tonight's Gospel and in the elements of tonight's liturgy.

Date: _____

HOMILY WORKSHEET for Holy Thursday

1. SEEDS

What today's readings say *to me*: _____

_____

_____

PARABLES, STORIES and EXPERIENCES that speak to the themes of today's readings: _____

_____

_____

SPECIAL CONSIDERATIONS this week: Audience? Events in the community? Unique dimensions to this celebration?

_____

_____

_____

What RESPONSE do I seek from my listeners?
❏ to affirm/enlighten them in their faith?
❏ to teach/inform them about _____

_____

❏ to have them take a specific action _____

_____

2. PLANTING

The point I want to make in this homily (*ONE sentence*): _____

_____

_____

HOMILY OUTLINE

OPENING (*introductory STORY*): _____

_____

_____

_____

_____

_____

Point 1. APPLICATION of STORY to Scripture themes: _____

_____

_____

_____

_____

_____

Point 2. CONNECTION between Scriptural themes and the listeners' life experience: _____

_____
_____
_____
_____
_____

Point 3. RESPONSE/CONSIDERATION sought from listeners: _____

_____
_____
_____
_____
_____

CLOSING STATEMENT (*refers back to STORY*): _____

_____
_____
_____
_____
_____

3. HARVEST—A Checklist:

❑ Does my completed homily make the point I articulated above (*under PLANTING*)?

❑ Am I excited about this homily. Am I readily able to convey my own enthusiasm, my sincere conviction of what I am going to say?

❑ Am I ready to preach this homily? Have I rehearsed this homily out loud until:

    ❑ I am comfortable with the *flow* of this homily: I can make the *transitions* from point to point, from idea to idea, smoothly and clearly;

    ❑ I am using *words* and *expressions* that my listeners can understand and appreciate: I am not speaking in theological jargon or "holy card" talk;

    ❑ my *delivery* (voice, gestures, speaking rate, pronunciation and enunciation, pauses, etc.) and

    ❑ my *inflection* and *emphasis* of key words and phrases are natural and effective?

❑ My homily lasts _____ minutes. Is it ❑ too long? ❑ too short? ❑ just about right?

4. GLEANINGS—Thoughts and notes AFTER the Homily

What worked, what didn't work in this homily; response and reactions from the community; ideas for next time; etc.

_____
_____
_____
_____
_____
_____
_____
_____
_____
_____
_____

Good Friday

The Readings:

READING 1: Isaiah 52: 13 - 53: 12

He was pierced for our offenses,
crushed for our sins;
Like a lamb led to the slaughter
or a sheep before the shearers,
he was silent and opened not his mouth.

Isaiah's fourth and final oracle of the "servant of God" is a hauntingly accurate description of the sufferings that the innocent servant will endure to atone for the sins of his people. Only in Jesus Christ is Isaiah's prophecy perfectly fulfilled.

READING 2: Hebrews 4: 14-16; 5: 7-9

Son though he was, he learned obedience from what he suffered; and when perfected, he became the source of eternal salvation for all who obey him.

The priesthood and sacrifice of Jesus are the themes of the letter to the Hebrews (scholars are unanimous in their belief that this letter, while reflecting Pauline Christology, was not written by Paul himself). The verses taken for today's second reading acclaim Jesus, Son of God and Son of Man, as the perfect mediator between God and humankind.

GOSPEL: John 18: 1 - 19: 42

The Passion of Our Lord Jesus Christ.

John's deeply theological Gospel portrays a Jesus who is very much aware of what is happening to him. His self-assurance unnerves the high priest and intimidates Pilate ("You have no power over me"). Hanging on the cross, he entrusts his mother to his beloved disciple, thus leaving behind the core of a believing community. He did not cry out "My God, why have you forsaken me?" because the Father was always with him. His final words are words of decision and completion: "It is finished." The crucifixion of Jesus, as narrated by John, is not a tragic end but the means to victory.

Themes:

• the broken body of Christ

The broken body of Jesus—humiliated, betrayed, scourged, abused, slain—is the central image of today's liturgy. Today, Jesus teaches us through his own broken body.

As a Church, as a community of faith, we are the body of Christ. But we are a broken body. Archbishop Rembert Weakland put it this way: "We are not perfect. The Church is a broken society. We live in a community of broken people. We minister as broken people to broken people." The suffering, the alienated, the rejected, the troubled, the confused, all are part of this body—the broken body of Christ.

This is the day to reflect on the reality of pain and suffering. This is the day to realize that the source of brokenness in our world—sin—is also a reality. But the "goodness" of "Good" Friday teaches us that there are other realities. For us who believe, the broken body of Christ is forever transformed into the full and perfect life of the Risen Christ. In conquering life's injustices and difficulties, we are healed and made whole in the reality of the Resurrection.

• the tree of the cross

Actually, it is a plank hoisted up on a pole anchored into the ground, but the wood of the cross is nevertheless a life-giving tree.

The tree of Good Friday repulses us, drives us away in horror and fear and, possibly, shame. The tree that is the center of today's liturgy confronts us with death and humiliation, with the injustice and betrayal of which we are all capable.

But through the tree of the cross we are reborn. The tree of defeat becomes the tree of victory. Where life was lost, there life will be restored. The tree of Good Friday will blossom anew, bringing life, not death; bringing light that shatters centuries of darkness; bringing Paradise, not destruction.

For Reflection:

• Have you experienced, in your own life, suffering that has been, somehow, life-giving?

• How is each one of us a member of the broken body of Christ?

• Where is the crucifixion of Jesus taking place in our own time and world?

Date: _____

HOMILY WORKSHEET for Good Friday

1. SEEDS

What today's readings say *to me*: _____

_____

_____

PARABLES, STORIES and EXPERIENCES that speak to the themes of today's readings: _____

_____

_____

SPECIAL CONSIDERATIONS this week: Audience? Events in the community? Unique dimensions to this celebration?

_____

_____

_____

What RESPONSE do I seek from my listeners?
❏ to affirm/enlighten them in their faith?
❏ to teach/inform them about _____

_____

❏ to have them take a specific action _____

_____

2. PLANTING

The point I want to make in this homily (*ONE sentence*): _____

_____

_____

HOMILY OUTLINE

OPENING (*introductory STORY*): _____

_____

_____

_____

_____

_____

Point 1. APPLICATION of STORY to Scripture themes: _____

_____

_____

_____

_____

_____

Point 2. CONNECTION between Scriptural themes and the listeners' life experience: _____

_____

_____

_____

_____

_____

Point 3. RESPONSE/CONSIDERATION sought from listeners: _____

_____

_____

_____

_____

_____

CLOSING STATEMENT (*refers back to STORY*): _____

_____

_____

_____

_____

_____

3. HARVEST—A Checklist:

❑ Does my completed homily make the point I articulated above (*under PLANTING*)?

❑ Am I excited about this homily. Am I readily able to convey my own enthusiasm, my sincere conviction of what I am going to say?

❑ Am I ready to preach this homily? Have I rehearsed this homily out loud until:

   ❑ I am comfortable with the *flow* of this homily: I can make the *transitions* from point to point, from idea to idea, smoothly and clearly;

   ❑ I am using *words* and *expressions* that my listeners can understand and appreciate: I am not speaking in theological jargon or "holy card" talk;

   ❑ my *delivery* (voice, gestures, speaking rate, pronunciation and enunciation, pauses, etc.) and

   ❑ my *inflection* and *emphasis* of key words and phrases are natural and effective?

❑ My homily lasts _____ minutes. Is it ❑ too long? ❑ too short? ❑ just about right?

4. GLEANINGS—Thoughts and notes AFTER the Homily

What worked, what didn't work in this homily; response and reactions from the community; ideas for next time; etc.

_____

_____

_____

_____

_____

_____

_____

_____

_____

_____

_____

The Easter Vigil

The Readings:

OLD TESTAMENT READINGS:

1. Genesis 1: 1 - 2:2 (or 1:1, 26-31)
   God looked at everything he had made, and found it very good.

2. Genesis 22: 1-18 (or 22: 1-2, 9, 10-13, 15-18)
   "Take your son, Isaac, your only one, whom you love and go to the land of Moriah, where you shall offer him up as a holocaust."

3. Exodus 14: 15 - 15: 1
   The Israelites marched into the midst of the sea on dry land, with the water like a wall to their right and to the left.

4. Isaiah 54: 5-14
   For a brief moment I abandoned you, but with great tenderness I will take you back.

5. Isaiah 55: 1-11
   I will renew with you the everlasting covenant.

6. Baruch 3: 9-15, 32 - 4: 4
   Wisdom is the book of the precepts of God, the law that endures forever. All who cling to her will live, but those will die who forsake her.

7. Ezekiel 36: 16-28
   I will sprinkle clean water upon you to cleanse you from all your impurities. I will give you a new heart and place new spirit within you.

EPISTLE: Romans 6: 3-11

Through baptism into Christ's death we were buried with him, so that, just as Christ was raised from the dead by the glory of the Father, we too might live a new life.

GOSPEL: Matthew 28: 1-10

"Do not be frightened. I know you are looking for Jesus of the crucified, but he is not here. He has been raised, exactly as he promised."

Theme:

• new creation

Did the universe begin with a bang or a whimper? Is God the master firemaker who ignited a big bang that set creation on its journey through the cosmos? Or is God the meticulous craftsman who carefully formed one single cell—a thousandfold smaller than a single particle of dust—that contained within its microscopic walls the power to give birth to planets and stars and plants and animals—and us? The scientists among us journey to the last frontiers of thought to discover how creation began. But the point is: it began.

• The First Genesis

Nobody saw Jesus leave the tomb. Nobody saw life return to the crucified body. Nobody saw the massive stone roll away. Theories abound, scenarios have been devised to explain it away. Some say that the apostles stole the body—but could that band of hapless fishermen and peasants perpetrate such a hoax? Be serious. Maybe Jesus didn't die—maybe he revived three days later. Re-read the events of Good Friday. He didn't have a chance. Ponder the whys and hows, but you cannot escape the reality. The empty tomb. The wrappings left behind—not torn off, but remaining folded as if the body they bound simply evaporated out of them. The eyewitness accounts of his appearances to Mary, Peter, the disciples traveling to Emmaus, the Eleven. Jesus is risen.

• The Second Genesis

On this night in early spring, we celebrate God's new creation. Death is no longer the ultimate finality but the ultimate beginning. The Christ who taught forgiveness, who pleaded for reconciliation, who handed himself over to his executioners for the sake of justice and mercy, has been raised up by God. We leave behind in the grave our sinfulness, our dark side, our selfishness, our pettiness—the evil that mars God's first creation.

"Our lives . . . are filled with ambiguity and uncertainty, but they at least have a starting point. It is that Jesus died and rose, and that he is Lord. On that cornerstone all else is built," wrote our American bishops in their 1983 pastoral letter, *The Challenge of Peace.*

Tonight, we join our renewed hearts and re-createdvoices in the "Alleluia!" of the new creation.

For Reflection:

• Tonight we celebrate with symbols: fire (light), story (Scripture), water (baptism) and bread (Eucharist). What do these symbols teach us about the Paschal mystery?

• "The Lord has been raised from the dead and now goes ahead of you to Galilee, where you will see him," the angel reports. How do we "see" the Risen Lord today in our own "Galilee?"

• How would our lives be different if tonight had not happened?

Date: _____

HOMILY WORKSHEET for The Easter Vigil

1. SEEDS

What today's readings say *to me*: _____
_____
_____

PARABLES, STORIES and EXPERIENCES that speak to the themes of today's readings: _____
_____
_____

SPECIAL CONSIDERATIONS this week: Audience? Events in the community? Unique dimensions to this celebration?
_____
_____
_____

What RESPONSE do I seek from my listeners?
❑ to affirm/enlighten them in their faith?
❑ to teach/inform them about _____
_____

❑ to have them take a specific action _____
_____

2. PLANTING

The point I want to make in this homily (*ONE sentence*): _____
_____
_____

HOMILY OUTLINE

OPENING (*introductory STORY*): _____
_____
_____
_____
_____

Point 1. APPLICATION of STORY to Scripture themes: _____
_____
_____
_____
_____

Point 2. CONNECTION between Scriptural themes and the listeners' life experience: _____

_____
_____
_____
_____
_____

Point 3. RESPONSE/CONSIDERATION sought from listeners: _____

_____
_____
_____
_____
_____

CLOSING STATEMENT (*refers back to STORY*): _____

_____
_____
_____
_____
_____

3. HARVEST—A Checklist:

❑ Does my completed homily make the point I articulated above (*under PLANTING*)?

❑ Am I excited about this homily. Am I readily able to convey my own enthusiasm, my sincere conviction of what I am going to say?

❑ Am I ready to preach this homily? Have I rehearsed this homily out loud until:

    ❑ I am comfortable with the *flow* of this homily: I can make the *transitions* from point to point, from idea to idea, smoothly and clearly;

    ❑ I am using *words* and *expressions* that my listeners can understand and appreciate: I am not speaking in theological jargon or "holy card" talk;

    ❑ my *delivery* (voice, gestures, speaking rate, pronunciation and enunciation, pauses, etc.) and

    ❑ my *inflection* and *emphasis* of key words and phrases are natural and effective?

❑ My homily lasts _____ minutes. Is it ❑ too long? ❑ too short? ❑ just about right?

4. GLEANINGS—Thoughts and notes AFTER the Homily

What worked, what didn't work in this homily; response and reactions from the community; ideas for next time; etc.

_____
_____
_____
_____
_____
_____
_____
_____
_____

Easter Sunday

The Readings:

READING 1: Acts 10: 34, 37-43

Peter's sermon to Cornelius' household:

> *"They killed him finally, 'hanging him on a tree,' only to have God raise him up on the third day and grant that he be seen, not by all, but only by those witnesses as had been chosen beforehand by God—by us who ate and drank with him after he rose from the dead."*

In this sermon recorded in Luke's Acts, Peter preaches the good news of the "Christ event" to the Gentile household of Cornelius. The resurrection of Jesus is the ultimate sign of God's love for all of humankind. The apostles' mandate to preach the Gospel is about to cross into the Gentile world from the Jerusalem matrix.

READING 2: Colossians 3: 1-4

> *Since you have been raised up in company with Christ, set your heart on what pertains to higher realms where Christ is seated at God's right hand.*

The imprisoned Paul writes that because we are baptized into Christ's death and resurrection, our lives should be re-centered in new values, in the things of heaven.

OR: Corinthians 5: 6-8

> *Christ our Passover has been sacrificed. Let us celebrate not with the old yeast but with the unleavened bread of sincerity and truth.*

This is one of the earliest Easter homilies in Christian literature. The Passover custom in many Jewish households was to discard old yeast (leaven) and bake unleavened bread for the feast. For Paul, this is a fitting symbol for the Christian community at Corinth: they must rid themselves of the self-centeredness and corruption which destroys their community and, together, share "the unleavened bread of sincerity and truth."

GOSPEL: John 20: 1-9

> *While it was still dark, Mary Magdalene saw that the stone had been moved away, so she ran off to Simon Peter and the other disciple (the one Jesus loved) and told them, "The Lord has been taken from the tomb."*

John's Easter Gospel relates two episodes concerning the empty tomb: its discovery by Mary Magdalene and the race of Peter and John to get there and look inside. Notice the different reactions of the three: Mary Magdalene fears that someone has "taken" Jesus' body; Peter does not know what to make of the news; but the other disciple immediately understands what had taken place. So great are the disciple's love and depth of faith that all of the strange remarks and dark references of Jesus now become clear to him.

(NOTE: The Gospel from the Easter Vigil—Matthew 28: 1-10—may be read in place of this Gospel.)

Themes:

• Easter resurrection

The novelist John Updike, in his 1961 collection *Telephone Polls and Other Poems*, includes a piece titled "Seven Stanzas at Easter." In the poem, Updike reflects on the physical dimensions of Jesus' resurrection. For the poet, Jesus' resurrection is a real event, not a metaphysical or spiritual parable. Updike concludes the poem:

> Let us not seek to make it less monstrous,
> for our own convenience,
>   our own sense of beauty,
> lest, awakened in one unthinkable hour,
> we are embarrassed by the miracle.*

Today we stand, with Peter and John and Mary, at the entrance to the empty tomb. With them, we wonder what this means. The Christ who challenged us to love one another is risen and walks among us! All that he taught—compassion, love, forgiveness, reconciliation, sincerity, selflessness for the sake of others—is vindicated and affirmed if he is truly risen. The empty tomb should not only console us and elate us, it should challenge us to embrace the life of the Gospel. May we travel through this life with an Easter faith, not "embarrassed by the miracle" but confident of the promise of the empty tomb.

• the Resurrection community

Every summer the doctors, nurses and medical technicians who are members of "Por Christo"—"For Christ"—spend two weeks in the poorest villages of South America setting up clinics and hospitals for the poorest of the poor. *Christ is risen!*

A city councilor fights on behalf of a low income housing project, despite the fact that his support might very well cost him his seat in the next election. Asked why he puts his political career in jeopardy to support such an unpopular cause, he says simply, "They elect you to lead." *Christ is risen!*

A supermarket cashier organizes her co-workers to collect the still good but unsellable food their market discards every day to distribute to food pantries and soup kitchens for the poor. *Christ is risen!*

The empty tomb should inspire us to bring resurrection into this life of ours: to rise above life's sufferings and pain to give love and life to others, to renew and re-create our relationships with others, to proclaim the Gospel of *Christ who died, Christ who is risen, Christ who will come again.*

For Reflection:

• Have any stories in the news this week struck you as examples of resurrection in our own time—of bringing hope, new life, new possibilities to formerly dark, hopeless places?

• How is the good news of the Risen Jesus proclaimed in the actions of people around you? Where is the Risen Lord present among us?

• So, was it a good Lent?

*"Seven Stanzas at Easter" by John Updike. Copyright 1961 by John Updike. Reprinted from *Telephone Polls* by John Updike, by permission of Random House, Inc.

Date: _____

HOMILY WORKSHEET for Easter Sunday

1. SEEDS

What today's readings say *to me*: _____

_____

_____

PARABLES, STORIES and EXPERIENCES that speak to the themes of today's readings: _____

_____

_____

SPECIAL CONSIDERATIONS this week: Audience? Events in the community? Unique dimensions to this celebration?

_____

_____

_____

What RESPONSE do I seek from my listeners?
❑ to affirm/enlighten them in their faith?
❑ to teach/inform them about _____

_____

❑ to have them take a specific action _____

_____

2. PLANTING

The point I want to make in this homily (*ONE sentence*): _____

_____

_____

HOMILY OUTLINE

OPENING (*introductory STORY*): _____

_____

_____

_____

_____

_____

Point 1. APPLICATION of STORY to Scripture themes: _____

_____

_____

_____

_____

_____

Point 2. CONNECTION between Scriptural themes and the listeners' life experience: _____

_____
_____
_____
_____
_____

Point 3. RESPONSE/CONSIDERATION sought from listeners: _____

_____
_____
_____
_____
_____

CLOSING STATEMENT (*refers back to STORY*): _____

_____
_____
_____
_____
_____

3. HARVEST—A Checklist:

❑ Does my completed homily make the point I articulated above (*under PLANTING*)?

❑ Am I excited about this homily. Am I readily able to convey my own enthusiasm, my sincere conviction of what I am going to say?

❑ Am I ready to preach this homily? Have I rehearsed this homily out loud until:

> ❑ I am comfortable with the *flow* of this homily: I can make the *transitions* from point to point, from idea to idea, smoothly and clearly;

> ❑ I am using *words* and *expressions* that my listeners can understand and appreciate: I am not speaking in theological jargon or "holy card" talk;

> ❑ my *delivery* (voice, gestures, speaking rate, pronunciation and enunciation, pauses, etc.) and

> ❑ my *inflection* and *emphasis* of key words and phrases are natural and effective?

❑ My homily lasts _____ minutes. Is it ❑ too long? ❑ too short? ❑ just about right?

4. GLEANINGS—Thoughts and notes AFTER the Homily

What worked, what didn't work in this homily; response and reactions from the community; ideas for next time; etc.

_____
_____
_____
_____
_____
_____
_____
_____
_____
_____
_____

Second Sunday of Easter

The Readings:

READING 1: Acts 2: 42-47

The brethren devoted themselves to the apostles' instruction and the communal life, to the breaking of bread and the prayers.

The first reading on all the Sundays of the Easter season is taken from Luke's Acts of the Apostles. Acts has been called the "Gospel of the Holy Spirit" because it recounts how the Spirit of God was at work forming from this small group on the fringes of Judaism a new Israel, the Church of the Risen Christ. In today's reading, Luke presents an idealized picture of the first Christian community in Jerusalem—the first parish. Instruction, sharing, Eucharist and prayer were the hallmarks of this first church.

READING 2: 1 Peter 1: 3-9

Praised be the God and Father of our Lord Jesus Christ,
he who in his great mercy gave us a new birth;
a birth unto hope which draws its life
from the resurrection of Jesus Christ from the dead.

On Sundays during this (cycle A) Easter season the second reading will be taken from the first letter attributed to Peter (although the letters were probably written by Silvanus, a companion of Paul's). The letter, addressed to converts from paganism and the predominantly Gentile Christian communities of Asia Minor, is a collection of exhortations, especially on faithfulness in the midst of persecution and suffering. It presents a beautiful catechesis on the Paschal dimensions of baptism.

Today's reading is a prayer of thanksgiving that outlines the major themes of Peter's message: God has given us a new birth in the resurrection of Jesus, which leads to a "heavenly inheritance" incapable of fading, despite the trials and persecutions of the world.

GOSPEL: John 20: 19-31

On the evening of that first day of the week, Jesus came and stood before them.
"Peace be with you," he said. It happened that one of the Twelve, Thomas (the name means
"Twin") was absent when Jesus came.

This is "Act Two" of John's Easter Gospel. In Jesus' breathing on the disciples, John clearly has the Genesis story of creation in mind: as God created man and woman by breathing life into them (Genesis 2:7), the Risen Lord re-creates humankind by breathing the Holy Spirit upon the apostles.

His fellow apostles' wondrous news makes no impact on Thomas. Only when he sees the Risen Jesus himself does he profess the faith of every Christian since, "My Lord and my God."

Themes:

• Easter faith: optimism/hope

Someone once said that a skeptic is someone who would ask God for an I.D. card. If that's the case, then Thomas is the premier skeptic in the Gospel. When Jesus announces that he is going to Lazarus' tomb, Thomas regards the trip as foolish (John 11: 16). Later in the Gospel, Thomas is not afraid to ask Jesus where this trip to Jerusalem is heading (John 14: 5). And, as we hear today, Thomas is not buying this outrageous story the others are telling him about seeing Jesus, who was very dead three days ago.

But the Easter event manages to melt even the skepticism of Thomas, so that Thomas articulates what is perhaps the most magnificent act of faith in the entire New Testament.

God bless skeptics—they help keep the rest of us honest. But skepticism can be tragically destructive, shutting us out from hope, from rebuilding our lives, from both forgiveness and forgiving. May the Easter event transform our skepticism into optimism and our despair into hope, so that we may experience and share resurrection with one another.

• the parish community: witness to the Resurrection

In today's Gospel, the disciples experience as a community the presence of the Risen Christ. The evangelist notes that Jesus "breathed" his spirit into them: Peace. As the Father has sent me, so do I send you. The first Christian community—the first parish—is formed. We trace our roots as a parish community to that Easter night.

Luke provides, in today's second reading, a "snapshot" of the first post-Pentecost community. Note the verbs Luke uses to describe the community: *devoted* themselves to the apostles' instruction . . . *shared* all things. . . *broke* bread . . . *praised* God . . . *won* the approval of all the people. To be a community of the Risen Christ means to center our lives, both as individuals and as a community, in the Word of God, in sharing what we have with others, in sacrament and in prayer.

For Reflection:

• Have you or someone you know ever experienced skepticism and despair so destructive that it almost destroyed you or that person? How was that skepticism transformed into hope, into belief?

• In what ways is your parish community like Luke's community in Acts?

• Imagine the Risen Christ appeared in our midst today. What would he say to us about our community?

Date: _____

HOMILY WORKSHEET for the First Sunday of Advent

1. SEEDS

What today's readings say *to me*: _____

_____

_____

PARABLES, STORIES and EXPERIENCES that speak to the themes of today's readings: _____

_____

_____

SPECIAL CONSIDERATIONS this week: Audience? Events in the community? Unique dimensions to this celebration?

_____

_____

_____

What RESPONSE do I seek from my listeners?

☐ to affirm/enlighten them in their faith?

☐ to teach/inform them about _____

_____

☐ to have them take a specific action _____

_____

2. PLANTING

The point I want to make in this homily (*ONE sentence*): _____

_____

_____

HOMILY OUTLINE

OPENING (*introductory STORY*): _____

_____

_____

_____

_____

_____

Point 1. APPLICATION of STORY to Scripture themes: _____

_____

_____

_____

_____

_____

Point 2. CONNECTION between Scriptural themes and the listeners' life experience: _____
_____
_____
_____
_____
_____
_____

Point 3. RESPONSE/CONSIDERATION sought from listeners: _____
_____
_____
_____
_____
_____
_____

CLOSING STATEMENT (*refers back to STORY*): _____
_____
_____
_____
_____
_____
_____

3. HARVEST—A Checklist:

❑ Does my completed homily make the point I articulated above (*under PLANTING*)?

❑ Am I excited about this homily. Am I readily able to convey my own enthusiasm, my sincere conviction of what I am going to say?

❑ Am I ready to preach this homily? Have I rehearsed this homily out loud until:

> ❑ I am comfortable with the *flow* of this homily: I can make the *transitions* from point to point, from idea to idea, smoothly and clearly;

> ❑ I am using *words* and *expressions* that my listeners can understand and appreciate: I am not speaking in theological jargon or "holy card" talk;

> ❑ my *delivery* (voice, gestures, speaking rate, pronunciation and enunciation, pauses, etc.) and

> ❑ my *inflection* and *emphasis* of key words and phrases are natural and effective?

❑ My homily lasts _____ minutes. Is it ❑ too long? ❑ too short? ❑ just about right?

4. GLEANINGS—Thoughts and notes AFTER the Homily

What worked, what didn't work in this homily; response and reactions from the community; ideas for next time; etc.

_____
_____
_____
_____
_____
_____
_____
_____
_____
_____
_____
_____

Third Sunday of Easter

The Readings:

READING 1: Acts 2: 14, 22-28

Peter's Pentecost sermon:

"God freed Jesus from death's bitter pangs and raised him up again, for it was impossible that death should keep its hold on him.

Today's reading from Acts is Peter's Pentecost sermon in which the apostle preaches that the Old Testament prophecies of a Messiah who will descend from David are fulfilled in Christ Jesus. Peter cites Psalm 16 (today's responsorial psalm) as David's own prophesy of the Messiah's resurrection.

READING 2: 1 Peter 1: 17-21

Conduct yourselves reverently during your sojourn in a strange land. You were delivered from the futile way of life your fathers handed on to you by Christ's blood beyond all price.

Delivered by God from the "futile ways" of their ancestors, the Gentile converts of Asia Minor are expected to be out of step with their former pagan culture ("your sojourn in a strange land"). Peter writes that they are to live lives "spotless and unblemished" like the Lamb who redeemed them.

GOSPEL: Luke 24: 13-35

The two disciples recognize him in the breaking of the bread.

It is three days after Good Friday. Having just completed the observance of the Passover Sabbath, two disciples of Jesus (one identified as Cleophas) are making the seven-mile trip to the village of Emmaus. By identifying them as disciples, Luke is emphasizing that these two were more than disinterested observers of the events of Holy Week.

Luke writes that their exchange was "lively"—we can well imagine! As well as anger at the great travesty of justice that had taken place, they must have felt emotionally shattered by what had befallen Jesus. He was their hope—and now he was gone. The two are suddenly joined by a stranger who asks the subject of their "lively" conversation. The stranger then explains, to their astonishment, the why of each of the events of the past week. When they reach the village, the two disciples ask the stranger to stay with them. And, in the words from Luke's Gospel that we have come to treasure, the two disciples "come to know (the Risen Christ) in the breaking of the bread."

Themes:

• Eucharist: "bread blessed and broken"

Luke's Easter night story parallels our own experience of the Eucharist. Sometimes we come to the Lord's table feeling angry, hurt, despairing, alone. But at this table, coming to "know him in the breaking of the bread," we can experience the peace and presence of the Risen Christ.

• Christian Community: bound by Christ's memory

It has been said that true friendship begins when people share a memory. The joy of friendship comes to life when one can say to another, "Do you remember the time when . . .?" The first Christian communities were bound together by the apostles' memories of Jesus, like the story we read in today's Gospel and the *kerygma* ("proclamation") of Peter in Acts. When we gather to celebrate the Eucharist, we too, are bound as a community by the same memory of Jesus.

For Reflection:

• How is this place (this altar, this church) a place of peace, of hope, of healing?

• What memories bind you as a parish community?

• Put yourself in the place of the two disciples in today's Gospel. What do you think they were saying and feeling? Can you identify with those emotions?

Date: _____

HOMILY WORKSHEET for the Third Sunday of Easter

1. SEEDS

What today's readings say *to me*: _____

_____
_____

PARABLES, STORIES and EXPERIENCES that speak to the themes of today's readings: _____

_____
_____

SPECIAL CONSIDERATIONS this week: Audience? Events in the community? Unique dimensions to this celebration?

_____
_____
_____

What RESPONSE do I seek from my listeners?
❑ to affirm/enlighten them in their faith?
❑ to teach/inform them about _____

_____

❑ to have them take a specific action _____

_____

2. PLANTING

The point I want to make in this homily (*ONE sentence*): _____

_____
_____

HOMILY OUTLINE

OPENING (*introductory STORY*): _____

_____
_____
_____
_____
_____

Point 1. APPLICATION of STORY to Scripture themes: _____

_____
_____
_____
_____
_____

Point 2. CONNECTION between Scriptural themes and the listeners' life experience: _____

_____
_____
_____
_____
_____
_____

Point 3. RESPONSE/CONSIDERATION sought from listeners: _____

_____
_____
_____
_____
_____
_____

CLOSING STATEMENT (*refers back to STORY*): _____

_____
_____
_____
_____
_____

3. HARVEST—A Checklist:

❑ Does my completed homily make the point I articulated above (*under PLANTING*)?

❑ Am I excited about this homily. Am I readily able to convey my own enthusiasm, my sincere conviction of what I am going to say?

❑ Am I ready to preach this homily? Have I rehearsed this homily out loud until:

   ❑ I am comfortable with the *flow* of this homily: I can make the *transitions* from point to point, from idea to idea, smoothly and clearly;

   ❑ I am using *words* and *expressions* that my listeners can understand and appreciate: I am not speaking in theological jargon or "holy card" talk;

   ❑ my *delivery* (voice, gestures, speaking rate, pronunciation and enunciation, pauses, etc.) and

   ❑ my *inflection* and *emphasis* of key words and phrases are natural and effective?

❑ My homily lasts _____ minutes. Is it ❑ too long? ❑ too short? ❑ just about right?

4. GLEANINGS—Thoughts and notes AFTER the Homily

What worked, what didn't work in this homily; response and reactions from the community; ideas for next time; etc.

_____
_____
_____
_____
_____
_____
_____
_____
_____
_____
_____

Fourth Sunday of Easter

The Readings:

READING 1: Acts 2: 14, 36-41

Peter's Pentecost sermon:

"You must reform and be baptized, each one of you, in the name of Jesus Christ, that your sins may be forgiven."

The reaction to Peter's Pentecost sermon parallels the response to John the Baptist's exhortation in Luke's Gospel (Luke 3: 10-11). Whereas John spoke of a baptism of Spirit to come, Peter proclaims that it is now a reality.

Luke describes salvation both in terms of community and individual commitment. Each person has to accept his/her call to salvation. But salvation never remains a private matter between the individual and God; rather, one is baptized into God's people ("added") and saved as a member of the Church.

READING 2: 1 Peter 2: 20-25

Christ suffered for you in just this way and left you an example.

Peter's words are addressed especially to slaves. Suffering is a bitter fact of the slave's life, but Peter attempts to give them hope by interpreting their experience in light of the suffering Christ. In verses 22-24, Peter repeats Isaiah's Song of the Servant (Isaiah 53: 1-12, Reading 1 for Good Friday): Christ was truly innocent, there was no justification for what he was forced to endure, but he endured it all for the sake of humankind. So Christians—even slaves—are called to imitate Christ. Peter uses the image of the shepherd to describe Christ's work of redemption ("the guardian of your souls").

GOSPEL: John 10: 1-10

"I am the sheepgate. All who came before me were thieves and marauders . . . I am the gate. Whoever enters through me will be safe. I came that they might have life and have it to the full."

Chapter 10 of John's Gospel is the "Good Shepherd" discourse. In today's Gospel reading, two kinds of sheepfolds or corrals are mentioned. In the community or town sheepfold, the real shepherd was recognized by the gatekeeper and his flock knew his voice and followed. Out in fields, the shepherd slept across the corral opening—his body became the corral opening. Both gates are beautiful images of the Redeeming Christ.

There is another important dimension to this discourse. John places these words of Jesus right after the curing of the man born blind (the Gospel read a few weeks ago on the Fourth Sunday of Lent). The evangelist uses these references about shepherds, sheep and sheepgates to underline the miserable job of "shepherding" being done by the Pharisees and the temple authorities as in the case of the blind man. John is writing in the spirit of the prophet Ezekiel (34): God will raise up a new shepherd to replace the irresponsible and thieving shepherds who feed themselves at the expense of the flock.

Themes:

• leadership

Today's Gospel is a lesson in leadership. To be a "shepherd" in the spirit of the Gospel means to stand up to the "thieves and marauders" who come "only to steal and slaughter and destroy." To truly imitate Christ demands both courage and selflessness.

• the hard demands of the gospel

The ancients told a story about Euclid, the great mathematician of the third century before Christ. Euclid was engaged by the royal family to tutor their young heir. Patiently, Euclid explained each step in proving the first few geometric theorems, but the prince was having a great deal of trouble following the process. In frustration, the prince burst out, "Is there no simple way you can get to the point? Surely the crown prince need not be expected to concern himself with such minutiae!" Euclid quietly but firmly replied to his royal student, "Sire, there is no royal road to learning."

Sometimes we look at the Gospel from our modern, sophisticated perspective and quietly dismiss what Jesus says as too unrealistic or too simplistic to deal with the complex problems we must face. We are too involved in finding high-tech answers to high-tech problems to be concerned with such "minutiae" like love for one another, forgiveness, compassion and justice. But, to paraphrase Euclid, there is no high-tech, comfortable, convenient road to living the Gospel. The Risen Christ is the only "gate" through which we can have life to the fullest.

For Reflection:

• Share stories about individuals who are true "shepherds"—leaders in the spirit of the Good Shepherd.

• What trends do you see in society today as running counter to the Gospel demands of selfless and compassionate giving to others?

• How do you reconcile the *personal* and the *communal* dimensions of faith?

Date: _____

HOMILY WORKSHEET for the Fourth Sunday of Easter

1. SEEDS

What today's readings say *to me*: _____

_____

_____

PARABLES, STORIES and EXPERIENCES that speak to the themes of today's readings: _____

_____

_____

SPECIAL CONSIDERATIONS this week: Audience? Events in the community? Unique dimensions to this celebration?

_____

_____

_____

What RESPONSE do I seek from my listeners?
❑ to affirm/enlighten them in their faith?
❑ to teach/inform them about _____

_____

❑ to have them take a specific action _____

_____

2. PLANTING

The point I want to make in this homily (*ONE sentence*): _____

_____

_____

HOMILY OUTLINE

OPENING (*introductory STORY*): _____

_____

_____

_____

_____

_____

Point 1. APPLICATION of STORY to Scripture themes: _____

_____

_____

_____

_____

Point 2. CONNECTION between Scriptural themes and the listeners' life experience: _____

_____

_____

_____

_____

_____

Point 3. RESPONSE/CONSIDERATION sought from listeners: _____

_____

_____

_____

_____

_____

CLOSING STATEMENT (*refers back to STORY*): _____

_____

_____

_____

_____

_____

3. HARVEST—A Checklist:

❑ Does my completed homily make the point I articulated above (*under PLANTING*)?

❑ Am I excited about this homily. Am I readily able to convey my own enthusiasm, my sincere conviction of what I am going to say?

❑ Am I ready to preach this homily? Have I rehearsed this homily out loud until:

> ❑ I am comfortable with the *flow* of this homily: I can make the *transitions* from point to point, from idea to idea, smoothly and clearly;

> ❑ I am using *words* and *expressions* that my listeners can understand and appreciate: I am not speaking in theological jargon or "holy card" talk;

> ❑ my *delivery* (voice, gestures, speaking rate, pronunciation and enunciation, pauses, etc.) and

> ❑ my *inflection* and *emphasis* of key words and phrases are natural and effective?

❑ My homily lasts _____ minutes.   Is it ❑ too long? ❑ too short? ❑ just about right?

4. GLEANINGS—Thoughts and notes AFTER the Homily

What worked, what didn't work in this homily; response and reactions from the community; ideas for next time; etc.

_____

_____

_____

_____

_____

_____

_____

_____

_____

_____

Fifth Sunday of Easter

The Readings:

READING 1: Acts 6: 1-7

"Look around among your own number for seven men acknowledged to be deeply spiritual and prudent, and we shall appoint them to this task."

The ordination of the first seven deacons is a watershed for the young Church: leadership is now being passed on to a new kind and generation of minister. The community recognizes that it is growing beyond just the Hebrew-speaking to include the Greek-speaking Christians. This is especially significant because Greek was one of the major world languages at the time.

The numbers twelve and seven are important symbols of the nature of the Church: the apostles, twelve in number like the tribes of Israel, are the leaders of the new Israel; the seven deacons (the same in number as the world's seas) are signs of the Church's outreach to the whole world.

READING 2: 1 Peter 2: 4-9

Come to the Lord, a living stone . . . you too are living stones, built as an edifice of spirit, into a holy priesthood.

Peter continues his baptismal catechesis, using the Old Testament images of the rejected stone and nationhood (community) to explain to new Christians the nature of their membership in the Church. To those who do not believe, Jesus is "a stumbling block" and an "obstacle," while for the faithful, Jesus is the "cornerstone." Baptized into Christ's death and resurrection, we too are living stones and share in the priesthood of the new covenant.

GOSPEL: John 14: 1-12

"I am indeed going to prepare a place for you."

The scene is the Last Supper. John's account of that night is the longest in the Gospels—five chapters in length (but with no account of the institution of the Eucharist). The evangelist uses a literary device common in Scripture: a leader (Moses, Joshua, David and Tobit) gathers his own (family, friends, disciples) to announce his imminent departure, offer advice and insight into the future and give final instructions.

At the time John is writing his Gospel, Christians are being harassed by both the Jews and the Romans. Proclaiming the crucified Jesus as the Messiah is blasphemy to Judaism, while accusing the Romans of judicial murder in the death of Jesus threatened the new faith's chances of survival as a "lawful religion" tolerated by their Roman occupiers.

The dominant themes here are consolation and encouragement: be faithful, remember and live what I have taught you, for better days are ahead for you.

Themes:

• the Church: the people of God

Our Church is not a passive social grouping or a cherished old museum piece; our Church, our parishes, should be living, active communities of faith. In working for reconciliation among peoples, in caring for one another, in bringing the values of the Gospel to our homes and workplaces, we exercise our "priesthood," we give witness to the Risen Christ, the "cornerstone" of our "edifice of spirit."

• Christ's revelation of the Father

To the Greeks of two millennia ago, God was "the Invisible." To Jews, it was an article of faith that no one had ever seen God. But we Christians have seen God, living our life: God has become real to us in the person of Jesus.

• our return "home"

A visitor traveled many days and many miles to meet the great Polish rabbi and teacher Hafez Hayyim. The visitor was astonished to see that the rabbi's home was only a simple room filled with books. The only furniture was a table and a bench.

> "Rabbi, where is your furniture?" the visitor asked.
> "Where is *your* furniture?" the rabbi asked in reply.
> "Mine? I'm only a visitor here."
> "So am I," said the rabbi.

Seldom do we think of death as a return home, but today's Gospel image of the "house with many dwelling places" helps us to realize that we were created for a life beyond this one—we were created by God for life in and with him. The Risen Jesus is the way to our return "home" to the Father.

For Reflection:

• How does Jesus' image of " many dwelling places" alter or change our childhood image of heaven?

• How is God, as revealed to us by Jesus, "real" to us today?

• Consider ways your parish is or should be an "edifice of spirit."

• What does the story of the first seven deacons teach today's parish communities about ministry?

Date: _____

HOMILY WORKSHEET for the Fifth Sunday of Easter

1. SEEDS

What today's readings say *to me*: _____

_____

_____

PARABLES, STORIES and EXPERIENCES that speak to the themes of today's readings: _____

_____

_____

SPECIAL CONSIDERATIONS this week: Audience? Events in the community? Unique dimensions to this celebration?

_____

_____

_____

What RESPONSE do I seek from my listeners?
❑ to affirm/enlighten them in their faith?
❑ to teach/inform them about _____

_____

❑ to have them take a specific action _____

_____

2. PLANTING

The point I want to make in this homily (*ONE sentence*): _____

_____

_____

HOMILY OUTLINE

OPENING (*introductory STORY*): _____

_____

_____

_____

_____

_____

Point 1. APPLICATION of STORY to Scripture themes: _____

_____

_____

_____

_____

_____

Point 2. CONNECTION between Scriptural themes and the listeners' life experience: _____
_____
_____
_____
_____
_____
_____

Point 3. RESPONSE/CONSIDERATION sought from listeners: _____
_____
_____
_____
_____
_____
_____

CLOSING STATEMENT (*refers back to STORY*): _____
_____
_____
_____
_____
_____
_____

3. HARVEST—A Checklist:

❑ Does my completed homily make the point I articulated above (*under PLANTING*)?

❑ Am I excited about this homily. Am I readily able to convey my own enthusiasm, my sincere conviction of what I am going to say?

❑ Am I ready to preach this homily? Have I rehearsed this homily out loud until:

   ❑ I am comfortable with the *flow* of this homily: I can make the *transitions* from point to point, from idea to idea, smoothly and clearly;

   ❑ I am using *words* and *expressions* that my listeners can understand and appreciate: I am not speaking in theological jargon or "holy card" talk;

   ❑ my *delivery* (voice, gestures, speaking rate, pronunciation and enunciation, pauses, etc.) and

   ❑ my *inflection* and *emphasis* of key words and phrases are natural and effective?

❑ My homily lasts _____ minutes. Is it ❑ too long? ❑ too short? ❑ just about right?

4. GLEANINGS—Thoughts and notes AFTER the Homily

What worked, what didn't work in this homily; response and reactions from the community; ideas for next time; etc.

_____
_____
_____
_____
_____
_____
_____
_____
_____
_____
_____
_____

Sixth Sunday of Easter

The Readings:

READING 1: Acts 8: 5-8, 14-17

Philip went down to the town of Samaria and there proclaimed the Messiah. When the apostles in Jerusalem had heard that Samaria had accepted the word of God, they sent Peter and John, who prayed that they might receive the Holy Spirit.

The universal mission of the Church takes its first steps outside of the Jewish world. Philip the deacon ("ordained" in last week's first reading) goes to Samaria, where his preaching about Jesus the Messiah is enthusiastically received. This was an unlikely and unexpected place for such a beginning: the Samaritans, remember, were the despised outcasts of Judaism. The acceptance of the Samaritans as equals in the Christian community was suspect by many of the Jewish members of the Church.

READING 2: 1 Peter 3: 15-18

Should anyone ask you the reason for this hope of yours, be ever ready to reply. Keep your conscience clear so that, whenever you are defamed, those who libel your way of life in Christ may be disappointed.

Peter tells his readers, many of whom are slaves, that the best witness to Christ is an honest and holy life that refutes defamation and libel by its clear and evident goodness.

GOSPEL: John 14: 15-21

"I will ask the Father
and he will give you another Paraclete—
to be with you always:
the Spirit of truth,
whom the world cannot accept,
but you can recognize him
because he remains with you
and will be within you."

A "paraclete" (from the Greek "parakletos," meaning "beside" and "to call") is one who intervenes and intercedes in favor of what is right or good. In legal terminology, a paraclete is an advocate who defends the accused on trial. For John, Christ is the first "Paraclete," who comes to liberate humanity from the slavery of sin. The second "Paraclete," promised by Jesus, is the Spirit of truth, who will live in the hearts of the faithful as they proclaim Jesus to the world despite great skepticism and rejection.

Themes:

• the Paraclete: faith perspective

Jesus acknowledges in his farewell to his disciples that their witness to him will be costly. He promises to send, from the Father, a paraclete who will stand by them (and us) during the difficult times ahead. The Paraclete, the Spirit within them, inspires them to forge ahead, as Philip does in his ministry to the hated Samaritans. The Paraclete advocates within us what is good, what is right and what is just, despite the skepticism and rejection of those who are blind to what is good.

The bishops of the United States wrote in their 1986 pastoral, *Economic Justice for All*: "After Jesus had appeared to them and when they received the gift of the Spirit, they became apostles of the good news to the ends of the earth. In the face of poverty and persecution they transformed human lives and formed communities which became signs of the power and presence of God. Sharing this same resurrect ion faith, contemporary followers of Christ can face the struggles and challenges that await those who bring the Gospel vision to bear on our complex economic world."

• "difficult" love

In his Gospel, John never allows love, as taught by Jesus, to remain at the level of sentiment or emotion. Its expression is always highly moral and is revealed in obedience to the will of the Father. To love as Jesus loved—in total and selfless obedience, without conditions and without expectation of that love ever being returned—is the "difficult" love that Jesus expects of those who claim to be his disciples. The world might say that only fools love like that, but such "difficult" love is the recognition of the Spirit of truth. In dying to our own interests we can become fully alive, fully human in the image of the Risen Christ.

For Reflection:

• In today's reading from Acts, Peter and John "impose hands on (the Samaritans) and they received the Holy Spirit." Recall your own confirmation, however many years ago. What images of that ceremony come to mind as you consider today's readings?

• Share an experience of "difficult love," when loving someone was painful or hard to do, or when following the instincts of the "Spirit" was met with opposition.

Date: _____

HOMILY WORKSHEET for the Sixth Sunday of Easter

1. SEEDS

What today's readings say *to me*: _____

_____

_____

PARABLES, STORIES and EXPERIENCES that speak to the themes of today's readings: _____

_____

_____

SPECIAL CONSIDERATIONS this week: Audience? Events in the community? Unique dimensions to this celebration?

_____

_____

_____

What RESPONSE do I seek from my listeners?
❑ to affirm/enlighten them in their faith?
❑ to teach/inform them about _____

_____

❑ to have them take a specific action _____

_____

2. PLANTING

The point I want to make in this homily (*ONE sentence*): _____

_____

_____

HOMILY OUTLINE

OPENING (*introductory STORY*): _____

_____

_____

_____

_____

_____

Point 1. APPLICATION of STORY to Scripture themes: _____

_____

_____

_____

_____

_____

Point 2. CONNECTION between Scriptural themes and the listeners' life experience: _____

_____
_____
_____
_____
_____

Point 3. RESPONSE/CONSIDERATION sought from listeners: _____

_____
_____
_____
_____
_____

CLOSING STATEMENT (*refers back to STORY*): _____

_____
_____
_____
_____
_____

3. HARVEST—A Checklist:

❑ Does my completed homily make the point I articulated above (*under PLANTING*)?

❑ Am I excited about this homily. Am I readily able to convey my own enthusiasm, my sincere conviction of what I am going to say?

❑ Am I ready to preach this homily? Have I rehearsed this homily out loud until:

  ❑ I am comfortable with the *flow* of this homily: I can make the *transitions* from point to point, from idea to idea, smoothly and clearly;

  ❑ I am using *words* and *expressions* that my listeners can understand and appreciate: I am not speaking in theological jargon or "holy card" talk;

  ❑ my *delivery* (voice, gestures, speaking rate, pronunciation and enunciation, pauses, etc.) and

  ❑ my *inflection* and *emphasis* of key words and phrases are natural and effective?

❑ My homily lasts _____ minutes. Is it ❑ too long? ❑ too short? ❑ just about right?

4. GLEANINGS—Thoughts and notes AFTER the Homily

What worked, what didn't work in this homily; response and reactions from the community; ideas for next time; etc.

_____
_____
_____
_____
_____
_____
_____
_____
_____
_____
_____

Solemnity of the Ascension

The Readings:

READING 1: Acts 1: 1-11

"You are to be my witnesses in Jerusalem, throughout Judea and Samaria, yes, even to the ends of the earth."

In his account of Jesus' return to the Father, Luke considers the time that the Risen Lord spent with his disciples especially important, expressing that interval in terms of the sacred number 40—like Moses' 40 years and Jesus' 40 days in the desert, their time with the Risen Lord is a "desert experience" for the apostles, to prepare them for their new ministry of preaching the Risen Christ.

READING 2: Ephesians 1: 17-23

May you know the great hope to which God has called you. He has put all things under Christ's feet and has made him thus exalted head of the Church, which is his body.

The union of all men and women in and with Christ, as members of his mystical body, is the theme of this letter, which in all probability circulated among many churches and not just to the Church at Ephesus. In this prayer of thanksgiving, Paul challenges his readers to realize their place as members of the body of the Risen Christ, the Church.

GOSPEL: Matthew 28: 16-20

"Go make disciples of all nations. Baptize them in the name of the Father, and of the Son and of the Holy Spirit."

The promise of "Emmanuel"—"God is with us"—is fulfilled and remains: Christ commissions his apostles to baptize and to teach, with the authority and encouragement of Christ's continued presence.

Theme:

• the commission to "teach" the Gospel

Before returning to the Father, Jesus leaves his Church the mandate to teach—teach all that I have taught you, share what I have revealed to you. When we hear those final words of Jesus, we tend to think of the "big" picture, the Church's global missionary campaigns. But those words are addressed to each one of us, almost 2,000 years later. We are called to "teach" the Gospel in our own small corners of the world, to hand on the story that has been handed on to us about Jesus and his Gospel of love and compassion.

The role of teacher is central to our vocation as Christians—that our lives "teach" the love Jesus taught. What exactly do we "teach" in the way we live our faith: How special and elite we are in being Catholic Christians? That Christianity is a "nice" thing to be, the "right" Church to belong to? Do we "teach" anything at all? Or do we "teach," in our relationships with others and our approach to life, the compassion and forgiveness of Jesus? May we be worthy and effective teachers of the good news of our liberation from sin, fear and hopelessness through the Risen Christ, who now sits at the right hand of the Father.

For Reflection:

• What emotions and feelings do you think the eleven apostles were experiencing as they walked down the mountain and returned to Jerusalem? Can we relate to such feelings?

• Who are the apostles to the small, hidden places on the earth?

• What are the different ways we "teach" the good news?

Date: _____

HOMILY WORKSHEET for the Solemnity of the Ascension

1. SEEDS

What today's readings say *to me*: _____

_____

_____

PARABLES, STORIES and EXPERIENCES that speak to the themes of today's readings: _____

_____

_____

SPECIAL CONSIDERATIONS this week: Audience? Events in the community? Unique dimensions to this celebration?

_____

_____

_____

What RESPONSE do I seek from my listeners?
❑ to affirm/enlighten them in their faith?
❑ to teach/inform them about _____

_____

❑ to have them take a specific action _____

_____

2. PLANTING

The point I want to make in this homily (*ONE sentence*): _____

_____

_____

HOMILY OUTLINE

OPENING (*introductory STORY*): _____

_____

_____

_____

_____

_____

Point 1. APPLICATION of STORY to Scripture themes: _____

_____

_____

_____

_____

_____

Point 2. CONNECTION between Scriptural themes and the listeners' life experience: _____

_____
_____
_____
_____
_____
_____

Point 3. RESPONSE/CONSIDERATION sought from listeners: _____

_____
_____
_____
_____
_____
_____

CLOSING STATEMENT (*refers back to STORY*): _____

_____
_____
_____
_____
_____
_____

3. HARVEST—A Checklist:

❑ Does my completed homily make the point I articulated above (*under PLANTING*)?

❑ Am I excited about this homily. Am I readily able to convey my own enthusiasm, my sincere conviction of what I am going to say?

❑ Am I ready to preach this homily? Have I rehearsed this homily out loud until:

   ❑ I am comfortable with the *flow* of this homily: I can make the *transitions* from point to point, from idea to idea, smoothly and clearly;

   ❑ I am using *words* and *expressions* that my listeners can understand and appreciate: I am not speaking in theological jargon or "holy card" talk;

   ❑ my *delivery* (voice, gestures, speaking rate, pronunciation and enunciation, pauses, etc.) and

   ❑ my *inflection* and *emphasis* of key words and phrases are natural and effective?

❑ My homily lasts _____ minutes. Is it ❑ too long? ❑ too short? ❑ just about right?

4. GLEANINGS—Thoughts and notes AFTER the Homily

What worked, what didn't work in this homily; response and reactions from the community; ideas for next time; etc.

_____
_____
_____
_____
_____
_____
_____
_____
_____
_____
_____
_____

Seventh Sunday of Easter

The Readings:

READING 1: Acts 1: 12-14

The apostles returned to Jerusalem from the mount called Olivet near Jerusalem. Together they devoted themselves to constant prayer. There were some women in their company and Mary the mother of Jesus and his brothers.

In this brief passage from Acts, the stage is set for the Pentecost event next week. Following Jesus' ascension, the small company returns to the upstairs room in Jerusalem. This reading also contains the last New Testament reference to Mary, the mother of God. Her role in Jesus' birth parallels her presence at the birth of the Church, the body of Christ.

READING 2: 1 Peter 4: 13-16

Whoever is made to suffer as a Christian should not be ashamed but glorify God because of that name.

In this final Easter reading from Peter's first letter, the writer concludes the letter with this exhortation for those who suffer and are persecuted. Their joy and hope in the promise of the Resurrection will not be in vain.

GOSPEL: John 17: 1-11

*I have made your name known
to those you gave me out of the world.
For those I pray—
for they are really yours.*

This reading from John's Gospel, the climax of the Last Supper discourse, is the "high priestly prayer" of Jesus. It is a prayer to the Father for the union of present and future disciples, a union rooted in the love of the Father and the Son.

The traditional "Our Father" that is recorded in the synoptics does not appear in John's Gospel, but echoes of that prayer are heard here: the invocation of God as Father, the honor of God's name, the hope that the Father's will ("work") be brought to completion, the plea for the protection of the faithful.

Themes:

• prayer: to be aware of God's presence

For Tevye the milkman and his family in the musical *Fiddler on the Roof*, life is a never-ending series of problems, challenges and catastrophes—from the marriages of his daughters (one to a poor tailor, one to a radical young student, the third to a Gentile) to their expulsion from their Russian village during a pogrom. But through it all, Tevye maintains his faith in God's presence in his life and in the life of his people.

Perhaps the most beautiful thing about Tevye's character is his awareness of God's presence around him and his sense of prayer. He is constantly aware of the presence of God in every moment and in every event around him. As he makes his daily milk deliveries, Tevye talks through his problems with God and asks God to help him to understand the Lord's purpose in the events that befall his family and friends. He gathers his family for prayer to begin the Sabbath ("May the Lord protect and defend you")

and his neighbors come together in prayer for the wedding of his daughter ("Sunrise, Sunset"). Even Tevye's "showstopper" song, "If I Were a Rich Man," is actually a prayer of hope and acceptance to the Lord.

For Tevye, prayer is not only rituals and formulas but it is an awareness of God's constant presence, an attitude of openness to seeing God in the people and events around him. To know God is not merely to have intellectual knowledge of him but to have an intimate, personal relationship with him, like the nearest and dearest relationship in life. In Jesus, God became approachable; he became "Father."

The Church as a community of prayer is at the heart of today's readings—prayer that is, first and foremost, an attitude of trust and acceptance of God's presence in the community, an attitude that is not occasional but constant and continuing, an attitude not limited to asking for something but of thanksgiving for what is and for what has been. Prayer speaks not in rituals alone but also in the silence of the heart. As St. Teresa of Avila taught her Carmelite sisters, all prayer is "the resolution to bring our wills in conformity with the will of God."

• "one, holy, Catholic and apostolic"

When Jesus left this world, he had little reason to hope. He seemed to have achieved so little and to have won so few. But Jesus was not afraid of the small beginning he had made with the eleven. With them, he changed the world; with us, Christ continues to change the world.

As Jesus returns to the Father, he leaves a portion of the Father's glory behind: the community of faith. Jesus' priestly prayer, which we hear on this Sunday before Pentecost, is that his followers will be united and consecrated in the truth Jesus has revealed. May Jesus' prayer be our prayer: that we may reveal to the world the love and care of the Father for all of the human family. With knowledge of "the one true God and the One whom he has sent" we are able to pass from death to life.

For Reflection:

• A monk asked his abbot: "Father Abbot, is it permissible to smoke while I pray?"

"Of course not!" the abbot said, unequivocally.

"Father Abbot, is it permissible to pray while I smoke?"

"Well, of course," the abbot replied.

What is a "person of prayer?" What does Luke mean when he describes the small community after the Ascension as "devoting themselves to constant prayer"? What do today's readings teach us about prayer?

• Is Jesus' priestly prayer "answered" in our parish? How?

Date: _____

HOMILY WORKSHEET for the Seventh Sunday of Easter

1. SEEDS

What today's readings say *to me*: _____

_____

_____

PARABLES, STORIES and EXPERIENCES that speak to the themes of today's readings: _____

_____

_____

SPECIAL CONSIDERATIONS this week: Audience? Events in the community? Unique dimensions to this celebration?

_____

_____

_____

What RESPONSE do I seek from my listeners?
❑ to affirm/enlighten them in their faith?
❑ to teach/inform them about _____

_____

❑ to have them take a specific action _____

_____

2. PLANTING

The point I want to make in this homily (*ONE sentence*): _____

_____

_____

HOMILY OUTLINE

OPENING (*introductory STORY*): _____

_____

_____

_____

_____

_____

Point 1. APPLICATION of STORY to Scripture themes: _____

_____

_____

_____

_____

_____

Point 2. CONNECTION between Scriptural themes and the listeners' life experience: _____
_____
_____
_____
_____
_____
_____

Point 3. RESPONSE/CONSIDERATION sought from listeners: _____
_____
_____
_____
_____
_____
_____

CLOSING STATEMENT (*refers back to STORY*): _____
_____
_____
_____
_____
_____

3. HARVEST—A Checklist:

❑ Does my completed homily make the point I articulated above (*under PLANTING*)?

❑ Am I excited about this homily. Am I readily able to convey my own enthusiasm, my sincere conviction of what I am going to say?

❑ Am I ready to preach this homily? Have I rehearsed this homily out loud until:

    ❑ I am comfortable with the *flow* of this homily: I can make the *transitions* from point to point, from idea to idea, smoothly and clearly;

    ❑ I am using *words* and *expressions* that my listeners can understand and appreciate: I am not speaking in theological jargon or "holy card" talk;

    ❑ my *delivery* (voice, gestures, speaking rate, pronunciation and enunciation, pauses, etc.) and

    ❑ my *inflection* and *emphasis* of key words and phrases are natural and effective?

❑ My homily lasts _____ minutes. Is it ❑ too long? ❑ too short? ❑ just about right?

4. GLEANINGS—Thoughts and notes AFTER the Homily

What worked, what didn't work in this homily; response and reactions from the community; ideas for next time; etc.

_____
_____
_____
_____
_____
_____
_____
_____
_____
_____
_____
_____

Pentecost

The Readings:

READING 1: Acts 2: 1-11

*All were filled with the Holy Spirit. They began to express themselves and make bold
proclamations as the Spirit prompted them.*

Pentecost was the Jewish festival of the harvest (also called the Feast of Weeks), celebrated 50 days
after Passover, when the first fruits of the corn harvest were offered to the Lord. A feast of pilgrimage
(hence the presence in Jerusalem of so many "devout Jews of every nation"), Pentecost also com-
memorated Moses' receiving of the Law on Mount Sinai.

Luke's descriptions of wind and fire are Old Testament images: God frequently revealed his
presence in fire (the pillar of fire in the Sinai) and in wind (the wind that sweeps over the earth to make
the waters of the Great Flood subside). The Hebrew word for spirit, "ruah," and the Greek word
"pneuma" also refer to the movement of air, not only as wind, but also of breath: as in God's creation of
man in Genesis 2 and the revivification of the dry bones in Ezekiel 37. Through his life-giving breath,
the Lord begins the era of the new Israel on Pentecost.

READING 2: 1 Corinthians 12: 3-7, 12-13

*There are different gifts but the same Spirit; there are different ministries but the same Lord;
there are different works but the same God.*

Appealing for unity in the badly-splintered Corinthian community, Paul reminds the Corinthians of
the presence of the Holy Spirit in their midst, which brings together the different charisms each possesses for the good of the whole community and the glory of God.

GOSPEL: John 20: 19-23

Jesus came and stood before them.
"Peace be with you . . .
As the Father has sent me, so I send you."
Jesus breathed on them and said:
"Receive the Holy Spirit."

This Gospel of the first appearance of the Risen Jesus before his ten dsiciples (remember Thomas is
not present) on Easter night is John's version of the Pentecost event. In "breathing" the Holy Spirit upon
them, Jesus imitates God's act of creation in Genesis. Just as Adam's life came from God, so the
disciples' new life of the Spirit comes from Jesus. By Christ's sending them forth, the disciples become
apostles—those sent."

Themes:

• the Spirit: the unity of the Church

In Steinbeck's *The Grapes of Wrath,* the old minister Jim Casey describes the "sperit" (sic) of God as
love: "Maybe it's all men an' all women we love; maybe that's the Holy Sperit—the human sperit—the
whole shebang. Maybe all men got one big soul ever'body's a part of."

The central teaching of Jesus is the love of God the Father for all of us and the love we should have
for one another as brothers and sisters. To embrace the Holy Spirit is to live this teaching—to see
humankind as having "one big soul."

• the Spirit: the life of the Church

Before directing his Oscar-winning film *Ordinary People*, Robert Redford knew very little about cinematography. The first morning on the set, he took the six cinematographers aside and played for them Pachelbel's "Canon in D Minor," the beautiful music that is heard at the beginning and throughout the film. "I want you to listen to this, and I want you to think about how a suburban scene would look like if it corresponded to the music," the director explained. The "Canon" became the "life," the style, of the movie.

The word "spirit" in Hebrew is "ruah," meaning "breath of life." Today's celebration of Pentecost celebrates Christ "breathing" into his new Church the new life of his resurrection. It is the Spirit of God that animates and strengthens us to do the work of the Gospel and that makes God's will our will. Through his Spirit, God lives in us, he becomes us, in order that we might bring his life and love to our broken world.

For Reflection:

• The Spirit of God reveals itself in today's readings in the forms of fire, wind and breath. What other images can help us understand the Spirit of God working within us?

• How does the presence of the Holy Spirit make your parish "different" from other groups and organizations of people?

• Share stories of God's Spirit alive around you. How would those stories be different if God's Spirit was not present there?

Date: _____

HOMILY WORKSHEET for Pentecost

1. SEEDS

What today's readings say *to me*: _____

_____

_____

PARABLES, STORIES and EXPERIENCES that speak to the themes of today's readings: _____

_____

_____

SPECIAL CONSIDERATIONS this week: Audience? Events in the community? Unique dimensions to this celebration?

_____

_____

_____

What RESPONSE do I seek from my listeners?
❑ to affirm/enlighten them in their faith?
❑ to teach/inform them about _____

_____

❑ to have them take a specific action _____

_____

2. PLANTING

The point I want to make in this homily (*ONE sentence*): _____

_____

_____

HOMILY OUTLINE

OPENING (*introductory STORY*): _____

_____

_____

_____

_____

_____

Point 1. APPLICATION of STORY to Scripture themes: _____

_____

_____

_____

_____

_____

Point 2. CONNECTION between Scriptural themes and the listeners' life experience: _____

_____
_____
_____
_____
_____
_____

Point 3. RESPONSE/CONSIDERATION sought from listeners: _____

_____
_____
_____
_____
_____
_____

CLOSING STATEMENT (*refers back to STORY*): _____

_____
_____
_____
_____
_____
_____

3. HARVEST—A Checklist:

❑ Does my completed homily make the point I articulated above (*under PLANTING*)?

❑ Am I excited about this homily. Am I readily able to convey my own enthusiasm, my sincere conviction of what I am going to say?

❑ Am I ready to preach this homily? Have I rehearsed this homily out loud until:

　　❑ I am comfortable with the *flow* of this homily: I can make the *transitions* from point to point, from idea to idea, smoothly and clearly;

　　❑ I am using *words* and *expressions* that my listeners can understand and appreciate: I am not speaking in theological jargon or "holy card" talk;

　　❑ my *delivery* (voice, gestures, speaking rate, pronunciation and enunciation, pauses, etc.) and

　　❑ my *inflection* and *emphasis* of key words and phrases are natural and effective?

❑ My homily lasts _____ minutes.　Is it ❑ too long? ❑ too short? ❑ just about right?

4. GLEANINGS—Thoughts and notes AFTER the Homily

What worked, what didn't work in this homily; response and reactions from the community; ideas for next time; etc.

_____
_____
_____
_____
_____
_____
_____
_____
_____
_____
_____

Trinity Sunday

The Readings:

READING 1: Exodus 34: 4-6, 8-9

The Lord passed before Moses and cried out, "The Lord, the Lord, a merciful and gracious God, slow to anger and rich in kindness and fidelity."

An angry and frustrated Moses returns to the summit of Mount Sinai. Having received the Law from God, Moses descended to the Israelite camp to find the people worshipping a golden calf. In his anger, Moses slammed the tablets to the ground, shattering them. God has instructed Moses to make a new set of tablets and return to the mountain, where the Lord will once again inscribe the Law on the new tablets. In his great mercy, God will forgive Israel and renew his covenant with them.

READING 2: 2 Corinthians 13: 11-13

Live in harmony and peace, and the God of love and peace be with you all.

Paul's second letter to the Corinthians is his most personal and stormiest epistle. As in 1 Corinthians, Paul confronts the troubled community at Corinth with the issues dividing it and its strained relationship with Paul. These verses are the conclusion of Paul's letter, a final greeting of peace and prayer for unity in the Father, Son and Spirit (we have adopted the final verse as one of the greetings for the Celebration of the Eucharist).

GOSPEL: John 3: 16-18

"God so loved the world
that he gave his only son
that whoever believes in him may not die
but may have eternal life."

Nicodemus, a Pharisee and member of the Sanhedrin, comes under the cover of darkness to meet the remarkable rabbi he has heard so much about. In their discussion Jesus speaks of the need to be reborn "from above" and of the great love of God who gives the world his own Son, not to condemn humankind but to save it.

Themes:

• God: giver and sustainer of life

Many metaphors have been used to explain and depict the Trinity. St. John of Damascus, the great Eastern theologian of the eighth century, suggested that we think "of the Father as a root, of the Son as a branch, and of the Spirit as a fruit, for the substance of these three is one." Today we celebrate the essence of our faith: our belief in the God who has revealed himself as Father, Lord and Giver of life; as Son, Jesus Christ, redeemer of humankind, who reveals to us the love of God; and as Spirit, the love of God living among us, giving life and vision to us, his people, his Church.

• the God of mercy and forgiveness

The three readings today all speak of a God who is motivated by a love we mortals cannot fathom. Despite our ignorance, displacement and sometimes outright rejection of him, God continues to call us back to him, always making the first move to welcome us back: God readily forgives Israel and renews his covenant with them (Exodus); God is the ultimate source of loving community, even for the deeply divided Corinthian church (2 Corinthians); God re-creates humankind in touching human history in the Christ event (John). Today's celebration is an invitation to share in God's work of reconciliation, of creating communion and community among all his people.

For Reflection:

• Share stories of people who have been able to re-create their lives because they have experienced the God who calls us back to him.

• The shamrock, the triangle and the fruit tree (St. John of Damascus, cited above) have all been used to depict the mystery of the Trinity. Are there any contemporary images that help you understand and appreciate the Triune God?

• How has God—Father, Son and Spirit—made his presence known to you? How would you explain this presence to a non-believer?

• John 3 tells the story of Jesus' meeting with Nicodemus, the Pharisee who comes at night to meet Jesus. In what ways do we approach God and the whole question of faith like Nicodemus approaches Jesus?

Date: _____

HOMILY WORKSHEET for Trinity Sunday

1. SEEDS

What today's readings say *to me*: _____

_____

_____

PARABLES, STORIES and EXPERIENCES that speak to the themes of today's readings: _____

_____

_____

SPECIAL CONSIDERATIONS this week: Audience? Events in the community? Unique dimensions to this celebration?

_____

_____

_____

What RESPONSE do I seek from my listeners?
❑ to affirm/enlighten them in their faith?
❑ to teach/inform them about _____

_____

❑ to have them take a specific action _____

_____

2. PLANTING

The point I want to make in this homily (*ONE sentence*): _____

_____

_____

HOMILY OUTLINE

OPENING (*introductory STORY*): _____

_____

_____

_____

_____

_____

Point 1. APPLICATION of STORY to Scripture themes: _____

_____

_____

_____

_____

_____

Point 2. CONNECTION between Scriptural themes and the listeners' life experience: _____

_____

_____

_____

_____

_____

_____

Point 3. RESPONSE/CONSIDERATION sought from listeners: _____

_____

_____

_____

_____

_____

_____

CLOSING STATEMENT (*refers back to STORY*): _____

_____

_____

_____

_____

_____

3. HARVEST—A Checklist:

❑ Does my completed homily make the point I articulated above (*under PLANTING*)?

❑ Am I excited about this homily. Am I readily able to convey my own enthusiasm, my sincere conviction of what I am going to say?

❑ Am I ready to preach this homily? Have I rehearsed this homily out loud until:

  ❑ I am comfortable with the *flow* of this homily: I can make the *transitions* from point to point, from idea to idea, smoothly and clearly;

  ❑ I am using *words* and *expressions* that my listeners can understand and appreciate: I am not speaking in theological jargon or "holy card" talk;

  ❑ my *delivery* (voice, gestures, speaking rate, pronunciation and enunciation, pauses, etc.) and

  ❑ my *inflection* and *emphasis* of key words and phrases are natural and effective?

❑ My homily lasts _____ minutes. Is it ❑ too long? ❑ too short? ❑ just about right?

4. GLEANINGS—Thoughts and notes AFTER the Homily

What worked, what didn't work in this homily; response and reactions from the community; ideas for next time; etc.

_____

_____

_____

_____

_____

_____

_____

_____

_____

_____

_____

The Body and Blood of the Lord

The Readings:

READING 1: Deuteronomy 8: 2-3, 14-16

Remember how for forty years now the Lord, your God, has directed all your journeying through the desert . . . The Lord let you be afflicted with hunger, and then fed you with manna, a food unknown to you, in order to show you that not by bread alone does man live, but by every word that comes forth from the mouth of God.

Today's reading is taken from Moses' second address in Deuteronomy, as Israel emerges from their 40-year journey through the desert to the Promised Land. Moses and his people are standing on the high plateaus of Moab; stretching below them is the land God gives them as his own. Before entering the Promised Land, Moses calls the Israelites together to consider again the Law and statutes that mark their covenant with God. At this moment of fulfillment, Moses exhorts Israel to remember forever the goodness and mercy of God during their sojourn and cites many examples of God's providence, including the gift of manna in the desert. Food from heaven and the importance of remembrance will also dominate the Passover of the new covenant, the Eucharist.

READING 2: 1 Corinthians 10: 16-17

Because the loaf of bread is one, we, many though we are, are one body for we all partake of the one loaf.

In appealing to the Corinthians to heal their divisions, Paul cites the gift of the Eucharist as the ultimate expression of the unity of the Christian community.

GOSPEL: John 6: 51-58

*"I myself am the living bread
come down from heaven.
He who feeds on my flesh
and drinks my blood
has life eternal."*

In the "bread of life" discourse in John's Gospel, Jesus' revelations concerning his Messianic ministry take on a Eucharistic theme. The image of Jesus as "bread from heaven" echoes two dimensions of the same Old Testament image: the wisdom of God's Law nourishing all who accept it and God's blessing of manna to feed the journeying Israelites.

Themes:

• Eucharist: becoming bread for one another

"If you have received worthily," St. Augustine wrote, "you are what you have received." The gift of the Eucharist comes with an important "string" attached: it must be shared. In the body of Christ, we the body of Christ. If we partake of the "one loaf" (Reading 2), then we must be willing to become Eucharist for others—to make the love of Christ real for all.

• Eucharist: "in memory of me"

"God gave us memory," the Scottish playwright and novelist James Barrie wrote, "so that we might have roses in December." Before entering the Promised Land, Moses admonished the Israelites to become a people bound together by the memory of the great things God has done for them. At the Last Supper, Jesus instituted the new Passover of the Eucharist "in memory of me." Our coming to the table of the Eucharist is even more than just reliving the memory of Christ's great sacrifice for our redemption—in sharing the Eucharist we re-enter the inexplicable love of God who gives us eternal life in his Son, the Risen Christ.

• Eucharist: the new manna, food for the journey

The God who breathed his life into each one of us also gives us a world filled with all that is necessary to maintain that life. The people of Israel remember, especially, how God sustained them during their sojourn through the Sinai with the gift of manna. In raising Christ from the dead, God has effectively re-created humankind: we live in the hope that we will share in the life of the Risen One. The Eucharist is the new manna which sustains us on our journey to the eternal life of the Resurrection.

For Reflection:

• How can we be "Eucharist" to one another? How can we bring the Eucharist from our church to our world?

• Of all the foods of the earth, why is bread the perfect food to become the body of Christ?

• Why do we "need" this feast of "Corpus Christi" when we already celebrate Holy Thursday, the night Jesus instituted the Eucharist?

Date: _____

HOMILY WORKSHEET for The Body and Blood of the Lord

1. SEEDS

What today's readings say *to me*: _____

_____

_____

PARABLES, STORIES and EXPERIENCES that speak to the themes of today's readings: _____

_____

_____

SPECIAL CONSIDERATIONS this week: Audience? Events in the community? Unique dimensions to this celebration?

_____

_____

_____

What RESPONSE do I seek from my listeners?
❑ to affirm/enlighten them in their faith?
❑ to teach/inform them about _____

_____

❑ to have them take a specific action _____

_____

2. PLANTING

The point I want to make in this homily (*ONE sentence*): _____

_____

_____

HOMILY OUTLINE

OPENING (*introductory STORY*): _____

_____

_____

_____

_____

_____

Point 1. APPLICATION of STORY to Scripture themes: _____

_____

_____

_____

_____

_____

Point 2. CONNECTION between Scriptural themes and the listeners' life experience: _____

_____
_____
_____
_____
_____

Point 3. RESPONSE/CONSIDERATION sought from listeners: _____

_____
_____
_____
_____
_____

CLOSING STATEMENT (*refers back to STORY*): _____

_____
_____
_____
_____
_____

3. HARVEST—A Checklist:

❑ Does my completed homily make the point I articulated above (*under PLANTING*)?

❑ Am I excited about this homily. Am I readily able to convey my own enthusiasm, my sincere conviction of what I am going to say?

❑ Am I ready to preach this homily? Have I rehearsed this homily out loud until:

    ❑ I am comfortable with the *flow* of this homily: I can make the *transitions* from point to point, from idea to idea, smoothly and clearly;

    ❑ I am using *words* and *expressions* that my listeners can understand and appreciate: I am not speaking in theological jargon or "holy card" talk;

    ❑ my *delivery* (voice, gestures, speaking rate, pronunciation and enunciation, pauses, etc.) and

    ❑ my *inflection* and *emphasis* of key words and phrases are natural and effective?

❑ My homily lasts _____ minutes. Is it ❑ too long? ❑ too short? ❑ just about right?

4. GLEANINGS—Thoughts and notes AFTER the Homily

What worked, what didn't work in this homily; response and reactions from the community; ideas for next time; etc.

_____
_____
_____
_____
_____
_____
_____
_____
_____
_____

The Proper of the Year

Second Sunday of the Year*

The Readings:

READING 1: Isaiah 49: 3, 5-6

The Lord said to me: you are my servant,
Israel, through whom I show my glory.
The Lord formed me as his servant from the womb,
That Jacob may be brought back to him
and Israel gathered to him.

The second of Isaiah's "Servant" songs, this oracle describes the mission of the servant: to bring Israel back to the Lord and, through her, extend the Lord's salvation to every nation and people on earth.

READING 2: 1 Corinthians: 1:1-3

(You) have been consecrated in Christ Jesus and called to be a holy people.

On the next seven Sundays of the year, the second reading will be taken from Paul's first letter to the Church at Corinth.

Corinth was one of the great cities of the ancient world, a commercial crossroads between east and west. The city was a melting pot of Jewish, Roman and Greek cultures, religions and influences. Corinth had all of the best and the worst of a bustling pagan capital: the high ideals of Greek spirituality existed side by side with a decadence and moral depravity that were reactions to the ancient Greek asectic scorn of the physical. Paul stayed in Corinth for almost two years during his second missionary journey. He wrote this letter, probably from Ephesus, in response to a communication he received outlining the problems and rivalry facing the Corinthian community.

In today's reading, the introduction to the letter, Paul describes the great dignity of those called to be part of the "consecrated. . . holy people" in Christ. Using Old Testament images, Paul targets the two major themes of his letter to the Corinthians: the common call to holiness and their unity in the same Lord.

GOSPEL: John 1: 29-34

"The one who sent me to baptize with water told me, 'When you see the Spirit descend and
rest on someone. It is he who is to baptize with the Holy Spirit.' Now I have seen for myself
and have testified, 'This is God's chosen One.' "

John's Gospel emphasizes the Baptizer's role as the last great prophet who identifies Jesus as the Messiah. John recognizes the Spirit of God "resting" within this Jesus. In Jesus, the Father's Spirit took up permanent abode.

*The First Sunday of the Year is the Feast of the Baptism of the Lord.

Themes:

• a "consecrated" people

In his book, *Man's Search for Meaning*, Viktor Frankl, a psychotherapist who was imprisoned in a concentration camp during World War II, points out that while many prisoners collapsed under the terror of the Nazi death camps, those who survived were men and women who believed that their lives—including their sufferings—had "ultimate meaning." When a prisoner had faith, that faith gave meaning to his or her existence. That conviction provided the survivors with the singular energy that helped them maintain their humanity.

The human life we are given is a gift from God "who formed (us) as his servant(s) from the womb." Jesus, who began his public ministry by submitting to the baptism of John, came to sanctify and "consecrate" all humanity. We are so consecrated in our own baptisms: we have been set apart as sacred, as holy, by our God. This sacred dimension of all human life should profoundly affect every human contact and relationship we have.

• the call to be witness and prophet

For most of us, John the Baptizer is an Advent character. He appears in the Advent readings admonishing us to prepare the way of the Lord who comes, of course, at Christmas. Although Christmas has been over for some weeks now, John is back in today's Gospel. Today's appearance bridges Christmas (Christ has come) and Eastertide (the Risen Christ will come again). Christ comes now to do the *work* of Christmas—to bring forgiveness and reconciliation to our hurting world.

We have been called, as John was called, to declare to our contemporaries that the "Lamb of God" has come. John declared his witness in preaching and baptizing; our witness can be declared in less vocal but no less profound vehicles: in our unfailing compassion for others, in our uncompromising moral and ethical convictions, in our everyday sense of joy and purpose.

For Reflection:

• Have there been times in your life when you have experienced the presence of the "Lamb of God" in the kindness, in the heroic charity, in the selfless attitude of someone?

• Who are the witnesses of Christ among us now, whose perseverance and suffering say to the world: "Look there! The Lamb of God!"?

• The word consecrate comes from the Latin words meaning to set apart for the use of the sacred or holy. If we are a "consecrated" people, what difference should that "setting apart for the sacred" make in our lives?

Date: _____

HOMILY WORKSHEET for the Second Sunday of the Year

1. SEEDS

What today's readings say *to me*: _____

_____

_____

PARABLES, STORIES and EXPERIENCES that speak to the themes of today's readings: _____

_____

_____

SPECIAL CONSIDERATIONS this week: Audience? Events in the community? Unique dimensions to this celebration?

_____

_____

_____

What RESPONSE do I seek from my listeners?
❑ to affirm/enlighten them in their faith?
❑ to teach/inform them about _____

_____

❑ to have them take a specific action _____

_____

2. PLANTING

The point I want to make in this homily (*ONE sentence*): _____

_____

_____

HOMILY OUTLINE

OPENING (*introductory STORY*): _____

_____

_____

_____

_____

_____

Point 1. APPLICATION of STORY to Scripture themes: _____

_____

_____

_____

_____

_____

Point 2. CONNECTION between Scriptural themes and the listeners' life experience: _____
_____
_____
_____
_____
_____

Point 3. RESPONSE/CONSIDERATION sought from listeners: _____
_____
_____
_____
_____
_____
_____

CLOSING STATEMENT (*refers back to STORY*): _____
_____
_____
_____
_____
_____

3. HARVEST—A Checklist:

❑ Does my completed homily make the point I articulated above (*under PLANTING*)?

❑ Am I excited about this homily. Am I readily able to convey my own enthusiasm, my sincere conviction of what I am going to say?

❑ Am I ready to preach this homily? Have I rehearsed this homily out loud until:

> ❑ I am comfortable with the *flow* of this homily: I can make the *transitions* from point to point, from idea to idea, smoothly and clearly;

> ❑ I am using *words* and *expressions* that my listeners can understand and appreciate: I am not speaking in theological jargon or "holy card" talk;

> ❑ my *delivery* (voice, gestures, speaking rate, pronunciation and enunciation, pauses, etc.) and

> ❑ my *inflection* and *emphasis* of key words and phrases are natural and effective?

❑ My homily lasts _____ minutes. Is it ❑ too long? ❑ too short? ❑ just about right?

4. GLEANINGS—Thoughts and notes AFTER the Homily

What worked, what didn't work in this homily; response and reactions from the community; ideas for next time; etc.

_____
_____
_____
_____
_____
_____
_____
_____
_____
_____
_____

Third Sunday of the Year

The Readings:

READING 1: Isaiah 8: 23 - 9: 3

> He has glorified the seaward road,
>> the land west of Jordan, the District of the Gentiles.
> The people who walked in darkness
>> have seen a great light.
> Upon those who dwelt in the land of gloom
>> a light has shone.

Preaching to the Jews who have been conquered and exiled from their homeland by the Assyrians, Isaiah prophesies that the region of Northern Palestine, including Galilee ("the District of the Gentiles") will be redeemed by Emmanuel, the "great light."

READING 2: 1 Corinthians 1: 10-13, 17

> *Let there be no factions; rather, be united in mind and judgement.*
> *This is what I mean: one of you will say, "I belong to Paul," another, "I belong to Apollos," still another, "Cephas has my allegiance," and the fourth, "I belong to Christ." Has Christ, then, been divided into parts?*

The Christian community at Corinth was terribly divided. The factions were set up along lines of allegiance to the individual ministers who introduced them to Christianity—and each side was proud of their loyalty. "Disciples" of Cephas (Peter) would tend to be Jews, while the Gentiles would look to Paul for leadership. Greek converts, raised in the ascetic philosophy of the ancients, were devoted to Apollos, a fellow Greek. There may have also been a few in the community who had actually seen Jesus and met him and might have lorded that fact over the rest of the community.

Paul minces no words in reminding them that the Church is one community by the cross of Christ, that Christ—not Paul or Apollos or Cephas or anyone else—redeemed them and brought them back to God.

GOSPEL: Matthew 4: 12-23 (or 4: 12-17)

> *Jesus toured all of Galilee. He taught in their synogogues, proclaimed the good news of the kingdom and cured peoples of every disease and illness.*

Galilee is the centerpiece of today's Gospel and Old Testament readings.

In Jesus' time, Galilee was the most populated and productive region of Palestine. The great roads of the world passed through Galilee, making it a strategic target for invasion. White-sailed ships crept up the Mediterranean coast from Alexandria and caravans traveled through the area from Mesopotamia and Egypt.

Galilee, unlike the rest of Palestine, had an "international perspective," in touch with many non-Jewish ideas and influences. Josephus, the Roman historian, wrote of the people of Galilee: "They were fond of innovation and, by nature, disposed to change and delighted in sedition . . . The Galileans were never destitute of courage. . . They were evermore anxious for honor than for gain."

Jesus' beginning his public ministry in Galilee is, for Matthew, yet another fulfillment of an ancient oracle concerning the Messiah: Jesus, the "great light," first appears in Galilee (Reading 1).

Themes:

• building dynamic Christian communities

Today's readings tell us about two very different groups of people: the Galileans, a people open to new ideas and change, and the Corinthians, a people torn apart by factionalism. Galilee and Corinth should challenge our parish families to be genuine Christian communities: may we hear the Gospel with inquisitive openness to change and renewal in our lives; may we recognize in one another the faith we share and the humanity we have in common, given to us by the same God, the Father of us all.

• being open to God's word

Today we begin a somewhat continuous reading of Matthew's Gospel. On Sundays this year we will hear Matthew's account of the wonders Jesus taught, the signs he worked, the stories he told and, finally, his Passion, death and Resurrection.

It is easy to dismiss the Gospel as too "simple" for our complex society: It's a nice thought, Jesus, but, hey, life just isn't like that anymore. It's a dog-eat-dog world out there. It's kill or be killed. Love one another? God, we'd get murdered. The kingdom of heaven? Tell that to my creditors and the I.R.S.

May we take to heart the Gospel with the openness that characterized the people of Galilee, the first people to hear and see Jesus. May we hear these words each Sunday with open minds and open hearts, not allowing our biases, suspicions and self-interests to dismiss or reject the clear voice of God in Matthew's account of Jesus of Galilee.

For Reflection:

• How does your parish community resemble the Galileans? How does your parish community resemble the Corinthians?

• We human beings have a knack for rationalizing—for devising plausible but superficial explanations (excuses) to explain the sometimes rotten things we do. How do we rationalize our beliefs, attitudes and actions to convince ourselves that we are justified in acting contrary to the spirit of the Gospel?

Date: _____

HOMILY WORKSHEET for the Third Sunday of the Year

1. SEEDS

What today's readings say *to me*: _____

_____

_____

PARABLES, STORIES and EXPERIENCES that speak to the themes of today's readings: _____

_____

_____

SPECIAL CONSIDERATIONS this week: Audience? Events in the community? Unique dimensions to this celebration?

_____

_____

_____

What RESPONSE do I seek from my listeners?

❑ to affirm/enlighten them in their faith?

❑ to teach/inform them about _____

_____

❑ to have them take a specific action _____

_____

2. PLANTING

The point I want to make in this homily (*ONE sentence*): _____

_____

_____

HOMILY OUTLINE

OPENING (*introductory STORY*): _____

_____

_____

_____

_____

_____

Point 1. APPLICATION of STORY to Scripture themes: _____

_____

_____

_____

_____

_____

Point 2. CONNECTION between Scriptural themes and the listeners' life experience: _____

_____
_____
_____
_____
_____
_____

Point 3. RESPONSE/CONSIDERATION sought from listeners: _____

_____
_____
_____
_____
_____
_____

CLOSING STATEMENT (*refers back to STORY*): _____

_____
_____
_____
_____
_____
_____

3. HARVEST—A Checklist:

❑ Does my completed homily make the point I articulated above (*under PLANTING*)?

❑ Am I excited about this homily. Am I readily able to convey my own enthusiasm, my sincere conviction of what I am going to say?

❑ Am I ready to preach this homily? Have I rehearsed this homily out loud until:

    ❑ I am comfortable with the *flow* of this homily: I can make the *transitions* from point to point, from idea to idea, smoothly and clearly;

    ❑ I am using *words* and *expressions* that my listeners can understand and appreciate: I am not speaking in theological jargon or "holy card" talk;

    ❑ my *delivery* (voice, gestures, speaking rate, pronunciation and enunciation, pauses, etc.) and

    ❑ my *inflection* and *emphasis* of key words and phrases are natural and effective?

❑ My homily lasts _____ minutes. Is it ❑ too long? ❑ too short? ❑ just about right?

4. GLEANINGS—Thoughts and notes AFTER the Homily

What worked, what didn't work in this homily; response and reactions from the community; ideas for next time; etc.

_____
_____
_____
_____
_____
_____
_____
_____
_____
_____
_____

Fourth Sunday of the Year

The Readings:

READING 1: Zephaniah 2: 3; 3: 12-13

I will leave as a remnant in your midst
a people humble and lowly,
Who shall take refuge in the name of the Lord:
the remnant of Israel.

This reading is not typical of the firebrand Zephaniah. Zephaniah preached passionately to a Jerusalem corrupted by a return to old pagan practices (such as worshiping the sun and moon and stars) and political intrigue with their Assyrian occupiers. The three chapters of Zephaniah are a terrifying warning of the coming Day of the Lord (Zephaniah's descriptions of the final judgment inspired the Christian hymn *Dies Irae*). But in today's reading, the doomsayer Zephaniah speaks of hope: the Lord will protect "the remnant of Israel," the "people humble and lowly" who remain faithful to their covenant with him.

READING 2: 1 Corinthians 1: 26-31

God chose those whom the world considers absurd to shame the wise; he singled out the weak of this world to shame the strong.

For the most part, the Christians in Corinth were non-entities. They were the most non-influential people in a very power-conscious city. But Paul assures them that worldly influence and wisdom do not matter. God did not choose the intellectual, the powerful and the noble for his own. To "boast in the Lord" (a favorite expression of Paul's) means to acknowledge that we live because of God's goodness and we live only for him.

GOSPEL: Matthew 5: 1-12

How blest are the poor in spirit: the reign of God is theirs.

The Gospel readings for the next few Sundays will be taken from the Sermon on the Mount, Matthew's compilation of the discourses of Jesus. Today's Gospel is the beautiful "Beatitudes" reading.

The word "blessed" as used by Jesus in the eight maxims was written in Greek as *makarios,* a word which indicates a joy that is God-like in its serenity and totality.

Specific Greek words used throughout the text indicate several important meanings:

• "the poor in spirit:" those who are detached from material things, who put their trust in God.

• "the sorrowing:" this Beatitude speaks of the value of caring and of compassion, hallmarks of Jesus' teaching.

• "the lowly:" the Greek word used here is *praotes*—true humility which banishes all pride; the "blest" who accept the necessity to learn and grow and the necessity to be forgiven.

• "they who show mercy:" the Greek word *eleymones* used here indicates the ability to get "inside a person's skin" until we can see things from his/her eyes, think things with his/her mind and feel things with his/her feelings.

• "the peacemakers:" peace is not merely the absence of trouble or discord; peace is a positive condition—it is everything which provides and makes for humanity's highest good. Note, too, that the "blest" are described as peace-*makers* and not simply peace-*lovers.*

Themes:

•. the Christian's system of values

The Beatitudes call us to a very different set of values than those of our dog-eat-dog-success-is-every-thing-get-them-before-they-get-you-bottom-line world. We are called, as Zephaniah preaches, "to seek the Lord in all things." Rabbi Harold Kushner writes in his book, *When All You've Ever Wanted Isn't Enough*: "Our souls are not hungry for fame, comfort, wealth or power. Those rewards create almost as many problems as they solve. Our souls are hungry for meaning, for the sense that we have figured out how to love so that our lives matter."*

• the "humble and lowly"

Today's readings describe the people of God in less-than-exhilarating terms: "a remnant, humble and lowly" (Reading 1); "absurd, weak, lowborn and despised" (Reading 2); and "poor, lowly, sorrowing and persecuted" (Gospel). The point is that as a people of faith we are called to focus our lives on the "blessedness" of the Sermon on the Mount: to seek God in all things.

For Reflection:

• The literary form used by Jesus in the Beatitudes, "Blessed are. . . for they. . ." is used frequently in the Old Testament, especially in the Wisdom literature and the Psalms. How would Jesus "compose" the Beatitudes if he were speaking to your parish community?

• How can we realistically and pragmatically be the people of the Beatitudes, "a remnant, humble and lowly" in the marketplaces of our world?

• Who are among the "remnant" of our world who remain faithful while living in a faithless world?

When All You've Ever Wanted Isn't Enough by Harold Kushner (New York: Summit Books, 1986) page 18.

Date: _____

HOMILY WORKSHEET for the Fourth Sunday of the Year

1. SEEDS

What today's readings say *to me*: _____

_____

_____

PARABLES, STORIES and EXPERIENCES that speak to the themes of today's readings: _____

_____

_____

SPECIAL CONSIDERATIONS this week: Audience? Events in the community? Unique dimensions to this celebration?

_____

_____

_____

What RESPONSE do I seek from my listeners?
❏ to affirm/enlighten them in their faith?
❏ to teach/inform them about _____

_____

❏ to have them take a specific action _____

_____

2. PLANTING

The point I want to make in this homily (*ONE sentence*): _____

_____

_____

HOMILY OUTLINE

OPENING (*introductory STORY*): _____

_____

_____

_____

_____

_____

Point 1. APPLICATION of STORY to Scripture themes: _____

_____

_____

_____

_____

_____

Point 2. CONNECTION between Scriptural themes and the listeners' life experience: _____

_____

_____

_____

_____

_____

Point 3. RESPONSE/CONSIDERATION sought from listeners: _____

_____

_____

_____

_____

_____

CLOSING STATEMENT (*refers back to STORY*): _____

_____

_____

_____

_____

_____

3. HARVEST—A Checklist:

❏ Does my completed homily make the point I articulated above (*under PLANTING*)?

❏ Am I excited about this homily. Am I readily able to convey my own enthusiasm, my sincere conviction of what I am going to say?

❏ Am I ready to preach this homily? Have I rehearsed this homily out loud until:

> ❏ I am comfortable with the *flow* of this homily: I can make the *transitions* from point to point, from idea to idea, smoothly and clearly;

> ❏ I am using *words* and *expressions* that my listeners can understand and appreciate: I am not speaking in theological jargon or "holy card" talk;

> ❏ my *delivery* (voice, gestures, speaking rate, pronunciation and enunciation, pauses, etc.) and

> ❏ my *inflection* and *emphasis* of key words and phrases are natural and effective?

❏ My homily lasts _____ minutes. Is it ❏ too long? ❏ too short? ❏ just about right?

4. GLEANINGS—Thoughts and notes AFTER the Homily

What worked, what didn't work in this homily; *response and reactions from the community; ideas for next time; etc.*

_____

_____

_____

_____

_____

_____

_____

_____

_____

_____

_____

Fifth Sunday of the Year

The Readings:

READING 1: Isaiah 58: 7-10

If you bestow your bread on the hungry
and satisfy the afflicted
Then light shall rise for you in the darkness,
and the gloom shall become for you like midday.

Isaiah exhorts his listeners to a life of sharing. If we hear and respond to the plight of the poor, the Lord God will hear us when we call upon him. In these verses, Isaiah (the "Christmas prophet") continues to speak of the Messiah's coming, not as a time of political or military victory for Israel, but as a time of justice, mercy and reconciliation.

READING 2: 1 Corinthians 2: 1-5

My message and my preaching had none of the persuasive force of "wise" argumentation,
but the convincing power of the Spirit.

Continuing his letter to the strife-torn Christian community at Corinth, Paul remembers his first disastrous preaching in Corinth. At first, Paul, as a distinguished member of the Pharisees, was invited to speak in the synagogue at Corinth. But his preaching on this Risen Jesus was not well received by his Jewish audience who summarily cast him out of the synagogue. The Acts of the Apostles reports that Paul's "weakness and fear" was in sharp contrast to the "eloquence" of Apollos. While the Corinthians responded favorably to Apollos' preaching, they were put off by Paul. The community began to splinter into factions.

But regardless of whose preaching they heard and accepted, whatever effect the Gospel has had on them, Paul writes, is not due to the preacher's own "wisdom" or "eloquence" but to the Spirit of God giving life to Paul's words.

GOSPEL: Matthew 5: 13-16

"You are the salt of the earth . . . You are the light of the world."

Unsalted popcorn and an electrical power outage are all that we need to appreciate Jesus' message in today's Gospel reading (the continuation of the Sermon on the Mount). Through the images of salt and light, Jesus impresses upon his listeners the vocation of Christians: as I am salt and light to the world, so you, as my disciples, must reflect me to the world.

Themes:

• the Christian vocation: "salt"

As well as being the best thing that ever happened to french fries, the chemical compound salt has literally thousands of other uses. Not only does salt flavor food, it also preserves food, such as meat and fish, by drawing up the moisture from microorganisms that cause decay in food (without moisture, the bacteria die thus keeping food from spoiling). Our bodies need about one-fourth of an ounce of salt a day. Salt, an element in our blood, sweat and tears, bathes the billions of cells in our bodies.

Salt has even more industrial uses: it is found in shoe leather and clothing dye; it softens water; it is used in making glass, building roads, manufacturing shampoo, bleaching paper and cooling nuclear reactors; it is used both in freezing and in de-icing.

133

There are over 14,000 uses of salt. But salt, by itself, is useless; only when it mixes with something else is the value of salt realized. When Jesus tells us that we are to be "salt for the earth," he presents us with a very difficult challenge. If we are to be like salt, then our belief must not be confined to Sunday Mass; it must be a part of every dimension of our lives: at home, at work, at school, at play.

• the Christian vocation: "light"

Since antiquity, darkness has symbolized sin, and light has symbolized goodness. Isaiah frequently uses light as a sign both of good conquering evil and of the Messiah. Jesus uses the image of light in the same way, but makes the additional point that we should not be afraid to be light to the world ("one does not light a lamp and then put it under a bushel basket"). Our simplest acts of charity can be a "light" for our world and unmistakable evidence of the presence of God among us.

For Reflection:

• Who are the "hungry. . . oppressed. . . homeless. . . and naked" among us? How would Isaiah preach the first reading to your community today?

• Do you know people who have been "light" to others?

• When and how are we salt-*less* Christians?

Date: _____

HOMILY WORKSHEET for the Fifth Sunday of the Year

1. SEEDS

What today's readings say *to me*: _____

_____

_____

PARABLES, STORIES and EXPERIENCES that speak to the themes of today's readings: _____

_____

_____

SPECIAL CONSIDERATIONS this week: Audience? Events in the community? Unique dimensions to this celebration?

_____

_____

_____

What RESPONSE do I seek from my listeners?

❑ to affirm/enlighten them in their faith?

❑ to teach/inform them about _____

_____

❑ to have them take a specific action _____

_____

2. PLANTING

The point I want to make in this homily (*ONE sentence*): _____

_____

_____

HOMILY OUTLINE

OPENING (*introductory STORY*): _____

_____

_____

_____

_____

_____

Point 1. APPLICATION of STORY to Scripture themes: _____

_____

_____

_____

_____

_____

Point 2. CONNECTION between Scriptural themes and the listeners' life experience: _____

_____
_____
_____
_____
_____
_____

Point 3. RESPONSE/CONSIDERATION sought from listeners: _____

_____
_____
_____
_____
_____
_____

CLOSING STATEMENT (*refers back to STORY*): _____

_____
_____
_____
_____
_____
_____

3. HARVEST—A Checklist:

❑ Does my completed homily make the point I articulated above (*under PLANTING*)?

❑ Am I excited about this homily. Am I readily able to convey my own enthusiasm, my sincere conviction of what I am going to say?

❑ Am I ready to preach this homily? Have I rehearsed this homily out loud until:

> ❑ I am comfortable with the *flow* of this homily: I can make the *transitions* from point to point, from idea to idea, smoothly and clearly;

> ❑ I am using *words* and *expressions* that my listeners can understand and appreciate: I am not speaking in theological jargon or "holy card" talk;

> ❑ my *delivery* (voice, gestures, speaking rate, pronunciation and enunciation, pauses, etc.) and

> ❑ my *inflection* and *emphasis* of key words and phrases are natural and effective?

❑ My homily lasts _____ minutes. Is it ❑ too long? ❑ too short? ❑ just about right?

4. GLEANINGS—Thoughts and notes AFTER the Homily

What worked, what didn't work in this homily; response and reactions from the community; ideas for next time; etc.

_____
_____
_____
_____
_____
_____
_____
_____
_____
_____
_____

Sixth Sunday of the Year

The Readings:

READING 1: Sirach 15: 15-20

Before man are life and death,
whichever he chooses shall be given to him.

Life is a series of choices: between light and darkness, between good and evil, between life and death. We must take responsibilities for the choices we make—we cannot claim that we were simply "led astray." True wisdom (Ben Sirach's theme throughout this Old Testament book) is seeking and choosing the things of God.

READING 2: 1 Corinthians 2: 6-10

God has revealed this wisdom to us through the Spirit.

The Corinthian Church is a broken community, divided by different loyalties and philosophies. These verses would appear to be addressed to the Greeks who were schooled in the philosophical approaches of Aristotle, Sophocles and Plato. Echoing Ben Sirach's theme, Paul writes that the source of true and eternal wisdom is God, who has revealed, in Christ Jesus, wisdom far beyond any "wisdom" the world teaches.

GOSPEL: Matthew 5: 17-37 (or 5: 20-22, 27-28, 33-34, 37)

"Unless your holiness surpasses that of the scribes and Pharisees you shall not enter the kingdom of heaven."

You have heard the commandment imposed on your forefathers, 'You shall not commit murder; every murderer will be liable to judgment.' What I say to you is: everyone who grows angry with his brother will be liable to judgment."

Today's Gospel is the first indication of trouble between Jesus and the leaders of the Jews. The role of the scribes evolved from being the recorders and codifiers of the Torah to that of the interpreters of the specific rules and regulations of the Torah. The Pharisees, whose name means "separated brethren," removed themselves from everyday activity in order to keep the Law assiduously, thereby serving as a model to the Jewish people who, consequently, held the Pharisees in esteem.

While the scribes and Pharisees were extreme legalists in their interpretation of the Law, Jesus is the ultimate *supra-legalist*. He takes their legalities a step further: the Spirit of God, which gives life and meaning to the Law, transcends the letter of the Law. We cannot be satisfied with merely avoiding the act of murder but must also curb the insults and anger that lead to murder; we cannot be satisfied with justifying separation and estrangement but must actively seek reconciliation and forgiveness; we cannot be satisfied just fulfilling contracts in order to avoid being sued but must seek to become honest and trustworthy persons in all our dealings. Jesus comes to teach an approach to life that is motivated neither by edict nor fear but by the recognition and celebration of the humanity we share with all men and women.

Themes:

• the "spirit" of law

It seemed so much more reassuring, if not easier, to be a Catholic when everything from the color of vestments to the severity of sins were clearly specified. Now we are more or less "on our own" to consciously make our own decisions based on our listening to the Spirit within us instead of unconsciously following custom and ritual. As St. Augustine wrote: "What else are the laws of God written on our hearts but the very presence of the Holy Spirit?"

• wisdom

We seem to be more comfortable with something when we can measure it or quantify it. Such can be said for our concepts of success (sales figures, rating points) and wisdom (data collected, facts tested and proven in the laboratory). Today's readings redefine that concept of wisdom: true wisdom begins and ends with the knowledge of God as Father and Creator of all, are that this life of ours is a passageway to eternity with him.

• responsibility for the choices we make

On his deathbed, the noted cynic and agnostic W.C. Fields was discovered reading a Bible. When asked why his sudden interest in the Good Book, Fields explained, "I'm looking for a loophole."

Ben Sirach's words (Reading 1) strike at the "loophole detector" in all of us. We must take responsibility for the choices we make in this life. Similarly, Jesus' sermon in today's Gospel makes clear that more is expected of us than the scrupulous following of the letter of the Law. God holds us accountable not only for what we do but for the sincerity of the love that motivates us. God looks beyond excuses and rationalizations to the selflessness (or the self-centeredness) within our hearts.

For Reflection:

• Have you experienced or witnessed love and commitment that transcended legal or moral expectations?

• How do we rationalize our way around or explain away ethical and moral dilemmas?

• How can getting "hung up" with technicalities and structure limit our ability to accomplish something good?

• Consider how the wisdom of God is at odds with what *Newsweek* magazine calls the "old CW" ("conventional wisdom").

Date: _____

HOMILY WORKSHEET for the Sixth Sunday of the Year

1. SEEDS

What today's readings say *to me*: _____

_____

_____

PARABLES, STORIES and EXPERIENCES that speak to the themes of today's readings: _____

_____

_____

SPECIAL CONSIDERATIONS this week: Audience? Events in the community? Unique dimensions to this celebration?

_____

_____

_____

What RESPONSE do I seek from my listeners?
❑ to affirm/enlighten them in their faith?
❑ to teach/inform them about _____

_____

❑ to have them take a specific action _____

_____

2. PLANTING

The point I want to make in this homily (*ONE sentence*): _____

_____

_____

HOMILY OUTLINE

OPENING (*introductory STORY*): _____

_____

_____

_____

_____

_____

Point 1. APPLICATION of STORY to Scripture themes: _____

_____

_____

_____

_____

_____

Point 2. CONNECTION between Scriptural themes and the listeners' life experience: _____

_____

_____

_____

_____

_____

_____

Point 3. RESPONSE/CONSIDERATION sought from listeners: _____

_____

_____

_____

_____

_____

_____

CLOSING STATEMENT (*refers back to STORY*): _____

_____

_____

_____

_____

_____

3. HARVEST—A Checklist:

❑ Does my completed homily make the point I articulated above (*under PLANTING*)?

❑ Am I excited about this homily. Am I readily able to convey my own enthusiasm, my sincere conviction of what I am going to say?

❑ Am I ready to preach this homily? Have I rehearsed this homily out loud until:

    ❑ I am comfortable with the *flow* of this homily: I can make the *transitions* from point to point, from idea to idea, smoothly and clearly;

    ❑ I am using *words* and *expressions* that my listeners can understand and appreciate: I am not speaking in theological jargon or "holy card" talk;

    ❑ my *delivery* (voice, gestures, speaking rate, pronunciation and enunciation, pauses, etc.) and

    ❑ my *inflection* and *emphasis* of key words and phrases are natural and effective?

❑ My homily lasts _____ minutes. Is it ❑ too long? ❑ too short? ❑ just about right?

4. GLEANINGS—Thoughts and notes AFTER the Homily

What worked, what didn't work in this homily; response and reactions from the community; ideas for next time; etc.

_____

_____

_____

_____

_____

_____

_____

_____

_____

_____

Seventh Sunday of the Year

The Readings:

READING 1: Leviticus 19: 1-2, 17-18

Take no revenge and cherish no grudge against your fellow countrymen. You shall love your neighbor as yourself.

The Book of Leviticus is the Torah's "Sacramentary." A good portion of this third book of the Bible consists of laws governing rituals and sacrifices prescribed for the priests of the tribe of Levi. These few verses reflect on charity towards one's "neighbor." Jews considered their "neighbors" to be exclusively Jewish; but Jesus made the concept of "neighbor" universal.

READING 2: 1 Corinthians 3: 16-23

The temple of God is holy, and you are that temple. If anyone of you thinks he is wise in a worldly way, he had better become a fool . . . for the wisdom of this world is aburdity with God.

Paul's words are targeted to the different factions which are crippling the Church in Corinth. Paul minces no words: regardless of who baptized you or whose "brand" of Christianity you find attractive, in the faith all Christians share we form *one* "temple of God"—and woe to anyone who tries to destroy that temple, Paul warns. The alleged superiority of one minister over another or one faction over another is absurd, in light of "true" wisdom.

Paul's cryptic remarks about becoming a "fool" are addressed to a people who are considered outsiders in their own city. Corinth is an influential, cosmopolitan capital—the Corinthians pride themselves on their sophistication and wisdom in the affairs of the world. But Paul reminds the Christians there that true wisdom is of God and not of this world. We should purposely seek to be "fools" in the eyes of the world in order to be "wise" for the sake of the kingdom of God.

GOSPEL: Matthew 5: 38-48

"You have heard the commandment, 'You shall love your countryman and hate your enemy.' My command to you is: love your enemies, pray for your persecutors."

Jesus continues to take the Law further than its official interpreters are comfortable taking it. The phrase, "and hate your enemy," does not appear in the Old Testament—the concept of "enemy" was an assumption on the part of the scribes and Pharisees, who defined an enemy as anyone not a Jew. But Jesus challenges that assumption: God's love unites all men and women, on whom the Father's "sun rises and sets as well." However justified retaliation might appear to be, Jesus calls us to seek reconciliation instead of vengeance.

Themes:

• the ministry of reconciliation

Christ calls us to be more than just "law abiding" people—he calls us to be a people of reconciliation: to love the unlovable, to reach out to the alienated, and to replace walls that divide and isolate people with bridges that bring people together. The challenge of the Gospel is to be ready and willing to take the first step in reconciliation—even towards people we are much more comfortable and happier having little or nothing to do with.

• forgiving our "enemies"

In the Greek text, the word used in today's Gospel for love is "agape." The word indicates not a romantic kind of love or the kind of love we have for the special ones in our lives but rather a state of benevolence and good will. To "love our enemies" means that no matter how he/she hurts us, we will never let bitterness close our hearts to that person nor will we seek anything but good for that "enemy." "Agape" begins with recognizing the humanity we share with all people who call God "Father."

For Reflection:

• How do factions destroy unity of purpose in any organization or community?

• How does Jesus' teaching on loving one's enemies square with today's headlines?

• Is retaliation or vengeance ever justified?

Date: _____

HOMILY WORKSHEET for the Seventh Sunday of the Year

1. SEEDS

What today's readings say *to me*: _____

_____

_____

PARABLES, STORIES and EXPERIENCES that speak to the themes of today's readings: _____

_____

_____

SPECIAL CONSIDERATIONS this week: Audience? Events in the community? Unique dimensions to this celebration?

_____

_____

_____

What RESPONSE do I seek from my listeners?
❏ to affirm/enlighten them in their faith?
❏ to teach/inform them about _____

_____

❏ to have them take a specific action _____

_____

2. PLANTING

The point I want to make in this homily (*ONE sentence*): _____

_____

_____

HOMILY OUTLINE

OPENING (*introductory STORY*): _____

_____

_____

_____

_____

_____

Point 1. APPLICATION of STORY to Scripture themes: _____

_____

_____

_____

_____

_____

Point 2. CONNECTION between Scriptural themes and the listeners' life experience: _____

_____
_____
_____
_____
_____
_____

Point 3. RESPONSE/CONSIDERATION sought from listeners: _____

_____
_____
_____
_____
_____
_____

CLOSING STATEMENT (*refers back to STORY*): _____

_____
_____
_____
_____
_____
_____

3. HARVEST—A Checklist:

❑ Does my completed homily make the point I articulated above (*under PLANTING*)?

❑ Am I excited about this homily. Am I readily able to convey my own enthusiasm, my sincere conviction of what I am going to say?

❑ Am I ready to preach this homily? Have I rehearsed this homily out loud until:

> ❑ I am comfortable with the *flow* of this homily: I can make the *transitions* from point to point, from idea to idea, smoothly and clearly;

> ❑ I am using *words* and *expressions* that my listeners can understand and appreciate: I am not speaking in theological jargon or "holy card" talk;

> ❑ my *delivery* (voice, gestures, speaking rate, pronunciation and enunciation, pauses, etc.) and

> ❑ my *inflection* and *emphasis* of key words and phrases are natural and effective?

❑ My homily lasts _____ minutes. Is it ❑ too long? ❑ too short? ❑ just about right?

4. GLEANINGS—Thoughts and notes AFTER the Homily

What worked, what didn't work in this homily; response and reactions from the community; ideas for next time; etc.

_____
_____
_____
_____
_____
_____
_____
_____
_____
_____
_____
_____

Eighth Sunday of the Year

The Readings:

READING 1: Isaiah 49: 14-15

Can a mother forget her infant,
be without tenderness for the child of her womb?
Even should she forget,
I will never forget you.

Second Isaiah's prophetic mission was to give consolation to the Israelites who had been deported to Babylon by Nebuchadnezzar after the fall of Jerusalem in 597 B.C. Today's reading, from Isaiah's poems of return, assures Israel that Yahweh has not forgotten them and that he is about to free his people again. The passage beautifully uses the female experience to offer an important insight into humanity's relationship with God.

READING 2: 1 Corinthians 4: 1-5

The Lord is the one to judge me, so stop passing judgment before the time of his return. He will bring to light what is hidden in darkness and manifest the intentions of hearts.

In the final weekly reading in this series from Paul's first letter to the Corinthians, the apostle continues his appeal to the many factions within the Church at Corinth to put aside their differences and remember their common call to be servants to one another in Christ. Questioning one another's commitment to the Gospel and sincerity of faith is a meaningless and fruitless exercise; such judgments are the domain of Christ alone.

GOSPEL: Matthew 6: 24-34

"Seek first God's kingship over you, his way of holiness, and all things will be given you besides."

Jesus' homily on serving "two masters" and the parables of the birds and wild flowers challenge our scale of values: do we exist to acquire the holiness of God or the riches of life? Jesus does not deny the reality of basic human needs for food and clothing, but to displace the holiness of God with the perishables of wealth and power is the ultimate human tragedy.

Themes:

• values: becoming slaves to things

So much of our time and energy is spent worrying about and securing things. We can become so absorbed with the pursuit of money, prestige and power that we miss the sense of purpose God's presence gives our lives and the richness of the love of those who are most important to us. Jesus does not condemn work, but he places it all in perspective. This life is a passing stage. It is not an end in itself but a means to a greater end—the kingdom of God.

• the providence of God

All three readings today speak of the providence of God: the God who does not forget us but constantly loves us as a mother who loves her child (Isaiah); the Lord who knows the "intentions of hearts" (1 Corinthians); and the Father who will provide for us (Matthew). In realizing God's care for all his people, we should, in turn, realize our own worth and the worth of every man, woman and child, who are also loved and cared for by God. This understanding of God's providence should have a profound

impact on the values we embrace, helping us see the world as one human family and leading us to seek what is good and just for all of God's people.

For Reflection:

• We have come to "know" God primarily in male images (Father, King, etc.). Taking a cue from Second Isaiah, consider the "feminine" qualities of God.

• Do you know of individuals whose climb up the ladder of success left them feeling empty, jaded, unfulfilled?

• We all know incessant worriers—people who deprive themselves of so much joy because of their often needless anxieties and groundless fears. What does today's Gospel say to them?

• How can we make life "simpler" in this high-tech world of ours?

• What are the "warning signs" that one's pursuit of fame and fortune is out of control, that one is losing perspective of what is genuinely important and of value in this life God has given him/her?

Date: _____

HOMILY WORKSHEET for the Eighth Sunday of the Year

1. SEEDS

What today's readings say *to me*: _____

_____

_____

PARABLES, STORIES and EXPERIENCES that speak to the themes of today's readings: _____

_____

_____

SPECIAL CONSIDERATIONS this week: Audience? Events in the community? Unique dimensions to this celebration?

_____

_____

_____

What RESPONSE do I seek from my listeners?
❏ to affirm/enlighten them in their faith?
❏ to teach/inform them about _____

_____

❏ to have them take a specific action _____

_____

2. PLANTING

The point I want to make in this homily (*ONE sentence*): _____

_____

_____

HOMILY OUTLINE

OPENING (*introductory STORY*): _____

_____

_____

_____

_____

_____

Point 1. APPLICATION of STORY to Scripture themes: _____

_____

_____

_____

_____

_____

Point 2. CONNECTION between Scriptural themes and the listeners' life experience: _____

_____
_____
_____
_____
_____

Point 3. RESPONSE/CONSIDERATION sought from listeners: _____

_____
_____
_____
_____
_____

CLOSING STATEMENT (*refers back to STORY*): _____

_____
_____
_____
_____
_____

3. HARVEST—A Checklist:

❏ Does my completed homily make the point I articulated above (*under PLANTING*)?

❏ Am I excited about this homily. Am I readily able to convey my own enthusiasm, my sincere conviction of what I am going to say?

❏ Am I ready to preach this homily? Have I rehearsed this homily out loud until:

   ❏ I am comfortable with the *flow* of this homily: I can make the *transitions* from point to point, from idea to idea, smoothly and clearly;

   ❏ I am using *words* and *expressions* that my listeners can understand and appreciate: I am not speaking in theological jargon or "holy card" talk;

   ❏ my *delivery* (voice, gestures, speaking rate, pronunciation and enunciation, pauses, etc.) and

   ❏ my *inflection* and *emphasis* of key words and phrases are natural and effective?

❏ My homily lasts _____ minutes. Is it ❏ too long? ❏ too short? ❏ just about right?

4. GLEANINGS—Thoughts and notes AFTER the Homily

What worked, what didn't work in this homily; response and reactions from the community; ideas for next time; etc.

_____
_____
_____
_____
_____
_____
_____
_____
_____
_____
_____

Ninth Sunday of the Year

The Readings:

READING 1: Deuteronomy 11: 18, 26-28

Moses told the Israelites:

"Take these words of mine into your heart and soul. Bind them at your wrist as a sign, and let them be a pendant on your forehead."

The Book of Deuteronomy is a collection of Moses' exhortations to the Israelites on the plains of Moab as they prepared to enter the Promised Land. Today's reading concludes Moses' explanation of the Covenant and its implications for the new nation of Israel. In their desert experience, Israel learned the great fidelity and power of God—despite their own infidelity and weakness. Now, as they are about to become a nation, Moses reminds his people that their very existence and identity as a people are dependent upon its response to the great love of God for them.

READING 2: Romans 3: 21-25, 28

All have sinned and hence are deprived of the glory of God. All are now undeservedly justified by the gift of God, through the redemption wrought in Christ Jesus.

For the next 16 consecutive Sundays of the year in Cycle A, the second reading will be taken from Paul's letter to the Christian community at Rome. The apostle wrote this, the longest of his letters, at the end of his third missionary journey. Writing from Corinth in 58 A.D., Paul is looking westward—all the way to what is now Spain—to new missionary challenges. This epistle was written to prepare the way for a journey to the imperial city, to introduce himself and his teaching to a Christian community he did not know.

Paul's letter to the Romans is a systematic treatise explaining how God's plan of salvation, since Old Testament times, is fulfilled in Jesus Christ. Today's reading effectively summarizes a key theme of Romans: one's "justification" before God is not determined by the observance of all the detailed requirements of the Jewish Torah but by the depth of one's faith.

GOSPEL: Matthew 7:21-27

"Anyone who hears my words and puts them into practice is like the wise man who built his house on rock."

Jesus concludes the Sermon on the Mount exhorting his listeners to put the words of the Gospel into action. The depth of one's conviction of faith is the foundation of religion: the faith we actually live is the faith we really believe. One's sincerity is reflected in one's deeds; words can never substitute for deeds.

Themes:

• faith: the "rock" of personal conviction

Many older Catholics especially remember a Church where every detail of faith was codified, measured and outlined for us—from the amount of money one could steal before the theft became a mortal sin (we were taught that $5 was the limit, based on 1960 prices) to how much time we could save ourselves in Purgatory with the right combination and timing of prayers. The Jews of Jesus' time had the same experience: the rabbis had counted 613 separate laws and precepts specified in the Pentateuch, the Decalogue and Moses' explanation of them. To be a good and faithful Jew, then, was determined in one's observance of these 613 *mitzvoth.*

But Jesus says that authentic faith begins in the individual's heart. It begins with an understanding of God's love for us and the irrepressible longing to respond to that love. The Fathers at Vatican II saw this in terms of the dignity of one's conscience:

> "Man has in his heart a law inscribed by God. His dignity lies in observing this law, and by it he will be judged. His conscience is man's most secret core his sanctuary. There he is alone with God, whose voice echoes in his depths. In a wonderful way, conscience reveals that law which is fulfilled by love of God and neighbor." (*The Church in the Modern World*, 16)

• our covenant with God

A covenant is a very special kind of agreement or "testament" (*diatheke* in Greek) between two parties in which each solemnly bind themselves to the other.

But there is an important difference between the Scriptural concept of a covenant agreement and our understanding of contracted agreements. A contract is an agreement between two *equal* parties, each offering something to the other in return for something of equal value. But the Scriptural covenant was a compact between God and humankind—two very *unequal* parties. One of the central themes of Scripture is the covenant relationship between God and humankind—a free, loving binding of God to his creatures, with God demanding love and loyalty in return. Since Old Testament times, God freely offers humanity his love, despite humanity's unfaithfulness and rejection. Love is the foundation of our covenant with God; we accept God's offer of covenant in our love for one another.

For Reflection:

• What agreements do people make with one another that might be considered covenants in the Scriptural sense—a binding together that transcends the legal concept of contract? What moral dimensions of such covenants are similar to humankind's covenant with God?

• Like houses built on rock and on sand, some people's faith helps them withstand the storms of life, while others' faith fails them. Do you know stories of both kinds of faith? Why did faith remain? Why did it collapse?

• Recall times when your parish, as a whole, acted with the faith of "a house solidly set on rock."

Date: _____

HOMILY WORKSHEET for the Ninth Sunday of the Year

1. SEEDS

What today's readings say *to me*: _____

_____

_____

PARABLES, STORIES and EXPERIENCES that speak to the themes of today's readings: _____

_____

_____

SPECIAL CONSIDERATIONS this week: Audience? Events in the community? Unique dimensions to this celebration?

_____

_____

_____

What RESPONSE do I seek from my listeners?
❑ to affirm/enlighten them in their faith?
❑ to teach/inform them about _____

_____

❑ to have them take a specific action _____

_____

2. PLANTING

The point I want to make in this homily (*ONE sentence*): _____

_____

_____

HOMILY OUTLINE

OPENING (*introductory STORY*): _____

_____

_____

_____

_____

_____

Point 1. APPLICATION of STORY to Scripture themes: _____

_____

_____

_____

_____

_____

Point 2. CONNECTION between Scriptural themes and the listeners' life experience: _____

_____
_____
_____
_____
_____
_____

Point 3. RESPONSE/CONSIDERATION sought from listeners: _____

_____
_____
_____
_____
_____
_____

CLOSING STATEMENT (*refers back to STORY*): _____

_____
_____
_____
_____
_____

3. HARVEST—A Checklist:

❑ Does my completed homily make the point I articulated above (*under PLANTING*)?

❑ Am I excited about this homily. Am I readily able to convey my own enthusiasm, my sincere conviction of what I am going to say?

❑ Am I ready to preach this homily? Have I rehearsed this homily out loud until:

❑ I am comfortable with the *flow* of this homily: I can make the *transitions* from point to point, from idea to idea, smoothly and clearly;

❑ I am using *words* and *expressions* that my listeners can understand and appreciate: I am not speaking in theological jargon or "holy card" talk;

❑ my *delivery* (voice, gestures, speaking rate, pronunciation and enunciation, pauses, etc.) and

❑ my *inflection* and *emphasis* of key words and phrases are natural and effective?

❑ My homily lasts _____ minutes. Is it ❑ too long? ❑ too short? ❑ just about right?

4. GLEANINGS—Thoughts and notes AFTER the Homily

What worked, what didn't work in this homily; response and reactions from the community; ideas for next time; etc.

_____
_____
_____
_____
_____
_____
_____
_____
_____
_____
_____

Tenth Sunday of the Year

The Readings:

READING 1: Hosea 6:3-6

For it is love that I desire, not sacrifice, and knowledge of God rather than holocausts.

One of the 12 "minor prophets" of the Old Testament, Hosea was the first to describe the relationship between Yahweh and Israel in terms of marriage. Hosea preached in the eighth century before Christ in the northern kingdom of Israel, which he refers to as Ephraim (Judah is the southern kingdom). In today's reading the prophet warns the Israelites that their worship of God is meaningless if it is not genuine. Public worship, such as the offering of sacrifices and holocausts, should reflect the community's interior spirit of obedience and adoration. Without love and knowledge of God, such worship is a sham.

READING 2: Romans 4:18-25

Abraham believed hoping against hope. He never questioned or doubted God's promise; rather, he was strengthened in faith and gave glory to God, fully persuaded that God could do whatever he had promised.

Both Abraham and we Christians know a God who brings forth life out of death. For Abraham, God brought life out of Sarah's dead womb; in raising Jesus from the dead, God restored us to life. Abraham is a model of faith for us who have witnessed God's covenant promises to the Old Testament patriarchs and prophets fulfilled in the Risen Christ.

GOSPEL: Matthew 9: 9-13

The call of Matthew the tax collector:
"I have come to call not the self-righteous, but sinners."

Tax collectors like Matthew were despised by the Jews of Palestine. Tax collectors, also known as publicans, amassed huge fortunes through a taxation system that effectively legalized corruption, extortion and bribery.

Realizing it could never efficiently collect taxes from every subject in its far-flung empire, the Roman government auctioned off the right to collect taxes in a given area. Whoever bought that right was responsible to the Roman government for the agreed upon sum; whatever the purchaser could collect over and above that sum was his commission. How he "collected" those taxes was of little concern to the Romans. The Jews considered tax collectors collaborators with their nation's conquerors who became wealthy men by taking advantage of their people's misfortune.

That Jesus should invite a tax collector to join his closest circle, as well as welcoming known sinners into his company, scandalized the Pharisees. Citing the words of the prophet Hosea (today's first reading), Jesus states unequivocally that his Messianic mission is universal in nature and spirit, not limited to the coldly orthodox and piously self-righteous of Israel. Christ comes to call all men and women—Jew and Gentile, rich and poor, saint and sinner—back to the Father.

Themes:

• worship: celebrating faith as a community

Each week we gather around this altar to celebrate, in word and sacrament, our relationship with God. God calls us here not by imposing upon us an obligation but by inviting us to celebrate with him. Our worship means very little if we are conscious of our faith only for this one hour each week. (Sometimes our sense of Christian love and community doesn't even make it out of the church parking lot!) Our worship should reflect and celebrate the joy and love we live every day of every week; otherwise, as Hosea says, our worship is "like the dew that early passes away."

• to rejoice in what is good and right

Jesus came to show fishermen and farmers, peasants and prostitutes, tax collectors and shepherds, widows and children that they are all special in God's eyes. The sad thing about the incident recorded in today's Gospel is the Pharisees' inability to rejoice with them and for them. These "professional religious" could not accept the fact that God loves these people as much as he does those who considered themselves the "separated brethren" because of their fastidious keeping of the Law. Because of their concern with criticism instead of encouragement and condemnation instead of forgiveness, the Pharisees failed to understand that God speaks, not through legal entities and impersonal theological treatises, but through compassion and reconciliation directly to human hearts.

For Reflection:

• How should our celebration of the Eucharist each week affect the everyday dimensions of our lives?

• What do Hosea's words in today's first reading say to the planners of liturgy? To musicians? To celebrants and preachers? To the community?

• Have you ever found yourself suspicious over someone's "conversion"? What made you suspicious? Did it turn to anger? Why?

• When do we become a society of "Pharisees," critical and intolerant of other individuals and groups we consider "different" and "unworthy" to be part of our community?

Date: _____

HOMILY WORKSHEET for the Tenth Sunday of the Year

1. SEEDS

What today's readings say *to me*: _____

_____

_____

PARABLES, STORIES and EXPERIENCES that speak to the themes of today's readings: _____

_____

_____

SPECIAL CONSIDERATIONS this week: Audience? Events in the community? Unique dimensions to this celebration?

_____

_____

_____

What RESPONSE do I seek from my listeners?
❏ to affirm/enlighten them in their faith?
❏ to teach/inform them about _____

_____

❏ to have them take a specific action _____

_____

2. PLANTING

The point I want to make in this homily (*ONE sentence*): _____

_____

_____

HOMILY OUTLINE

OPENING (*introductory STORY*): _____

_____

_____

_____

_____

_____

Point 1. APPLICATION of STORY to Scripture themes: _____

_____

_____

_____

_____

_____

Point 2. CONNECTION between Scriptural themes and the listeners' life experience: _____

_____
_____
_____
_____
_____

Point 3. RESPONSE/CONSIDERATION sought from listeners: _____

_____
_____
_____
_____
_____
_____

CLOSING STATEMENT (*refers back to STORY*): _____

_____
_____
_____
_____
_____

3. HARVEST—A Checklist:

❑ Does my completed homily make the point I articulated above (*under PLANTING*)?

❑ Am I excited about this homily. Am I readily able to convey my own enthusiasm, my sincere conviction of what I am going to say?

❑ Am I ready to preach this homily? Have I rehearsed this homily out loud until:

    ❑ I am comfortable with the *flow* of this homily: I can make the *transitions* from point to point, from idea to idea, smoothly and clearly;

    ❑ I am using *words* and *expressions* that my listeners can understand and appreciate: I am not speaking in theological jargon or "holy card" talk;

    ❑ my *delivery* (voice, gestures, speaking rate, pronunciation and enunciation, pauses, etc.) and

    ❑ my *inflection* and *emphasis* of key words and phrases are natural and effective?

❑ My homily lasts _____ minutes. Is it ❑ too long? ❑ too short? ❑ just about right?

4. GLEANINGS—Thoughts and notes AFTER the Homily

What worked, what didn't work in this homily; response and reactions from the community; ideas for next time; etc.

_____
_____
_____
_____
_____
_____
_____
_____
_____
_____
_____

11th Sunday of the Year

The Readings:

READING 1: Exodus 19:2-6

"If you hearken to my voice and keep my covenant, you shall be my special possession, dearer to me than all other people."

The covenant God makes with Israel during the Exodus transformed the Israelites from a band of ex-slaves into a nation. It gave them an identity and a destiny. The God who brought them out of the land of Egypt to a promised land now invites them to enter into a special relationship with him, a covenant of intimacy, holiness and freedom.

READING 2: Romans 5: 6-11

God proves his love for us: while we were still sinners, Christ died for us.

In light of today's first reading, this selection from Paul's letter to the Romans speaks of God's faithfulness in keeping his covenant with humankind. God continues to call humankind back to him, even sending his own Son to renew and re-create that covenant by his passion, death and resurrection.

GOSPEL: Matthew 9: 36—10:8

"The harvest is good but laborers are scarce . . . ." Jesus sent these men on mission as the Twelve.

These verses from Matthew's Gospel serve as a transition between Matthew's recounting of Jesus' miraculous deeds (chapters 8 and 9) and Jesus' missionary discourse (chapters 10 and 11). The missionary dimension of discipleship is brought out by two images: the people who are "like sheep without a shepherd" and the need for laborers to gather the harvest. Having established his great powers as a healer, Jesus now passes on to the Twelve the "gift" of their own call and mission to the people of Israel.

Themes:

• vocation: sharing the "gift" of faith

The Twelve whom Jesus "summons" in today's Gospel were very ordinary men. They possessed neither wealth, scholarship nor social standing. Yet they are given the "gift" of leadership to share with all people the Gospel they have received. Whether ordained or not all who are baptized share in this "priestly" work (Reading 1) of sharing the gift of faith with others.

• vocation: the ministry of reconciliation

In today's Gospel, Jesus commissions the apostles to a ministry of healing. But to see this commission as involving physical healing alone is to miss an important dimension of Jesus' ministry. Jesus commissions the apostles and his Church to heal hearts and souls in a ministry of reconciliation:

- "cure the sick": bring back to God those who are alienated, those who are weak in faith (the word used in the Greek text *asthenes* means "weak");

- "raise the dead": bring back those hopelessly and helplessly dead because of sin and blind and deaf to the goodness and love of God.

- "heal the leprous": bring back those who have been rejected or are separated from God's people;

- "expel demons": liberate those enslaved by sin and evil.

For Reflection:

• Would you consider your own call to ministry a gift?

• How is your parish community—both those ordained and those not ordained—a "kingdom of priests, a holy nation"?

• Is there one of the Twelve Apostles, listed by Matthew in today's Gospel, whom you especially relate to?

• What do today's readings tell us about God's love for the Jewish people? How should these insights affect your own relationships with your Jewish neighbors?

Date: _____

HOMILY WORKSHEET for the 11th Sunday of the Year

1. SEEDS

What today's readings say *to me*: _____

_____

_____

PARABLES, STORIES and EXPERIENCES that speak to the themes of today's readings: _____

_____

_____

SPECIAL CONSIDERATIONS this week: Audience? Events in the community? Unique dimensions to this celebration?

_____

_____

_____

What RESPONSE do I seek from my listeners?
❑ to affirm/enlighten them in their faith?
❑ to teach/inform them about _____

_____

❑ to have them take a specific action _____

_____

2. PLANTING

The point I want to make in this homily (*ONE sentence*): _____

_____

_____

HOMILY OUTLINE

OPENING (*introductory STORY*): _____

_____

_____

_____

_____

_____

Point 1. APPLICATION of STORY to Scripture themes: _____

_____

_____

_____

_____

_____

Point 2. CONNECTION between Scriptural themes and the listeners' life experience: _____

_____

_____

_____

_____

_____

_____

Point 3. RESPONSE/CONSIDERATION sought from listeners: _____

_____

_____

_____

_____

_____

_____

CLOSING STATEMENT (*refers back to STORY*): _____

_____

_____

_____

_____

_____

_____

3. HARVEST—A Checklist:

❑ Does my completed homily make the point I articulated above (*under PLANTING*)?

❑ Am I excited about this homily. Am I readily able to convey my own enthusiasm, my sincere conviction of what I am going to say?

❑ Am I ready to preach this homily? Have I rehearsed this homily out loud until:

❑ I am comfortable with the *flow* of this homily: I can make the *transitions* from point to point, from idea to idea, smoothly and clearly;

❑ I am using *words* and *expressions* that my listeners can understand and appreciate: I am not speaking in theological jargon or "holy card" talk;

❑ my *delivery* (voice, gestures, speaking rate, pronunciation and enunciation, pauses, etc.) and

❑ my *inflection* and *emphasis* of key words and phrases are natural and effective?

❑ My homily lasts _____ minutes. Is it ❑ too long? ❑ too short? ❑ just about right?

4. GLEANINGS—Thoughts and notes AFTER the Homily

What worked, what didn't work in this homily; response and reactions from the community; ideas for next time; etc.

_____

_____

_____

_____

_____

_____

_____

_____

_____

_____

_____

12th Sunday of the Year

The Readings:

READING 1: Jeremiah 20: 10-13

"Yes, I hear the whispers of many:
'Terror on every side!
Denounce! let us denounce him!'
But the Lord is with me, like a mighty champion."

Jeremiah recognized that the Babylonian empire rising in the north posed a serious threat to Judah. Jeremiah prophesied that Judah's pride and infidelity would lead to the fall of Jerusalem and the destruction of the temple. The king and people, enraged that Jeremiah could suggest such an unthinkable thing, had the prophet whipped and placed in the stocks. Though denounced and persecuted by the people he loved, the deeply sensitive Jeremiah remains faithful to his prophetic call, confident that God is with him and his persecutors will not triumph.

READING 2: Romans 5: 12-15

If by the offense of the one man all died, much more did the grace of God and the gracious gift of the one man, Jesus Christ, abound for all.

In today's reading from Romans, Paul contrasts the figures of Adam and Christ. For Paul, Adam is the first man who unleashed the power of sin into the world and, consequently, humankind's alienation from God. Jesus is the first man of God's new creation. By the gracious gift of Jesus Christ, sin and death fall and grace and life are restored.

GOSPEL: Matthew 10: 26-33

"Do not fear those who deprive the body of life but cannot destroy the soul . . . Whoever acknowledges me before men I will acknowledge before my Father in heaven."

In Matthew's missionary discourse, Jesus instills in his disciples the need for openness and courage in their preaching of the Gospel. The disciple who faithfully proclaims the Gospel will likely be denounced, ridiculed and abused; but the perseverance and courage of the faithful disciple will be rewarded in the kingdom of God.

Themes:

• the courage to proclaim the truth

Diogenes, the Greek philosopher, observed that for many, "truth is like light to sore eyes." Jesus does not sugarcoat his warning: the Gospel demands the courage to stand up for its principles in the face of society's skepticism and disapproval. Like the Jews' rejection of Jeremiah's unpopular message, many segments of society cannot abide the idea of unconditional love nor the constant call to forgive demanded by Jesus in the Gospel. If we take our role as disciples seriously, then we are probably going to do time in the "stocks" of public disapproval and derision for the Gospel we live.

Important to understand, too, is the call of Jesus to "acknowledge me before men." We can "disown" Jesus actively by our words and actions, but we can also "disown" him passively by our silence.

• "do not be afraid . . ."

Today's first reading and Gospel are powerful assurances that men and women of faith have nothing on earth to fear. Three times in today's Gospel Jesus tells his disciples not to be afraid. Imagine living your life fearing no person, group or institution anywhere, fearing only God—God who has already proven his love and acceptance of you unreservedly. Such a realization is the ultimate liberation and empowerment. As the late Dr. Martin Luther King Jr. preached:

"Courage is an inner resolution to go forward despite obstacles; cowardice is submissive surrender to circumstances. Courage breeds creative self-affirmation; cowardice produces destructive self-abnegation. Courage faces fear and masters it; cowardice represses fear and is mastered by it."

For Reflection:

• How do we "disown" Jesus by silence?

• Consider the lives and deaths of those who, since the days of the apostles, have gone to their deaths for their faith. Who among these martyrs do you find especially inspiring?

• In what ways are today's readings "liberating"?

• What community and national concerns today need the perseverance and faith of a Jeremiah?

Date: _____

HOMILY WORKSHEET for the 12th Sunday of the Year

1. SEEDS

What today's readings say *to me*: _____

_____

_____

PARABLES, STORIES and EXPERIENCES that speak to the themes of today's readings: _____

_____

_____

SPECIAL CONSIDERATIONS this week: Audience? Events in the community? Unique dimensions to this celebration?

_____

_____

_____

What RESPONSE do I seek from my listeners?
❏ to affirm/enlighten them in their faith?
❏ to teach/inform them about _____

_____

❏ to have them take a specific action _____

_____

2. PLANTING

The point I want to make in this homily (*ONE sentence*): _____

_____

_____

HOMILY OUTLINE

OPENING (*introductory STORY*): _____

_____

_____

_____

_____

_____

Point 1. APPLICATION of STORY to Scripture themes: _____

_____

_____

_____

_____

_____

Point 2. CONNECTION between Scriptural themes and the listeners' life experience: _____

_____

_____

_____

_____

_____

Point 3. RESPONSE/CONSIDERATION sought from listeners: _____

_____

_____

_____

_____

_____

CLOSING STATEMENT (*refers back to STORY*): _____

_____

_____

_____

_____

_____

3. HARVEST—A Checklist:

❑ Does my completed homily make the point I articulated above (*under PLANTING*)?

❑ Am I excited about this homily. Am I readily able to convey my own enthusiasm, my sincere conviction of what I am going to say?

❑ Am I ready to preach this homily? Have I rehearsed this homily out loud until:

   ❑ I am comfortable with the *flow* of this homily: I can make the *transitions* from point to point, from idea to idea, smoothly and clearly;

   ❑ I am using *words* and *expressions* that my listeners can understand and appreciate: I am not speaking in theological jargon or "holy card" talk;

   ❑ my *delivery* (voice, gestures, speaking rate, pronunciation and enunciation, pauses, etc.) and

   ❑ my *inflection* and *emphasis* of key words and phrases are natural and effective?

❑ My homily lasts _____ minutes. Is it ❑ too long? ❑ too short? ❑ just about right?

4. GLEANINGS—Thoughts and notes AFTER the Homily

What worked, what didn't work in this homily; response and reactions from the community; ideas for next time; etc.

_____

_____

_____

_____

_____

_____

_____

_____

_____

_____

_____

13th Sunday of the Year

The Readings:

READING 1: 2 Kings 4: 8-11, 14-16

Elisha promised the kind woman of Shunem:
  "This time next year you will be fondling a baby son."

Elisha was ordained by God to be the successor of the great prophet Elijah (1 Kings 19: 15-21). Today's reading is one of several delightful Old Testament tales about Elisha the "miracle worker" and his assistant Gehazi. The woman of Shunem recognizes the sacred nature of Elisha's calling and assists him as she is able, offering him the hospitality of her home. Elisha, in turn, rewards her for her kindness with the promise of a child.

READING 2: Romans 6: 3-4, 8-11

You must consider yourselves dead to sin but alive for God in Christ Jesus.

In today's reading from the letter to the Romans, Paul writes that our baptism liberates us from the hostile force of sin. Although sin is still very much a reality in our lives, Paul writes that it is no longer a permanent, hopeless condition. We Christians live always in the hope and power of the resurrection.

GOSPEL: Matthew 10: 37-42

"He who will not take up his cross and come after me is not worthy of me. Whoever gives a
cup of cold water to one of these lowly ones because he is a disciple will not want for his
reward."

Today's Gospel is the conclusion of Matthew's collection of Jesus' missionary discourses, in which Jesus speaks of the sacrifice demanded of his disciples and the suffering they will endure for their faith. In today's reading, Jesus clearly is not attacking family life; he is warning his disciples of the conflict they will experience. To be an authentic disciple of Jesus means embracing suffering, humility, pain and total selflessness; to be an authentic disciple of Jesus means taking on the often unpopular role of prophet for the sake of the kingdom; to be an authentic disciple of Jesus means welcoming and support-ing other disciples who do the work of the Gospel.

Themes:

• a Christian approach to conflict

The true disciple of Christ takes a very different approach to resolving conflict—an approach totally at odds with the win-at-all-costs philosophy of the world. We are called to work for reconciliation. Christ's challenge to us is to look beyond stereotypes and labels to see, instead, brothers and sisters. Christ calls his disciples to rise from the grave of self-centeredness, the needs of others first and our own interests last.

• welcoming prophets

Christ calls us to bring to the role of disciple all that we have and are. God gives to some the talent and courage to challenge society's institutions for the sake of the kingdom of God; to others, he gives the grace to hear that message and re-create society in the Spirit of that kingdom; and some are called by God to support that work by giving "a cup of cold water." May we accept the challenge of welcoming the prophets and the holy men and women who bless this age.

For Reflection:

• When was the last time you experienced a genuine crisis of conscience—a situation when you felt social convention pressuring you to act in a way contrary to your sense of the Gospel?

• How and when can we welcome the prophets present among us today?

• What would you see as the "Christian" approach to resolving conflict?

Date: _____

HOMILY WORKSHEET for the 13th Sunday of the Year

1. SEEDS

What today's readings say *to me*: _____
_____
_____

PARABLES, STORIES and EXPERIENCES that speak to the themes of today's readings: _____
_____
_____

SPECIAL CONSIDERATIONS this week: Audience? Events in the community? Unique dimensions to this celebration?
_____
_____
_____

What RESPONSE do I seek from my listeners?
❏ to affirm/enlighten them in their faith?
❏ to teach/inform them about _____
_____

❏ to have them take a specific action _____
_____

2. PLANTING

The point I want to make in this homily (*ONE sentence*): _____
_____
_____

HOMILY OUTLINE

OPENING (*introductory STORY*): _____
_____
_____
_____
_____
_____

Point 1. APPLICATION of STORY to Scripture themes: _____
_____
_____
_____
_____
_____

Point 2. CONNECTION between Scriptural themes and the listeners' life experience: _____

_____

_____

_____

_____

_____

Point 3. RESPONSE/CONSIDERATION sought from listeners: _____

_____

_____

_____

_____

_____

CLOSING STATEMENT (*refers back to STORY*): _____

_____

_____

_____

_____

_____

3. HARVEST—A Checklist:

❑ Does my completed homily make the point I articulated above (*under PLANTING*)?

❑ Am I excited about this homily. Am I readily able to convey my own enthusiasm, my sincere conviction of what I am going to say?

❑ Am I ready to preach this homily? Have I rehearsed this homily out loud until:

    ❑ I am comfortable with the *flow* of this homily: I can make the *transitions* from point to point, from idea to idea, smoothly and clearly;

    ❑ I am using *words* and *expressions* that my listeners can understand and appreciate: I am not speaking in theological jargon or "holy card" talk;

    ❑ my *delivery* (voice, gestures, speaking rate, pronunciation and enunciation, pauses, etc.) and

    ❑ my *inflection* and *emphasis* of key words and phrases are natural and effective?

❑ My homily lasts _____ minutes. Is it ❑ too long? ❑ too short? ❑ just about right?

4. GLEANINGS—Thoughts and notes AFTER the Homily

What worked, what didn't work in this homily; response and reactions from the community; ideas for next time; etc.

_____

_____

_____

_____

_____

_____

_____

_____

_____

_____

_____

14th Sunday of the Year

The Readings:

READING 1: Zechariah 9: 9-10

Your king shall come to you,
a just savior is he,
Meek, and riding an ass.
The warrior's bow shall be banished,
and he shall proclaim peace to the nations.

This prophecy by Zechariah was cited by the evangelists of the New Testament as fulfilled in Jesus's entry into Jerusalem. The prophecy is not only fulfilled literally but, more importantly, in spirit: the Messiah comes not in fire and fury but in quiet humility; he comes, not armed with military might, but with peace and justice, banishing the implements of war forever.

The image of a king riding an ass strikes today's listener as a contradiction, but, in Zechariah's time, a ruler riding on an ass was a symbol of great dignity and authority (hence, Jesus is hailed as a king in the Palm Sunday Gospel). There is also an irony in this image that is not lost on Zechariah's hearers: the Jews were despised by their Persian and Egyptian enemies who ridiculed the Jews as "donkey drivers." Among this nation of "donkey drivers" God's own Light will dawn for the world.

READING 2: Romans 8: 9, 11-13

You are not in the flesh; you are in the spirit.

We are people of the Spirit of God—we live constantly in the hope of the Resurrection, not in the hopelessness of this world of ours.

GOSPEL: Matthew 11: 25-30

"No one knows the Father but the Son—and anyone to whom the Son wishes to reveal him.

"Come to me, all you who are weary and find life burdensome, and I will refresh you. Take my yoke upon your shoulders and learn from me, for I am gentle and humble of heart."

Rarely outside of John's Gospel is Jesus' intimacy with the Father so clearly portrayed. We can only appreciate this intimacy within the divinity in terms of a father's love for a favorite son. Christ is the revelation of God's great love for humanity: Jesus reveals to us that our Creator loves us like a father loves his children and he invites humankind to come to know the wisdom of God through him.

Religion as a "yoke" was exactly how Jesus' Jewish listeners saw the Law. They saw their faith as a burden, a submission to a set of endless rules and regulations dictating every dimension of their lives. But Jesus describes his "yoke" as "easy." The Greek word used here that we translate as "easy" more accurately means "well-fitting." In Palestine, ox yokes were custom-made of wood, cut and measured to fit the particular animal. Jesus is proposing here a radical change in attitude regarding faith: our relationship with God is not based on how meticulously we keep an endless series of rules and regulations (a direct challenge to the long-held view of the scribes and Pharisees) but in the depth of our love of God, reflected in our love for others. Our relationship with God is not based on subjugation and weariness but on hope and joy.

There is also an important political dimension to these verses. Matthew's Gospel was written a short time after the destruction of Jerusalem in the year 70 A.D. by the soldier-emperor Vespasian. For both the Jewish and the new Christian communities, it was a time of painful introspection: would Israel's hope for the political restoration of the Jewish state never be realized? While orthodox Jews maintained unwavering fidelity to their people, language and sense of nationalism, the Christian "cult" among them saw their ultimate destiny not in the political restoration of Israel but in the coming of the kingdom of God—a kingdom that embraced not just Jews but all men and women, even Israel's most despised enemies. Jewish suspicion of the Christian community was growing as the new group would have no part of the Jewish political agenda. Jesus' words on gentleness and humility set off sparks between loyal Jews and Christians who were abandoning the cause.

Themes:

• the burden of discipleship: service

At the entrance to Father Flanagan's Boys' Town, there is a sculpture of an older boy carrying a younger child on his shoulders. The inscription at the base of the statue reads, "He ain't heavy, Father, he's my brother" (the inscription was also the title of a popular song recorded by Neil Diamond and by the Hollies in the early 1970s). The statue (and song) are the perfect responses to the "burden" Christ proposes for us. To love one another, to serve one another as Christ the Savior serves God's people, is a yoke that is "easy" in its sense of fulfillment and "light" in its sense of joy.

• the perspective of discipleship: humility

In calling us to be "gentle" and "humble of heart," Jesus is not calling us to be simpletons and anti-intellectuals. He is calling us, instead, to embrace his attitude and spirit of open-heartedness and open-handedness, to create understanding and community among all people (the vision of Reading 1), to seek the welfare of others before our own.

For Reflection:

• How do we needlessly approach our faith as a "burden"? How do we take the joy out of religion?

• How is the disciple of Christ to be a strong and tireless witness to the Gospel and, at the same time, "gentle and humble of heart"?

• What does the image of the "king riding on an ass" teach us about the crises and challenges facing our world at the threshold of the 20th century?

Date: _____

HOMILY WORKSHEET for the 14th Sunday of the Year

1. SEEDS

What today's readings say *to me*: _____

_____

_____

PARABLES, STORIES and EXPERIENCES that speak to the themes of today's readings: _____

_____

_____

SPECIAL CONSIDERATIONS this week: Audience? Events in the community? Unique dimensions to this celebration?

_____

_____

_____

What RESPONSE do I seek from my listeners?
❑ to affirm/enlighten them in their faith?
❑ to teach/inform them about _____

_____

❑ to have them take a specific action _____

_____

2. PLANTING

The point I want to make in this homily (*ONE sentence*): _____

_____

_____

HOMILY OUTLINE

OPENING (*introductory STORY*): _____

_____

_____

_____

_____

_____

Point 1. APPLICATION of STORY to Scripture themes: _____

_____

_____

_____

_____

_____

Point 2. CONNECTION between Scriptural themes and the listeners' life experience: _____

_____

_____

_____

_____

_____

Point 3. RESPONSE/CONSIDERATION sought from listeners: _____

_____

_____

_____

_____

_____

_____

CLOSING STATEMENT (*refers back to STORY*): _____

_____

_____

_____

_____

_____

3. HARVEST—A Checklist:

❑ Does my completed homily make the point I articulated above (*under PLANTING*)?

❑ Am I excited about this homily. Am I readily able to convey my own enthusiasm, my sincere conviction of what I am going to say?

❑ Am I ready to preach this homily? Have I rehearsed this homily out loud until:

❑ I am comfortable with the *flow* of this homily: I can make the *transitions* from point to point, from idea to idea, smoothly and clearly;

❑ I am using *words* and *expressions* that my listeners can understand and appreciate: I am not speaking in theological jargon or "holy card" talk;

❑ my *delivery* (voice, gestures, speaking rate, pronunciation and enunciation, pauses, etc.) and

❑ my *inflection* and *emphasis* of key words and phrases are natural and effective?

❑ My homily lasts _____ minutes. Is it ❑ too long? ❑ too short? ❑ just about right?

4. GLEANINGS—Thoughts and notes AFTER the Homily

What worked, what didn't work in this homily; response and reactions from the community; ideas for next time; etc.

_____

_____

_____

_____

_____

_____

_____

_____

_____

_____

_____

15th Sunday of the Year

The Readings:

READING 1: Isaiah 55: 10-11

Just as the rain and snow water the earth
making it fertile and fruitful,
So shall my word be
that goes from my mouth.

Deutero-Isaiah, the prophet of the exile, concludes his section of the Book of Isaiah with this description of God's word enriching our lives like the rains of heaven enrich the earth for the harvest.

READING 2: Romans 8: 18-23

I consider the sufferings of the present to be as nothing compared with the glory to be revealed in us.

The glory that awaits Christ's faithful far exceeds the sufferings of the present. All of creation, which "groans (in) agony," joins humanity in anticipation of the completion of the redemption of our bodies.

GOSPEL: Matthew 13: 1-23 (or 13: 1-9)

The parable of the sower.

Chapter 13 of Matthew's Gospel is the evangelist's collection of Jesus' parables. The word parable comes from the Greek word *parabole* which means putting two things side by side in order to confront or compare them. And that is exactly how Jesus uses parables: he places a simile from life or nature against the abstract idea of the kingdom of God. The comparison challenges the hearer to consider ideas and possibilities greater and larger than those to which they were accustomed. Jesus' hearers expected God's kingdom to be the restoration of Israel to great political and economic power; the Messiah would be a great warrior-king who would lead Israel to this triumph. Jesus' parables subtly and delicately led people, without crushing or disillusioning them, to rethink their concept of God's kingdom.

In Palestine, sowing was done before the ploughing. Seed was not carefully and precisely placed in the ground. The farmer scattered the seed in all directions, knowing that, even though much will be wasted, enough will be sown in good earth to ensure a harvest nonetheless. The parable of the sower (which appears in all three synoptic gospels) teaches that the seed's fruitfulness (God's word) depends on the the soil's openness (the willingness of the human heart to embrace it).

Themes:

• the harvest: opening our hearts to God

In order to grow, a seed must be placed *inside* the earth so that its roots may take hold as its stem reaches for the sun above the surface. The parable of the sower challenges us to see how deeply the word of God has taken root in our lives, how central God is to the very fabric of our day-to-day existence. Are we too obtuse to understand the meaning of God's word in our lives (the seed on the footpath)? Maybe our faith is a "Sunday mornings only" experience and has no practical application in the real world of Monday through Saturday (the seed on the rocky soil). Or perhaps we're too intent on "making it" in the world that we refuse to allow the presence of God to alter our agenda for wealth and power (the seed among the briers). As the dry earth yearns for the water to bring forth the harvest (Reading 1), so must our hearts be open to receive the word of God.

• the unexpected harvest: hope

The farmer of the parable confidently seeds his fields knowing that, although some seed will be lost to the footpaths, rocks and thorns, a harvest will come. God's word of love and healing will go forth and be fruitful (Reading 1)—sometimes in soil in which such growth is unexpected. We must not be discouraged or intimidated from what is right or good because it might be misinterpreted, misunderstood or rejected. Sometimes we may never realize what good will be realized from the smallest "seed" of kindness we plant.

For Reflection:

• Consider how different people react to the messages of the Gospel. Why the different reactions? What dimensions of people's backgrounds and experiences affect how—and how much—of the Gospel takes root?

• Share stories of how a simple act of kindness—a good word, a smile, a moment to listen—yielded an unexpected harvest of growth and goodness.

Date: _____

HOMILY WORKSHEET for the 15th Sunday of the Year

1. SEEDS

What today's readings say *to me*: _____

_____

_____

PARABLES, STORIES and EXPERIENCES that speak to the themes of today's readings: _____

_____

_____

SPECIAL CONSIDERATIONS this week: Audience? Events in the community? Unique dimensions to this celebration?

_____

_____

_____

What RESPONSE do I seek from my listeners?
❑ to affirm/enlighten them in their faith?
❑ to teach/inform them about _____

_____

❑ to have them take a specific action _____

_____

2. PLANTING

The point I want to make in this homily (*ONE sentence*): _____

_____

_____

HOMILY OUTLINE

OPENING (*introductory STORY*): _____

_____

_____

_____

_____

_____

Point 1. APPLICATION of STORY to Scripture themes: _____

_____

_____

_____

_____

_____

Point 2. CONNECTION between Scriptural themes and the listeners' life experience: _____

_____

_____

_____

_____

_____

Point 3. RESPONSE/CONSIDERATION sought from listeners: _____

_____

_____

_____

_____

_____

CLOSING STATEMENT (*refers back to STORY*): _____

_____

_____

_____

_____

_____

3. HARVEST—A Checklist:

❑ Does my completed homily make the point I articulated above (*under PLANTING*)?

❑ Am I excited about this homily. Am I readily able to convey my own enthusiasm, my sincere conviction of what I am going to say?

❑ Am I ready to preach this homily? Have I rehearsed this homily out loud until:

❑ I am comfortable with the *flow* of this homily: I can make the *transitions* from point to point, from idea to idea, smoothly and clearly;

❑ I am using *words* and *expressions* that my listeners can understand and appreciate: I am not speaking in theological jargon or "holy card" talk;

❑ my *delivery* (voice, gestures, speaking rate, pronunciation and enunciation, pauses, etc.) and

❑ my *inflection* and *emphasis* of key words and phrases are natural and effective?

❑ My homily lasts _____ minutes. Is it ❑ too long? ❑ too short? ❑ just about right?

4. GLEANINGS—Thoughts and notes AFTER the Homily

What worked, what didn't work in this homily; response and reactions from the community; ideas for next time; etc.

_____

_____

_____

_____

_____

_____

_____

_____

_____

_____

_____

16th Sunday of the Year

The Readings:

READING 1: Wisdom 12:13, 16-19

For your might is the source of justice;
your mastery over all things makes you lenient to all.
And you taught your people, by these deeds,
that those who are just must be kind.

The Old Testament Book of Wisdom, written less than 100 years before Christ, is addressed to the Jewish community that settled in Alexandria, Egypt, as a result of the exile. The author makes Solomon, the wise king of Hebrew tradition, his mouthpiece in order to give more credence to his teachings. The Book of Wisdom exhorts Greek-speaking Jews who have abandoned their faith to enter the mainstream of Greek philosophy and thought to seek again the true wisdom of God.

Today's reading speaks of the mercy and justice of God as signs of his great power. The author reminds his readers that as the chosen of God they are to be compassionate and merciful as God has been merciful and compassionate toward Israel through the centuries. The truly powerful do not intimidate others with displays of might, but use their power to inspire others to do what is good and right.

READING 2: Romans 8:26-27

The Spirit helps us in our weakness, for we do not know how to pray as we ought . . . The Spirit intercedes for the saints as God himself wills.

In today's reading from his letter to the Romans, Paul reflects on the role of the Spirit as an inspiration to prayer. The awareness of God's Spirit within us gives both meaning and focus to our prayers.

GOSPEL: Matthew 13: 24-42 (or 13:24-30)

"The reign of God may be likened to a man who sowed good seed in his field . . . to a mustard seed . . . to yeast kneaded into flour . . . ."

Matthew's Gospel has been called the "Gospel of the Kingdom," containing some 51 references to the kingdom or reign of God. Three of Jesus' "kingdom" parables make up today's gospel:

The parable of the wheat and the weeds: God's kingdom will be "harvested" from among the good which exists side-by-side with the bad. Palestinian farmers were plagued by *tares*—weeds that were very difficult to distinguish from good grain. The two would often grow together and become so intertwined that it was impossible to separate them without ripping both weed and plant from the ground.

The parable of the mustard seed: The smallest and humblest are enabled by the Spirit of God to do great things in the kingdom of God. From small and humble beginnings, God's kingdom will grow.

The parable of the yeast: Although unseen, God's reign is a powerful force. A small amount of yeast mixed with three measures of flour can make enough bread to feed over one hundred.

Matthew's Gospel was written some 50 years after Jesus' death and 15 years after the destruction of Jerusalem. By this time it is clear to the community of Christians that Jesus is not going to be accepted by all of Israel as the Messiah. In citing these parables, the writer encouraged the largely Jewish Christian community to see itself as the legitimate heir to God's promises to Israel. They were the good wheat existing side by side with the weeds that would destroy it, the small mustard seed that would give rise to the great and mighty tree of the Church, the small amount of yeast that would become bread for the world.

Themes:

• mustard seeds: small beginnings

On a December day in 1951, a Montgomery, Alabama seamstress named Rosa Parks started a revolution in this country. Just as she did every day, Mrs. Parks got on the Cleveland Street bus in downtown Montgomery for the trip home. When Mrs. Park, a black, was instructed to give up her seat for a white, she refused. She was arrested and fined $10. Her action triggered a 381-day bus boycott in Montgomery (a boycott organized and led by a young black minister by the name of Martin Luther King, Jr.). Rosa Parks' case went all the way to the U.S. Supreme Court, which ruled that racial segregation violated the 15th amendment of the Constitution. One black woman's single act of refusing to deny her own rights and dignity is regarded by many as a turning point in the battle for civil rights in America—from one small "mustard seed" of courage and conviction, the great "tree" of the civil rights movement took root.

• yeast and grain: the Christian vocation

The parables of the yeast and the wheat growing amid the weeds speak to us of our vocation as Christians in the world:

In baptism, we accept God's call to be "yeast," giving life to our world which is often lifeless in its despair and aimlessness.

The call to holiness becomes more and more difficult as society becomes less and less tolerant of the spiritual. What the world values as good and valuable is often at odds with Christ's call to selflessness and simplicity. Our faith in the God of forgiveness and redemption gives us the courage to carry on until the harvest.

For Reflection:

• Share stories you have found especially inspiring of small "seeds" giving rise to great things, of individuals who have realized the full potential of the Gospel mustard seed.

• Looking through today's newspaper, do you see, in the midst of war, terrorism, poverty, etc., traces of the "yeast" of the kingdom of God?

• In light of today's first reading from the Book of Wisdom, if we are the "wheat of the field," how should we deal with "the weeds"?

Date: _____

HOMILY WORKSHEET for the 16th Sunday of the Year

1. SEEDS

What today's readings say *to me*: _____

_____

_____

PARABLES, STORIES and EXPERIENCES that speak to the themes of today's readings: _____

_____

_____

SPECIAL CONSIDERATIONS this week: Audience? Events in the community? Unique dimensions to this celebration?

_____

_____

_____

What RESPONSE do I seek from my listeners?
❑ to affirm/enlighten them in their faith?
❑ to teach/inform them about _____

_____

❑ to have them take a specific action _____

_____

2. PLANTING

The point I want to make in this homily (*ONE sentence*): _____

_____

_____

HOMILY OUTLINE

OPENING (*introductory STORY*): _____

_____

_____

_____

_____

_____

Point 1. APPLICATION of STORY to Scripture themes: _____

_____

_____

_____

_____

_____

Point 2. CONNECTION between Scriptural themes and the listeners' life experience: _____

_____
_____
_____
_____
_____
_____

Point 3. RESPONSE/CONSIDERATION sought from listeners: _____

_____
_____
_____
_____
_____
_____

CLOSING STATEMENT (*refers back to STORY*): _____

_____
_____
_____
_____
_____
_____

3. HARVEST—A Checklist:

❑ Does my completed homily make the point I articulated above (*under PLANTING*)?

❑ Am I excited about this homily. Am I readily able to convey my own enthusiasm, my sincere conviction of what I am going to say?

❑ Am I ready to preach this homily? Have I rehearsed this homily out loud until:

   ❑ I am comfortable with the *flow* of this homily: I can make the *transitions* from point to point, from idea to idea, smoothly and clearly;

   ❑ I am using *words* and *expressions* that my listeners can understand and appreciate: I am not speaking in theological jargon or "holy card" talk;

   ❑ my *delivery* (voice, gestures, speaking rate, pronunciation and enunciation, pauses, etc.) and

   ❑ my *inflection* and *emphasis* of key words and phrases are natural and effective?

❑ My homily lasts _____ minutes. Is it ❑ too long? ❑ too short? ❑ just about right?

4. GLEANINGS—Thoughts and notes AFTER the Homily

What worked, what didn't work in this homily; response and reactions from the community; ideas for next time; etc.

_____
_____
_____
_____
_____
_____
_____
_____
_____
_____

17th Sunday of the Year

The Readings:

READING 1: 1 Kings 3: 5, 7-12

Solomon asks the Lord for the gift of wisdom:

"Give your servant an understanding heart to judge your people and to distinguish right from wrong."

Solomon succeeded his father David in 961 B.C. to become the third and last king of the twelve tribes. Today's passage underscores the promise of the young king, who requests from the Lord the wisdom and understanding to fulfill his role as a kind and just ruler of God's people.

READING 2: Romans 8: 28-30

God makes all things work together for the good of those who love him, who have been called according to his decree.

These verses outline the Christian vocation as it was designed by God: to be conformed to the image of his Son. The references to "predestination" do not refer to an arbitrary decision by God of who will and who will not be saved; it refers to the fact that God's offer to salvation to all of humanity transcends the confines of time.

GOSPEL: Matthew 13: 44-52 (13: 44-46)

"The reign of God is like a buried treasure found in a field . . . like a merchant's search for fine pearls . . . like a dragnet thrown into the lake . . . ."

The first two parables in today's Gospel—the parables of the buried treasure and the pearl—are lessons in the total dedication demanded of the disciple to make the reign of God a reality. The parable of the dragnet is similar in theme to last week's parable of the wheat. Again, Matthew makes the point that the kingdom of God is not an instant happening nor a static event, but a dynamic movement forward which Jesus set into motion.

Themes:

• the values of God

Today's readings are about the discovery for the "meaning of life," the search for lasting values. As Solomon understood in asking the Lord for wisdom and "an understanding heart" (Reading 1), the treasures and pearls of life are the things of God: the love of family and friends, the support of community, the sense of fulfillment from serving and giving for the sake of others.

• wisdom: the search for God in all things

In the comic strip *Bloom County*, Opus the penguin is suffering from a crisis of faith. While standing in front of a television set, Opus says, "I believe in our government," only to have the television newscaster report that "today the President admitted sending a personally-inscribed copy of Leo Buscaglia's *Living, Loving and Hugging* to Khadafy."

Opus walks into the next room and says, "I have faith in American captitalism." Just then Milo reads from the newspaper, "Today on Wall Street everybody but the hot dog vendors were busted."

Continuing into the next room, Opus says "Well, there's always religion." And Steve Dallas reads from a magazine, "Oral Roberts strangled Jimmy Swaggart and ran off with Tammy Bakker's drug counselor."

Stepping outside onto the back porch, Opus asks, "What can a fellow believe in any more? Are there no more bastions of purity?"

Just then Opus sees a pregnant woman and happily embraces her. "Motherhood!" Opus delights. "Surrogate," she dead pans.

The institutions and beliefs in which we place our faith can let us down. The present confounds us and the future bewilders us. As today's readings make clear, true wisdom begins with seeking God in all things.

For Reflection:

• Do you know of individuals who have discovered a "treasure" of insight that remained hidden to others around them?

• How have your values changed over the years?

• When God offers Solomon anything he wants, Solomon asks God for wisdom; in the parable of the buried treasure, the finder sells every possession he has to buy the field. Consider the high cost of embracing the wisdom and values of God.

Date: _____

HOMILY WORKSHEET for the 17th Sunday of the Year

1. SEEDS

What today's readings say *to me*: _____
_____
_____

PARABLES, STORIES and EXPERIENCES that speak to the themes of today's readings: _____
_____
_____

SPECIAL CONSIDERATIONS this week: Audience? Events in the community? Unique dimensions to this celebration?
_____
_____
_____

What RESPONSE do I seek from my listeners?
❏ to affirm/enlighten them in their faith?
❏ to teach/inform them about _____
_____

❏ to have them take a specific action _____
_____

2. PLANTING

The point I want to make in this homily (*ONE sentence*): _____
_____
_____

HOMILY OUTLINE

OPENING (*introductory STORY*): _____
_____
_____
_____
_____
_____

Point 1. APPLICATION of STORY to Scripture themes: _____
_____
_____
_____
_____
_____

Point 2. CONNECTION between Scriptural themes and the listeners' life experience: _____

_____
_____
_____
_____
_____
_____

Point 3. RESPONSE/CONSIDERATION sought from listeners: _____

_____
_____
_____
_____
_____
_____

CLOSING STATEMENT (*refers back to STORY*): _____

_____
_____
_____
_____
_____
_____

3. HARVEST—A Checklist:

❏ Does my completed homily make the point I articulated above (*under PLANTING*)?

❏ Am I excited about this homily. Am I readily able to convey my own enthusiasm, my sincere conviction of what I am going to say?

❏ Am I ready to preach this homily? Have I rehearsed this homily out loud until:

❏ I am comfortable with the *flow* of this homily: I can make the *transitions* from point to point, from idea to idea, smoothly and clearly;

❏ I am using *words* and *expressions* that my listeners can understand and appreciate: I am not speaking in theological jargon or "holy card" talk;

❏ my *delivery* (voice, gestures, speaking rate, pronunciation and enunciation, pauses, etc.) and

❏ my *inflection* and *emphasis* of key words and phrases are natural and effective?

❏ My homily lasts _____ minutes. Is it ❏ too long? ❏ too short? ❏ just about right?

4. GLEANINGS—Thoughts and notes AFTER the Homily

What worked, what didn't work in this homily; response and reactions from the community; ideas for next time; etc.

_____
_____
_____
_____
_____
_____
_____
_____
_____
_____
_____

18th Sunday of the Year

The Readings:

READING 1: Isaiah 55: 1-3

All you who are thirsty,
come to the water!
You who have no money,
come, receive grain and eat;
Come, without paying and without cost,
drink wine and milk!
Heed me, and you shall eat well,
you shall delight in rich fare.

King Cyrus of Persia defeated the Babylonians in 539 B.C. Unlike conquerors before him, Cyrus did not deport defeated peoples for slave labor nor did he suppress their religious traditions; instead, he allowed them to remain in their home land and he himself honored what his people held as sacred. And so Cyrus permitted the Jews who were exiled by the Babylonians to return to Jerusalem and rebuild the temple the Babylonians sacked and destroyed five decades before. Deutero-Isaiah, the prophet of the exile, rejoices in the repatriation of his people. Using the image of a great feast, the prophet preaches that the land God gave Israel will once again be fruitful if God's justice and mercy are allowed to prevail.

READING 2: Romans 8: 35, 37-39

Neither death nor life, neither angels nor principalities, neither the present nor the future, nor powers, neither height nor depth not any other creature, will be able to separate us from the love of God that comes to us in Christ Jesus.

Today's reading from Paul's letter to the Romans is a hymn of praise to Christ, the supreme hope of the Christian community. Nothing in this world nor outside of it has the power or authority to "separate" us from the love of Christ.

GOSPEL: Matthew 14: 13-21

Jesus took the five loaves and two fishes, looked up to heaven, blessed and broke them and gave the loaves to his disciples, who in turn gave them to the people.

The multiplication of the loaves and fishes is the only one of Jesus' miracles recorded in all four Gospels. Today we read Matthew's account. This story was especially cherished by the early Christian community, who saw this event as anticipating the Eucharist and the final banquet in the kingdom of God. This miracle also has strong roots in the Old Testament: just as the merciful God feeds the wandering Israelites with manna in the desert, Jesus, "his heart moved with pity," feeds the crowds who have come to hear him; a similar miracle was performed by the prophet Elisha (2 Kings 4: 42-44), when the prophet fed 100 poor men with only 20 barley loaves.

Themes:

• the banquet of heaven

For the peoples of both the Old and New Testament, the image of a great banquet was an important visualization of the reign of God: the gifts of the land were unmistakable signs of their God's great Providence; Jesus also spoke of the kingdom of God as a wedding feast to which all the faithful are invited; the miracle of the loaves and fishes is a clear affirmation in God's providence. The bread of the

Eucharist, which we share together in charity and faith, is a prelude to the great banquet of the next world to which our loving Father invites us.

• the "miracle" of sharing

In today's Gospel, Jesus feeds the crowds with the little that the apostles could scrape together—five pieces of bread and two fish. Because someone was willing to share what he or she had, Jesus was able to make a miracle happen. And the miracle of sharing made of that crowd community. St. Basil the Great put it this way:

> "The bread which you do not use is the bread of the hungry;
> the garment hanging in your wardrobe is the garment of the naked;
> the shoes you do not wear are the shoes of the one who is barefoot;
> the money you keep locked away is the money of the poor';
> the acts of charity you do not perform are so many injustices you commit."

For Reflection:

• Is our contemporary concept of a banquet still a fitting image for the providence of God, for the reign of God to come?

• Consider the ways we misuse food and drink—from self-destruction to exploitation.

• How is the crowd in today's Gospel like your own parish community?

Date: _____

HOMILY WORKSHEET for the 18th Sunday of the Year

1. SEEDS

What today's readings say *to me*: _____

_____

_____

PARABLES, STORIES and EXPERIENCES that speak to the themes of today's readings: _____

_____

_____

SPECIAL CONSIDERATIONS this week: Audience? Events in the community? Unique dimensions to this celebration?

_____

_____

_____

What RESPONSE do I seek from my listeners?
❑ to affirm/enlighten them in their faith?
❑ to teach/inform them about _____

_____

❑ to have them take a specific action _____

_____

2. PLANTING

The point I want to make in this homily (*ONE sentence*): _____

_____

_____

HOMILY OUTLINE

OPENING (*introductory STORY*): _____

_____

_____

_____

_____

_____

Point 1. APPLICATION of STORY to Scripture themes: _____

_____

_____

_____

_____

_____

Point 2. CONNECTION between Scriptural themes and the listeners' life experience: _____
_____
_____
_____
_____
_____
_____

Point 3. RESPONSE/CONSIDERATION sought from listeners: _____
_____
_____
_____
_____
_____
_____

CLOSING STATEMENT (*refers back to STORY*): _____
_____
_____
_____
_____
_____
_____

3. HARVEST—A Checklist:

❑ Does my completed homily make the point I articulated above (*under PLANTING*)?

❑ Am I excited about this homily. Am I readily able to convey my own enthusiasm, my sincere conviction of what I am going to say?

❑ Am I ready to preach this homily? Have I rehearsed this homily out loud until:

❑ I am comfortable with the *flow* of this homily: I can make the *transitions* from point to point, from idea to idea, smoothly and clearly;

❑ I am using *words* and *expressions* that my listeners can understand and appreciate: I am not speaking in theological jargon or "holy card" talk;

❑ my *delivery* (voice, gestures, speaking rate, pronunciation and enunciation, pauses, etc.) and

❑ my *inflection* and *emphasis* of key words and phrases are natural and effective?

❑ My homily lasts _____ minutes. Is it ❑ too long? ❑ too short? ❑ just about right?

4. GLEANINGS—Thoughts and notes AFTER the Homily

What worked, what didn't work in this homily; response and reactions from the community; ideas for next time; etc.

_____
_____
_____
_____
_____
_____
_____
_____
_____
_____
_____

19th Sunday of the Year

The Readings:

READING 1: 1 Kings 19: 9, 11-13

Elijah recognized the Lord in a tiny, whispering sound.

Elijah is on the run. His preaching against the idolatrous practices of King Ahab and Queen Jezebel made him a marked man. Forced into hiding, Elijah is a broken man. He begs God to take his life, but instead, God saw that he had whatever food he needed and sent him on a 40-day journey to Horeb, the same mountain upon which Moses encountered God. Elijah does not hear God in the tornado, earthquake and fire, but in a "tiny whispering sound" that speaks not to the senses but to the heart.

READING 2: Romans 9: 1-5

I could even wish to be separated from Christ for the sake of my kinsmen the Israelites. Theirs were the adoption, the glory, the covenants, the lawgiving, the worship, and the promises; theirs were the patriarchs, and from them came the Messiah.

These five verses reveal Paul's deep sensitivity to his Jewish roots and his anguish over his people's inability to see Jesus as the Messiah and the fulfillment of the God's promise of old. Paul says he would gladly undergo some curse himself for the sake of his kinsmen's coming to the knowledge of Christ.

GOSPEL: Matthew 14: 22-33

Jesus, walking on the waters, saves his disciples during a storm.

This event immediately followed the multiplication of the loaves and fishes. The depth of Peter's love for Jesus is not matched by a depth of faith.

Themes:

• the God of peace

Like his disciples and the Jews of Jesus' time, we expect a God of power, a God who will save us from every cataclysm. But as Elijah discovers in the first reading, the Lord's voice is often heard most distinctly in the quiet. God speaks and works his wonders through individuals who recognize him as a light in the midst of darkness, who hear him as the "whisper" in the midst of a storm. May the quiet power of the Lord inspire us to do powerful things in bringing his love and compassion to our world.

• calming the storms of our lives

We have all experienced "storms" in our lives when things seemed especially hopeless, when the pressure is on to suspend our values and what we know is right, when charity, compassion and forgiveness just don't seem to work. But Jesus is present to us if we have both the faith and the courage to see him. Just as he was there to catch the faltering Peter during the storm, so he is there for us, if we do not abandon the values he teaches us in the Gospel.

For Reflection:

• When have you heard the voice of God "in a tiny whispering sound"?

• Consider stories of men and women whose faith and values have calmed humanity's storms.

• How are we like Peter in today's Gospel—strong in love but weak in our faith?

Date: _____

HOMILY WORKSHEET for the 19th Sunday of the Year

1. SEEDS

What today's readings say *to me*: _____

_____

_____

PARABLES, STORIES and EXPERIENCES that speak to the themes of today's readings: _____

_____

_____

SPECIAL CONSIDERATIONS this week: Audience? Events in the community? Unique dimensions to this celebration?

_____

_____

_____

What RESPONSE do I seek from my listeners?
❑ to affirm/enlighten them in their faith?
❑ to teach/inform them about _____

_____

❑ to have them take a specific action _____

_____

2. PLANTING

The point I want to make in this homily (*ONE sentence*): _____

_____

_____

HOMILY OUTLINE

OPENING (*introductory STORY*): _____

_____

_____

_____

_____

_____

Point 1. APPLICATION of STORY to Scripture themes: _____

_____

_____

_____

_____

_____

Point 2. CONNECTION between Scriptural themes and the listeners' life experience: _____

_____
_____
_____
_____
_____
_____

Point 3. RESPONSE/CONSIDERATION sought from listeners: _____

_____
_____
_____
_____
_____
_____

CLOSING STATEMENT (*refers back to STORY*): _____

_____
_____
_____
_____
_____
_____

3. HARVEST—A Checklist:

❏ Does my completed homily make the point I articulated above (*under PLANTING*)?

❏ Am I excited about this homily. Am I readily able to convey my own enthusiasm, my sincere conviction of what I am going to say?

❏ Am I ready to preach this homily? Have I rehearsed this homily out loud until:

❏ I am comfortable with the *flow* of this homily: I can make the *transitions* from point to point, from idea to idea, smoothly and clearly;

❏ I am using *words* and *expressions* that my listeners can understand and appreciate: I am not speaking in theological jargon or "holy card" talk;

❏ my *delivery* (voice, gestures, speaking rate, pronunciation and enunciation, pauses, etc.) and

❏ my *inflection* and *emphasis* of key words and phrases are natural and effective?

❏ My homily lasts _____ minutes. Is it ❏ too long? ❏ too short? ❏ just about right?

4. GLEANINGS—Thoughts and notes AFTER the Homily

What worked, what didn't work in this homily; response and reactions from the community; ideas for next time; etc.

_____
_____
_____
_____
_____
_____
_____
_____
_____
_____
_____

20th Sunday of the Year

The Readings:

READING 1: Isaiah 56: 1, 6-7

My house shall be called a house of prayer for all peoples.

As the Israelites return to Jerusalem from exile, the prophet Isaiah announces a new, "international" vision of salvation that includes, not only Jews, but "foreigners" and non-Jews who believe in the Lord's goodness and keep his commandments.

READING 2: Romans 11: 13-15, 29-32

God's gifts and his call are irrevocable.

Paul acknowledges his joy over the acceptance of the Gospel by the Gentiles, but he expresses his hope that his own people, the Jews, will realize that Christ is not the rejection of Israel's covenant with God but the fulfillment of that covenant.

GOSPEL: Matthew 15: 21-28

The Canaanite woman begs Jesus to cure her daughter.

This story was very important to the Christians of predominately Gentile communities. The woman is not only a Gentile, but a descendent of one of Israel's ancient enemies, the Canaanites. Despite Jesus' rebuff of her (equating Gentiles with dogs, as Jews referred to anyone who was not a Jew), the woman has the presence of mind to point out that "even dogs are given crumbs and scraps from their masters' tables." She displays both great faith in Jesus (addressing him by the Messianic title of "Son of David") and great love for her daughter (subjecting herself to possible ridicule and retaliation for approaching Jesus) that should inspire both Jew and Gentile—and Christian.

Themes:

• "subtle" bigotry as opposed to being "human together"

Bishop Desmond Tutu gives this simple but telling insight into the turmoil in his South African homeland:

> "Many years ago. . .we (blacks) were thought to be human, but not quite as human as white people, for we lacked what seemed indispensable to that humanity—a particular skincolor. We have a wonderful country with truly magnificent people, if only we could be allowed to be human together."

Most of us would consider ourselves fair-minded and unbiased, neither bigots nor racists; but, if we're honest, we would probably recognize times we have treated people as if they were "a little less human" because they did not possess some quality or ingredient we consider imperative. We underestimate people because they are somehow different. We treat them as inferiors because they don't quite measure up to what we think they should or should not be. The Lord does not measure his people by our standards but welcomes to his holy mountain all who do what is "right" and "just." The Canaanite woman possesses the depth of faith and compassion by which we can be "human together."

• salvation: God's invitation to all humankind

As a Canaanite, the woman in today's Gospel is despised by the Jewish community. But Jesus does not see in her an old enemy: he sees, in her great compassion and love for her sick daughter, a loving mother; he sees, in her courage to approach Jesus in the face of imminent rejection and denunciation, a woman of great faith. The Lord calls every person who possesses such compassion and love, regardless of nationality or heritage or stereotype or label, to his holy mountain.

For Reflection:

• The Canaanite woman in today's Gospel is a figure of great courage, love and perseverance. Do you know of individuals who have possessed the same depth of courage, love and perseverance?

• We all think of ourselves as open-minded, fair and tolerant, without bias or prejudice. But can we be prejudiced, biased and intolerant of others without even realizing it?

• How can your own parish be a "house of prayer for all peoples"?

Date: _____

HOMILY WORKSHEET for the 20th Sunday of the Year

1. SEEDS

What today's readings say *to me*: _____

_____

_____

PARABLES, STORIES and EXPERIENCES that speak to the themes of today's readings: _____

_____

_____

SPECIAL CONSIDERATIONS this week: Audience? Events in the community? Unique dimensions to this celebration?

_____

_____

_____

What RESPONSE do I seek from my listeners?
❑ to affirm/enlighten them in their faith?
❑ to teach/inform them about _____

_____

❑ to have them take a specific action _____

_____

2. PLANTING

The point I want to make in this homily (*ONE sentence*): _____

_____

_____

HOMILY OUTLINE

OPENING (*introductory STORY*): _____

_____

_____

_____

_____

_____

Point 1. APPLICATION of STORY to Scripture themes: _____

_____

_____

_____

_____

_____

Point 2. CONNECTION between Scriptural themes and the listeners' life experience: _____
_____
_____
_____
_____
_____
_____

Point 3. RESPONSE/CONSIDERATION sought from listeners: _____
_____
_____
_____
_____
_____
_____

CLOSING STATEMENT (*refers back to STORY*): _____
_____
_____
_____
_____
_____
_____

3. HARVEST—A Checklist:

❑ Does my completed homily make the point I articulated above (*under PLANTING*)?

❑ Am I excited about this homily. Am I readily able to convey my own enthusiasm, my sincere conviction of what I am going to say?

❑ Am I ready to preach this homily? Have I rehearsed this homily out loud until:

❑ I am comfortable with the *flow* of this homily: I can make the *transitions* from point to point, from idea to idea, smoothly and clearly;

❑ I am using *words* and *expressions* that my listeners can understand and appreciate: I am not speaking in theological jargon or "holy card" talk;

❑ my *delivery* (voice, gestures, speaking rate, pronunciation and enunciation, pauses, etc.) and

❑ my *inflection* and *emphasis* of key words and phrases are natural and effective?

❑ My homily lasts _____ minutes. Is it ❑ too long? ❑ too short? ❑ just about right?

4. GLEANINGS—Thoughts and notes AFTER the Homily

What worked, what didn't work in this homily; response and reactions from the community; ideas for next time; etc.

_____
_____
_____
_____
_____
_____
_____
_____
_____
_____
_____
_____

21st Sunday of the Year

The Readings:

READING 1: Isaiah 22: 15, 19-23

> *He shall be a father to the inhabitants of Jerusalem*
> *and to the house of Judah.*
> *I will place the key of the house of David on his shoulders;*
> *when he opens, no one shall shut,*
> *when he shuts, no one shall open.*

Shebna is scribe to King Hezekiah and superintendent of the palace. With the Assyrians threatening Jerusalem's borders, Shebna has advised the king to enter into a conspiracy of agreements with the Egyptians, despite God's promise to protect his people. Isaiah is incensed at Shebna's refusal to trust God, as well as the scribe's ostentatiousness (the opulent tomb Shebna has built for himself) and his obsession with chariots and armaments. Isaiah prophesies how Shebna will be replaced by the faithful Eliakim, Hezekiah's royal chamberlain. This passage parallels the description of the office Jesus intends for Peter.

READING 2: Romans 11: 33-36

> *How deep are the riches and wisdom and knowledge of God! How inscrutable his judgements,*
> *how unsearchable his ways!*

This meditation concludes Paul's treatise on Christ as Redeemer of Jew and Gentile alike. Quoting Isaiah 40: 13, Paul praises God's goodness and grace as defying human comprehension; all we can do is praise him and accept his wondrous invitation to faith.

GOSPEL: Matthew 16: 13-20

> *"Blest are you, Simon son of John! No mere man has revealed this to you, but my heavenly Father. I for my part declare to you, you are 'Rock,' and on this rock I will build my church, I will entrust to you the keys of the kingdom of heaven."*

In Matthew's Gospel, Peter's confession of faith is a turning point in the ministry of Jesus. Jesus will now concentrate on preparing his disciples to take on the teaching ministry and leadership of the Church he will establish.

The scene of today's Gospel, Caesarea Philippi, was the site of temples dedicated to no less than 14 different pagan gods, ranging from the Syrian god Baal to Pan, the Greek god of nature. In the middle of the city was a great white temple built by Herod and dedicated to the "divinity" of Caesar (hence the name of the city). In the midst of this marketplace of gods and temples, Jesus first indicates his plans and hopes for his church.

Jesus "sets up" Peter's declaration of faith by asking his disciples what people are saying about him. Current popular opinion is that Jesus is the reincarnation of John the Baptizer or the long-awaited return of the prophet Elijah or Jeremiah (Malachi 4: 5-6), signalling the restoration of Israel. Simon, however, has been given the gift of faith ("no mere man has revealed this to you") and unequivocally states that Jesus is the Messiah.

Jesus blesses Simon with the new name of "rock" (*Kepha* in Aramaic, *Petros* in Greek), the foundation for Jesus' new Church. Peter is entrusted with the keys of the kingdom of heaven (an image probably drawn from Isaiah 22: 15-25, today's first reading) and the mission to bring sins to consciousness and to proclaim to sinners the love and forgiveness of God.

Themes:

• "You are rock . . ."

Peter is the first of the disciples to grasp the divinity of Christ. On the faith of Peter "the rock" Christ establishes his Church. Peter becomes, then, the first stone of the foundation of the Church. We who are baptized into the faith handed down to us by Peter and the apostles become stones in this "edifice of Spirit," the Church.

• "the keys of the kingdom of heaven"

Christ entrusts to Peter and the apostles the "keys of the kingdom of heaven." Our vision as a Church is therefore always focused not on the present but on the age to come; we live in constant hope of the kingdom of heaven and the reign of God. In our every moment of our lives, we proclaim to the world the promise of the resurrection and the life of the world to come.

For Reflection:

• Jesus tells Simon Peter that his realization of Jesus' divinity is a gift from God—"no mere man has revealed this to you." How can such faith be considered a "gift?"

• How does the Church today "declare bound on earth (what) shall be bound in heaven" and "loosed on earth (what) shall be loosed in heaven"?

• Since Biblical times, to entrust someone with keys is the ultimate sign of trust. To accept such a trust demands authority, responsibility, courage and strength—perhaps more so in ancient times, when keys were so large and heavy one had to carry it on one's shoulder (Reading 1). What past or present leaders of the Church have been especially heroic and effective custodians of the "keys of the kingdom of heaven"?

Date: _____

HOMILY WORKSHEET for the 21st Sunday of the Year

1. SEEDS

What today's readings say *to me*: _____

_____

_____

PARABLES, STORIES and EXPERIENCES that speak to the themes of today's readings: _____

_____

_____

SPECIAL CONSIDERATIONS this week: Audience? Events in the community? Unique dimensions to this celebration?

_____

_____

_____

What RESPONSE do I seek from my listeners?
❏ to affirm/enlighten them in their faith?
❏ to teach/inform them about _____

_____

❏ to have them take a specific action _____

_____

2. PLANTING

The point I want to make in this homily (*ONE sentence*): _____

_____

_____

HOMILY OUTLINE

OPENING (*introductory STORY*): _____

_____

_____

_____

_____

_____

Point 1. APPLICATION of STORY to Scripture themes: _____

_____

_____

_____

_____

_____

Point 2. CONNECTION between Scriptural themes and the listeners' life experience: _____

_____

_____

_____

_____

_____

_____

Point 3. RESPONSE/CONSIDERATION sought from listeners: _____

_____

_____

_____

_____

_____

_____

CLOSING STATEMENT (*refers back to STORY*): _____

_____

_____

_____

_____

_____

3. HARVEST—A Checklist:

❑ Does my completed homily make the point I articulated above (*under PLANTING*)?

❑ Am I excited about this homily. Am I readily able to convey my own enthusiasm, my sincere conviction of what I am going to say?

❑ Am I ready to preach this homily? Have I rehearsed this homily out loud until:

   ❑ I am comfortable with the *flow* of this homily: I can make the *transitions* from point to point, from idea to idea, smoothly and clearly;

   ❑ I am using *words* and *expressions* that my listeners can understand and appreciate: I am not speaking in theological jargon or "holy card" talk;

   ❑ my *delivery* (voice, gestures, speaking rate, pronunciation and enunciation, pauses, etc.) and

   ❑ my *inflection* and *emphasis* of key words and phrases are natural and effective?

❑ My homily lasts _____ minutes. Is it ❑ too long? ❑ too short? ❑ just about right?

4. GLEANINGS—Thoughts and notes AFTER the Homily

What worked, what didn't work in this homily; response and reactions from the community; ideas for next time; etc.

_____

_____

_____

_____

_____

_____

_____

_____

_____

_____

_____

_____

22nd Sunday of the Year

The Readings:

READING 1: Jeremiah 20: 7-9

You duped me, O Lord, and I let myself be duped;
*   you were too strong for me, and you triumphed.*
I say to myself, I will not mention him,
*   I will speak his name no more.*
But then it becomes like a fire burning in my heart.

Jeremiah has just about had it with being a prophet. His warnings of Jerusalem's fall and the destruction of the temple at the hands of the Babylonians on their northern border are met first with ridicule, derision and then anger—Jeremiah is imprisoned and beaten for his unpopular oracles. In this passage from Jeremiah's "Confessions," the prophet opens his soul to God with a bluntness and boldness seldom read in Scripture. He considers abandoning his office of prophet, but admits that God's word is too powerful to be ignored.

READING 2: Romans 12: 1-2

I beg you through the mercy of God to offer your bodies as a living sacrifice holy and acceptable to God, your spiritual worship. Do not conform yourselves to this age, but be transformed by the renewal of your mind.

In chapter 12 of his letter to the Romans, Paul discusses the practical implications of the Gospel in everyday life. Paul begins the chapter by pointing out that, while the Mosaic code included elaborate directions on sacrifices and other rituals, the Gospel invites believers to present their very selves as a "living sacrifice of praise" to God.

GOSPEL: Matthew 16: 21-27

"Whoever wishes to come after me, he must deny his very self, take up his cross, and begin to follow in my footsteps."

Peter's confession of faith (last Sunday's Gospel) begins a new phase of Matthew's Gospel. Jesus' teachings will now be addressed primarily to his disciples, as Jesus makes his way to Jerusalem. The hostility between Jesus and the leaders of Judaism is about to reach the crisis stage.

Jesus proclaims unambiguously that his mission as the Messiah includes suffering and death. Peter's seemingly innocent remark is sharply rebuked by Jesus, who sees Peter's refusal to accept the fact that such a fate could be part of God's plan as a "satanic" attempt to deflect the Messiah from his mission of redemption. To avoid suffering and hardship in order to opt for the easy and safe course is purely human thinking, an obstacle to experiencing the life of the Spirit. Authentic discipleship involves taking on the cross and "denying oneself"—disowning ourselves as the center of our existence and realize that God is the object and purpose of our lives.

Themes:

• discipleship: "it don't come easy"

One is not a Christian only because he/she claims to be one. There is no mistaking Jesus' point in today's Gospel: If you wish to be considered my follower, you must make yourself second for the sake of others, take up your cross and follow in my footsteps. The cross we are asked to take up is not easy: it

represents a value system that runs counter to our own; it compels us to make choices we would rather not make or opt for. The life of the true disciple of Christ is one of generous, selfless and sacrificial service for the sake of the kingdom of God.

• self denial: to discover God

"The diamond cannot be polished without friction," says the Chinese proverb, "nor the individual perfected without trials." As the despairing Jeremiah confesses in Reading 1 and the disciples will soon discover, to seek God means "not conforming to this age, but (to) be transformed. . . so that you may judge what is God's will, what is right" (Reading 2). The selflessness demanded by Jesus in the Gospel places us on a collision course with many of today's values and attitudes. But in letting go of our own selves and our own needs, we come to experience the true joy and freedom of a mind and heart "renewed" and "perfected" in Christ.

For Reflection:

• What experiences in your life reflect the wisdom of the Chinese proverb: "The diamond cannot be polished without friction, nor the individual perfected without trials"?

• Do you empathize with Jeremiah's despair in today's first reading? How does "the fire in your heart" keep you from being defeated by such hopelessness?

• What "crosses" are we called to take up today?

• Do you know of people who have accomplished or taught great things because of the suffering they endured?

Date: _____

HOMILY WORKSHEET for the 22nd Sunday of the Year

1. SEEDS

What today's readings say *to me*: _____
_____
_____

PARABLES, STORIES and EXPERIENCES that speak to the themes of today's readings: _____
_____
_____

SPECIAL CONSIDERATIONS this week: Audience? Events in the community? Unique dimensions to this celebration?
_____
_____
_____

What RESPONSE do I seek from my listeners?
❑ to affirm/enlighten them in their faith?
❑ to teach/inform them about _____
_____

❑ to have them take a specific action _____
_____

2. PLANTING

The point I want to make in this homily (*ONE sentence*): _____
_____
_____

HOMILY OUTLINE

OPENING (*introductory STORY*): _____
_____
_____
_____
_____
_____

Point 1. APPLICATION of STORY to Scripture themes: _____
_____
_____
_____
_____
_____

Point 2. CONNECTION between Scriptural themes and the listeners' life experience: _____

_____

_____

_____

_____

_____

Point 3. RESPONSE/CONSIDERATION sought from listeners: _____

_____

_____

_____

_____

_____

CLOSING STATEMENT (*refers back to STORY*): _____

_____

_____

_____

_____

_____

3. HARVEST—A Checklist:

❑ Does my completed homily make the point I articulated above (*under PLANTING*)?

❑ Am I excited about this homily. Am I readily able to convey my own enthusiasm, my sincere conviction of what I am going to say?

❑ Am I ready to preach this homily? Have I rehearsed this homily out loud until:

    ❑ I am comfortable with the *flow* of this homily: I can make the *transitions* from point to point, from idea to idea, smoothly and clearly;

    ❑ I am using *words* and *expressions* that my listeners can understand and appreciate: I am not speaking in theological jargon or "holy card" talk;

    ❑ my *delivery* (voice, gestures, speaking rate, pronunciation and enunciation, pauses, etc.) and

    ❑ my *inflection* and *emphasis* of key words and phrases are natural and effective?

❑ My homily lasts _____ minutes. Is it ❑ too long? ❑ too short? ❑ just about right?

4. GLEANINGS—Thoughts and notes AFTER the Homily

What worked, what didn't work in this homily; response and reactions from the community; ideas for next time; etc.

_____

_____

_____

_____

_____

_____

_____

_____

_____

_____

_____

23rd Sunday of the Year

The Readings:

READING 1: Ezekiel 33: 7-9

"You I have appointed watchman for the house of Israel . . . if I tell the wicked man that he shall surely die and you do not speak out to dissuade the wicked man from his way, the wicked shall die for his guilt, but I will hold you responsible for his death."

Ezekiel, who preached to the Jews exiled from their homeland by the Babylonians (after the fall of Jerusalem in 587 B.C.), is called by God to be Israel's "watchman"—not to warn of a coming military invasion but to proclaim the forgiveness of God to an Israel defeated by its loss of faith and sinfulness.

READING 2: Romans 13: 8-10

Love is the fulfillment of the law.

Paul repeats the teaching of Jesus that so infuriated the Jewish leaders of his time: that all 613 commandments derived from the Torah are fulfilled if one's spiritual and moral outlook is directed by the Christian virtue of love. The one thing we owe one another as Christians is to love one another as Christ has loved us.

GOSPEL: Matthew 18: 15-20

"If your brother should commit some wrong against you, go point out his fault, but keep it between the two of you . . . If he does not listen, however, summon another, so that every case may stand on the word of two or three witnesses . . . "Where two or three are gathered in my name, there am I in their midst."

Chapter 18 of Matthew's Gospel is a collection of Jesus' sayings on the practical challenges facing the Christian community, such as status-seeking, scandal, forgiveness and, the topic of today's reading, reconciliation (this chapter has been called the "church order discourse" of Jesus).

This Gospel reading sounds more like the regulations of an ecclesiastical committee than a discourse by Jesus. But the point of Jesus' exhortation is that we must never tolerate any breech of personal relationship between us and another member of the Christian community. At each stage of the process— personal discussion, discussion before witnesses, discussion before the whole community—the aim is to win the erring Christian back to the community (the three-step process of reconciliation outlined by Jesus here corresponds to the procedure of the Qumran community).

Jesus' exhortation closes with a promise of God's presence and support for every community, regardless of size, bound together by faith.

Themes:

• community: the ministry of reconciliation

All three of today's readings contain "rules" and "procedures" for bringing sinners back to the community. Excommunication is always a last resort—in a very real sense, excommunication is an indication of failure on both the individual's and the community's part . The Lord calls us to build communities that are *inclusive*, not *exclusive*. We are called to bring the lost back, not out of pride or zealousness, but out of "the debt that binds us to love one another."

Very often we voice what we see as wrong—we gossip, backbite, criticize, slander, moan and complain. But do we proclaim what is good? Do we work toward reconciliation? If our Church is to preach the love of Christ with credibility, then, we must show by our actions that this love of Christ can build up a just society in ways that other groups and institutions cannot. Pope Paul VI put it beautifully when he said:

"A love of reconciliation is not weakness or cowardice. It demands courage, nobility, generosity, sometimes heroism, an overcoming of oneself rather than one's adversary. At times it may even seem like dishonor (but) in reality, reconciliation is the patient, wise art of peace, of loving, of living with one's (brothers and sisters), after the example of Christ."

• community: Christ present for all of us

C.S. Lewis offers this insight in *Mere Christianity,* as to how theology started:

"People already knew about God in a vague way. Then came a man who claimed to be God; and yet he was not the sort of man you could dismiss as a lunatic. He made them believe him. They met him again after they had seen him killed. And then after they had been formed into a little society or community, they found God somehow inside them as well: directing them, making them able to do things they could never do before."*

Christ is present to us, in times of joy and sorrow, if our hearts and minds are open to his presence. We find affirmation and direction in his healing presence when we come together in his name.

For Reflection:

• Consider the situations and crises in the world that cry out for reconciliation.

• How is today's Gospel a lesson in "conflict management"?

• Have you ever experienced Christ's presence in some special or unique way in another?

• Is there anyone you know of who could be considered a "hero" of reconciliation?

* *Mere Christianity* by C.S. Lewis (New York: MacMillan Publishing Company, 1952), page 143.

Date: _____

HOMILY WORKSHEET for the 23rd Sunday of the Year

1. SEEDS

What today's readings say *to me*: _____

_____

_____

PARABLES, STORIES and EXPERIENCES that speak to the themes of today's readings: _____

_____

_____

SPECIAL CONSIDERATIONS this week: Audience? Events in the community? Unique dimensions to this celebration?

_____

_____

_____

What RESPONSE do I seek from my listeners?
❑ to affirm/enlighten them in their faith?
❑ to teach/inform them about _____

_____

❑ to have them take a specific action _____

_____

2. PLANTING

The point I want to make in this homily (*ONE sentence*): _____

_____

_____

HOMILY OUTLINE

OPENING (*introductory STORY*): _____

_____

_____

_____

_____

_____

Point 1. APPLICATION of STORY to Scripture themes: _____

_____

_____

_____

_____

_____

Point 2. CONNECTION between Scriptural themes and the listeners' life experience: _____

_____
_____
_____
_____
_____
_____

Point 3. RESPONSE/CONSIDERATION sought from listeners: _____

_____
_____
_____
_____
_____
_____

CLOSING STATEMENT (*refers back to STORY*): _____

_____
_____
_____
_____
_____
_____

3. HARVEST—A Checklist:

❏ Does my completed homily make the point I articulated above (*under PLANTING*)?

❏ Am I excited about this homily. Am I readily able to convey my own enthusiasm, my sincere conviction of what I am going to say?

❏ Am I ready to preach this homily? Have I rehearsed this homily out loud until:

   ❏ I am comfortable with the *flow* of this homily: I can make the *transitions* from point to point, from idea to idea, smoothly and clearly;

   ❏ I am using *words* and *expressions* that my listeners can understand and appreciate: I am not speaking in theological jargon or "holy card" talk;

   ❏ my *delivery* (voice, gestures, speaking rate, pronunciation and enunciation, pauses, etc.) and

   ❏ my *inflection* and *emphasis* of key words and phrases are natural and effective?

❏ My homily lasts _____ minutes. Is it ❏ too long? ❏ too short? ❏ just about right?

4. GLEANINGS—Thoughts and notes AFTER the Homily

What worked, what didn't work in this homily; response and reactions from the community; ideas for next time; etc.

_____
_____
_____
_____
_____
_____
_____
_____
_____
_____
_____

24th Sunday of the Year

The Readings:

READING 1: Sirach 27: 30 - 28: 7

Should a man nourish anger against his fellows and expect healing from the Lord?

In this meditation on anger and vengeance, the holy teacher Ben Sirach, writing 200 years before Christ, challenges the ancient proscription of "an eye for an eye." We can only obtain mercy and forgiveness from God if we forgive our neighbors.

READING 2: Romans 14: 7-9

Both in life and in death we are the Lord's.

The weekly series of readings from Paul's letter to the Romans concludes with this meditation on the Lordship of Jesus. If God has accepted each one of us, how can we not accept one another as brothers and sisters?

GOSPEL: Matthew 18: 21-35

"The reign of God may be said to be like a king who decided to settle accounts with his officials . . ."

It is ironic that Peter should ask the question about forgiveness that introduces the parable of the merciless steward, since Peter himself will be so generously forgiven by Jesus for his denial of Jesus on Good Friday. It was common rabbinical teaching that one must forgive another three times; the fourth time, the offender was not to be forgiven. Perhaps Peter was anticipating Jesus' response in his question by suggesting seven rather than the conventional three times; but Jesus responds that there should be no limit to the number of times we must be ready to forgive those who wrong us ("seventy times seven times"), just as there is no limit to the Father's forgiveness of us. As the king in the parable withdraws his forgiveness of his official because of the official's failure to forgive another, so will God withdraw his forgiveness of the unforgiving and merciless among us.

Theme:

• forgiveness

In his journal *Markings*, the late Dag Hammarskjold, the second secretary-general of the United Nations, wrote this revealing entry, dated Easter 1960:

"Forgiveness breaks the chain of causality, because he who 'forgives' you—out of love—takes upon himself the consequences of what you have done. Forgiveness, therefore, always entails sacrifice. The price you must pay for your own liberation through another's sacrifice is that you in turn must be willing to liberate in the same way, irrespective of the consequences to yourself."*

To forgive as God forgives means purging the evil that exists between us, healing the division and reconstructing broken relationships, and accepting unconditionally, totally and joyfully the good that the forgiven can offer us. Such forgiveness is sometimes painful; but Christ calls us to look beyond our own hurt to the other person's healing, to look beyond our own loss to the loss of relationship and the weakening of community, to look beyond our own pride to the dignity and goodness of those who wrong us.

* *Markings* by Dag Hammarskjold (New York: Alfred A. Knopf, Inc. and Faber and Faber, Ltd., 1964), page 173.

For Reflection:

• Share stories of heroic, extraordinary forgiveness.

• How is anger, of itself, a destructive, dehumanizing emotion?

• What are the practical implications of today's readings? Can forgiveness ever be withheld? When is restitution justified?

• When is forgiveness NOT forgiveness? When is forgiveness whole and complete?

Date: _____

HOMILY WORKSHEET for the 24th Sunday of the Year

1. SEEDS

What today's readings say *to me*: _____

_____

_____

PARABLES, STORIES and EXPERIENCES that speak to the themes of today's readings: _____

_____

_____

SPECIAL CONSIDERATIONS this week: Audience? Events in the community? Unique dimensions to this celebration?

_____

_____

_____

What RESPONSE do I seek from my listeners?
❑ to affirm/enlighten them in their faith?
❑ to teach/inform them about _____

_____

❑ to have them take a specific action _____

_____

2. PLANTING

The point I want to make in this homily (*ONE sentence*): _____

_____

_____

HOMILY OUTLINE

OPENING (*introductory STORY*): _____

_____

_____

_____

_____

_____

Point 1. APPLICATION of STORY to Scripture themes: _____

_____

_____

_____

_____

_____

Point 2. CONNECTION between Scriptural themes and the listeners' life experience: _____

_____
_____
_____
_____
_____
_____

Point 3. RESPONSE/CONSIDERATION sought from listeners: _____

_____
_____
_____
_____
_____
_____

CLOSING STATEMENT (*refers back to STORY*): _____

_____
_____
_____
_____
_____
_____

3. HARVEST—A Checklist:

❏ Does my completed homily make the point I articulated above (*under PLANTING*)?

❏ Am I excited about this homily. Am I readily able to convey my own enthusiasm, my sincere conviction of what I am going to say?

❏ Am I ready to preach this homily? Have I rehearsed this homily out loud until:

   ❏ I am comfortable with the *flow* of this homily: I can make the *transitions* from point to point, from idea to idea, smoothly and clearly;

   ❏ I am using *words* and *expressions* that my listeners can understand and appreciate: I am not speaking in theological jargon or "holy card" talk;

   ❏ my *delivery* (voice, gestures, speaking rate, pronunciation and enunciation, pauses, etc.) and

   ❏ my *inflection* and *emphasis* of key words and phrases are natural and effective?

❏ My homily lasts _____ minutes. Is it ❏ too long? ❏ too short? ❏ just about right?

4. GLEANINGS—Thoughts and notes AFTER the Homily

What worked, what didn't work in this homily; response and reactions from the community; ideas for next time; etc.

_____
_____
_____
_____
_____
_____
_____
_____
_____
_____
_____

25th Sunday of the Year

The Readings:

READING 1: Isaiah 55: 6-9

As high as the heavens are above the earth,
so high are my ways above your ways
and my thoughts above your thoughts.

Today's reading is from the collection of oracles and hymns composed by the writer known only as Deutero-Isaiah, who prophesied hope and salvation to Israel toward the end of the Babylonian exile. God's goodness, love and mercy defy human expectations and reasoning. We cannot understand why he continues to call us back to him, why he constantly forgives us, why he continues to love us.

READING 2: Philippians 1: 20-24, 27

To me, "life" means Christ; hence dying is so much gain.

Paul's letter to the Philippians has been called the "epistle of joy." He speaks with the pride of a founding father to his beloved community at Philippi (located in what is now Northern Greece), which Paul established in 50 A.D. The epistle to the Philippians is really three short letters which have been edited together somewhat haphazardly. Philippians (to be read over the next four Sundays) reveals a sensitive, tender, caring side of Paul that is seldom seen in his other letters.

Paul is writing to the community at Philippi from prison (probably in Ephesus). Conscious of the imminence of his own death, Paul finds consolation and joy in his faith that life is Christ.

GOSPEL: Matthew 20: 1-16

"The reign of God is like the case of the owner of an estate who went out at dawn to hire
workmen for his vineyard . . ."

This parable, which appears only in Matthew, is the first of several parables and exhortations challenging the Pharisees and scribes and those who criticized Jesus for preaching to tax collectors and sinners.

Two themes are contained in this parable:

First, it illustrates the universality of the new Church. The contracted workers, Israel, will be joined by the new "migrant workers," the Gentiles, who will share equally in the joy of the kingdom of God.

The parable also speaks of the primacy of compassion and mercy in the kingdom of God. The employer (God) responds to those who have worked all day that he has been just in paying them the agreed-upon wage; they have no grievance if he chooses to be generous to others. It is not the amount of service given but the attitude of love and generosity behind that service.

Themes:

• the ways of God versus our ways

Faith is a gift that should give joy and direction to our lives, but it fails as a standard for measuring or judging others. We have our scales, time clocks and computer print-outs to measure what is just and what is not; but God is generous, loving and forgiving with an extravagance that offends our sense of justice. Genuine forgiveness and reconciliation are the ways of God, no matter what our own sense of justice and fair play may tell us (Reading 1). Christ calls us to rejoice in those who have been healed, to welcome as co-workers those who have come to work in the vineyard. Let us celebrate the goodness

213

and mercy of God rather than feel slighted or cheated because others we consider "less worthy" find peace in him.

• welcoming all workers into the "vineyard"

Today's readings admonish those who consider themselves "pillars" of the Church that there is no elite or aristocracy in the kingdom of God. The faith we have received is a gift that should give joy and direction to our lives. Christ calls us to embrace the Gospel, not as ideologues or zealots, but as disciples who love him through our love for others. We are called to share Christ, not to manipulate or control others through him.

For Reflection:

• Oscar Wilde said that "a cynic is someone who knows the price of everything and the value of nothing." Would Isaiah and Matthew agree?

• Who are the "new" workers who come into the vineyard to work side-by-side with us? How do we "contract workers" patronize and diminish them?

• How can people be manipulated, used and controlled through Scripture? How can such misuse of Scripture be prevented?

Date: _____

HOMILY WORKSHEET for the 25th Sunday of the Year

1. SEEDS

What today's readings say *to me*: _____

_____

_____

PARABLES, STORIES and EXPERIENCES that speak to the themes of today's readings: _____

_____

_____

SPECIAL CONSIDERATIONS this week: Audience? Events in the community? Unique dimensions to this celebration?

_____

_____

_____

What RESPONSE do I seek from my listeners?
❏ to affirm/enlighten them in their faith?
❏ to teach/inform them about _____

_____

❏ to have them take a specific action _____

_____

2. PLANTING

The point I want to make in this homily (*ONE sentence*): _____

_____

_____

HOMILY OUTLINE

OPENING (*introductory STORY*): _____

_____

_____

_____

_____

_____

Point 1. APPLICATION of STORY to Scripture themes: _____

_____

_____

_____

_____

Point 2. CONNECTION between Scriptural themes and the listeners' life experience: _____

_____

_____

_____

_____

_____

Point 3. RESPONSE/CONSIDERATION sought from listeners: _____

_____

_____

_____

_____

_____

CLOSING STATEMENT (*refers back to STORY*): _____

_____

_____

_____

_____

_____

3. HARVEST—A Checklist:

❑ Does my completed homily make the point I articulated above (*under PLANTING*)?

❑ Am I excited about this homily. Am I readily able to convey my own enthusiasm, my sincere conviction of what I am going to say?

❑ Am I ready to preach this homily? Have I rehearsed this homily out loud until:

❑ I am comfortable with the *flow* of this homily: I can make the *transitions* from point to point, from idea to idea, smoothly and clearly;

❑ I am using *words* and *expressions* that my listeners can understand and appreciate: I am not speaking in theological jargon or "holy card" talk;

❑ my *delivery* (voice, gestures, speaking rate, pronunciation and enunciation, pauses, etc.) and

❑ my *inflection* and *emphasis* of key words and phrases are natural and effective?

❑ My homily lasts _____ minutes. Is it ❑ too long? ❑ too short? ❑ just about right?

4. GLEANINGS—Thoughts and notes AFTER the Homily

What worked, what didn't work in this homily; response and reactions from the community; ideas for next time; etc.

_____

_____

_____

_____

_____

_____

_____

_____

_____

_____

_____

26th Sunday of the Year

The Readings:

READING 1: Ezekiel 18: 25-28

But if the wicked, turning from the wickedness they have committted, do what is right and just, they shall preserve their lives.

Ezekiel writes during the wretched years of the Israelites' exile from Jerusalem (6th century B.C.). But the prophet admonishes his people to recognize that their exile from God—an exile they have imposed on themselves by their "wickedness"—is far more critical than their political exile from their homeland. The exiled Jews of Ezekiel's time blamed everyone from their ancestors to Yahweh for their plight. Ezekiel reminds them that each individual is responsible for his or her life, that each generation receives life or death according to its own actions; but God offers forgiveness and reconciliation to all people of all times.

READING 2: Philippians 2: 1-11 (or 2: 1-5)

I beg you; make my joy complete by your unanimity, possessing the one love, united in spirit and ideals . . . Your attitude must be Christ's.

Imprisoned in Ephesus and distressed by the divisions plaguing the Church at Corinth, Paul begs his beloved Philippians to be united in humility and selflessness, and quotes what many scholars believe was the text of an ancient hymn praising Christ as the supreme example of the selfless Servant of God.

GOSPEL: Matthew 21: 28-32

The parable of the two sons:
   "Let me make it clear that tax collectors and prostitutes are entering the kingdom of God before you."

Today's parable is a devastating condemnation of the Jewish religious leaders whose faith is confined to words and rituals—Jesus states unequivocally that the people they consider to be the very antithesis of religious are better than the "professional" religious.

Prostitutes and tax collectors were the most despised outcasts in Judaism. In light of the Old Testament image of God's relationship with Israel as a marriage and Israel's disloyalty as harlotry, prostitution was considered an especially heinous sin. Tax collectors were, in the eyes of Palestinian Jews, the very personification of corruption and theft. According to the Roman system of tax collection, publicans (tax collectors) would pay the state a fixed sum based on the theoretical amount of taxes due from a given region. The publican, in return, had the right to collect the taxes in that region—and they were not above using terrorism and extortion to collect. Tax collectors, as agents of the state, were also shunned as collaborators with Israel's Roman captors.

Jesus' declaration that those guilty of the most abhorrent of sins would enter God's kingdom before the self-righteous Jews deepened their animosity toward this country rabbi.

Themes:

• faith: the authority of deeds over words

Promises can never take the place of performance, words are never to be a substitute for deeds. The challenge of discipleship is to translate the many "good intentions" we have into the actual work of being Christ's followers.

• conversion of spirit: personal commitment of faith

"Man," Albert Schweitzer wrote, "must cease attributing his problems to his environment, and learn again to exercise his will—his personal responsibility in the realm of faith and morals." Both Jesus in today's Gospel and the prophet Ezekiel (Reading 1) teach that authentic faith begins with a conversion of spirit, a personal conviction and commitment to do the will of God in all things. We cannot take refuge in the mores of the tribe or bow to peer pressure. We cannot say we acted under orders. We cannot claim that our theft becomes a crime only when a judge or jury says so. True faith—embracing the Spirit of God—transcends the letter of law, the safety of social convention and the capriciousness of popular opinion.

For Reflection:

- Who, among us today, are among the unlikeliest but most certain to enter the kingdom of God?

- In what ways do we "exile" ourselves from God?

- In what ways do people tend to blame the Church, their parish, etc., for their lack of faith?

Date: _____

HOMILY WORKSHEET for the 26th Sunday of the Year

1. SEEDS

What today's readings say *to me*: _____

_____

_____

PARABLES, STORIES and EXPERIENCES that speak to the themes of today's readings: _____

_____

_____

SPECIAL CONSIDERATIONS this week: Audience? Events in the community? Unique dimensions to this celebration?

_____

_____

_____

What RESPONSE do I seek from my listeners?
❑ to affirm/enlighten them in their faith?
❑ to teach/inform them about _____

_____

❑ to have them take a specific action _____

_____

2. PLANTING

The point I want to make in this homily (*ONE sentence*): _____

_____

_____

HOMILY OUTLINE

OPENING (*introductory STORY*): _____

_____

_____

_____

_____

_____

Point 1. APPLICATION of STORY to Scripture themes: _____

_____

_____

_____

_____

_____

Point 2. CONNECTION between Scriptural themes and the listeners' life experience: _____

_____
_____
_____
_____
_____

Point 3. RESPONSE/CONSIDERATION sought from listeners: _____

_____
_____
_____
_____
_____

CLOSING STATEMENT (*refers back to STORY*): _____

_____
_____
_____
_____
_____

3. HARVEST—A Checklist:

❑ Does my completed homily make the point I articulated above (*under PLANTING*)?

❑ Am I excited about this homily. Am I readily able to convey my own enthusiasm, my sincere conviction of what I am going to say?

❑ Am I ready to preach this homily? Have I rehearsed this homily out loud until:

   ❑ I am comfortable with the *flow* of this homily: I can make the *transitions* from point to point, from idea to idea, smoothly and clearly;

   ❑ I am using *words* and *expressions* that my listeners can understand and appreciate: I am not speaking in theological jargon or "holy card" talk;

   ❑ my *delivery* (voice, gestures, speaking rate, pronunciation and enunciation, pauses, etc.) and

   ❑ my *inflection* and *emphasis* of key words and phrases are natural and effective?

❑ My homily lasts _____ minutes. Is it ❑ too long? ❑ too short? ❑ just about right?

4. GLEANINGS—Thoughts and notes AFTER the Homily

What worked, what didn't work in this homily; response and reactions from the community; ideas for next time; etc.

_____
_____
_____
_____
_____
_____
_____
_____
_____
_____

27th Sunday of the Year

The Readings:

READING 1: Isaiah 5: 1-7

My friend had a vineyard
on a fertile hillside;
He spaded it, cleared it of stones,
and planted the choicest vines;
Then he looked for the crop of grapes,
but what it yielded was wild grapes.

Imitating a popular folk song of the time, the prophet Isaiah sings of God as a friend who lavishes care on a vineyard (Israel), only to harvest a poor crop of wild grapes. Despite God's goodness, Israel has not been faithful to the covenant. Isaiah prophesies the destruction of the vineyard.

READING 2: Philippians 4: 6-9

Live according to what you have learned and accepted, what you have heard me say and seen me do. Then will the God of peace be with you.

Today's reading from Paul's letter to the Philippians continues his words of encouragement to his beloved converts at Philippi. In order that God's peace may reign in their lives they are to put into practice all that they have learned, received, heard and seen.

GOSPEL: Matthew 21: 33-43

The parable of the wicked tenant farmers:

"The kingdom of God will be taken away from you and given to a people that will yield a rich harvest."

Today's parable "updates" Isaiah's allegory of the friend's vineyard (Reading 1). God is the owner of the vineyard who has "leased" the property to the religious and political leaders of Israel. Many servants (prophets) were sent to the tenants, but all met the same fate. The owner finally sends his own Son, who is brutally murdered "outside" the vineyard (a prediction of his crucifixion outside the city of Jerusalem?). The owner comes himself and destroys the tenants and leaves the vineyard to others (the Church) who yield an abundant harvest. Clearly, this parable is intended to give hope and encouragement to the evangelist's Christian community, which is scorned and persecuted by its staunchly Jewish neighbors.

Themes:

• harvesting our section of the "vineyard"

Each one of us has been given a portion of God's vineyard to cultivate. Fear, selfishness and bigotry can kill whatever chances we have of turning our part of the vineyard into something productive; but, through justice, decency and compassion, we can reap a rich and fulfilling harvest, regardless of how small or poor or insignificant our piece of the vineyard is.

• the vineyard we share with the other "tenants"

God created the vineyard of this earth in order to sustain and nourish the life he gave to each one of us. We are all tenants of the vineyard of creation: the vineyard has been "leased" to us for the benefit and common good of all humanity. Through a recognition of the rights and needs of our fellow "tenants," through our respect for the earth and the fragility of nature, and through our quiet but most committed acts of charity, kindness and compassion, we plant the seeds which will reap an abundant harvest.

For Reflection:

- In what ways are we responsible and irresponsible "tenants" of the vineyard?

- Share stories of individuals who have made even the most "arid" sections of the "vineyard" bloom.

- How can your parish community become a more "productive" section of the vineyard?

Date: _____

HOMILY WORKSHEET for the 27th Sunday of the Year

1. SEEDS

What today's readings say *to me*: _____

_____

_____

PARABLES, STORIES and EXPERIENCES that speak to the themes of today's readings: _____

_____

_____

SPECIAL CONSIDERATIONS this week: Audience? Events in the community? Unique dimensions to this celebration?

_____

_____

_____

What RESPONSE do I seek from my listeners?
❑ to affirm/enlighten them in their faith?
❑ to teach/inform them about _____

_____

❑ to have them take a specific action _____

_____

2. PLANTING

The point I want to make in this homily (*ONE sentence*): _____

_____

_____

HOMILY OUTLINE

OPENING (*introductory STORY*): _____

_____

_____

_____

_____

_____

Point 1. APPLICATION of STORY to Scripture themes: _____

_____

_____

_____

_____

_____

Point 2. CONNECTION between Scriptural themes and the listeners' life experience: _____

_____

_____

_____

_____

_____

Point 3. RESPONSE/CONSIDERATION sought from listeners: _____

_____

_____

_____

_____

_____

_____

CLOSING STATEMENT (*refers back to STORY*): _____

_____

_____

_____

_____

_____

3. HARVEST—A Checklist:

❏ Does my completed homily make the point I articulated above (*under PLANTING*)?

❏ Am I excited about this homily. Am I readily able to convey my own enthusiasm, my sincere conviction of what I am going to say?

❏ Am I ready to preach this homily? Have I rehearsed this homily out loud until:

❏ I am comfortable with the *flow* of this homily: I can make the *transitions* from point to point, from idea to idea, smoothly and clearly;

❏ I am using *words* and *expressions* that my listeners can understand and appreciate: I am not speaking in theological jargon or "holy card" talk;

❏ my *delivery* (voice, gestures, speaking rate, pronunciation and enunciation, pauses, etc.) and

❏ my *inflection* and *emphasis* of key words and phrases are natural and effective?

❏ My homily lasts _____ minutes. Is it ❏ too long? ❏ too short? ❏ just about right?

4. GLEANINGS—Thoughts and notes AFTER the Homily

What worked, what didn't work in this homily; response and reactions from the community; ideas for next time; etc.

_____

_____

_____

_____

_____

_____

_____

_____

_____

_____

_____

28th Sunday of the Year

The Readings:

READING 1: Isaiah 25: 6-10

On this mountain the Lord of hosts
will provide for all peoples
A feast of rich food and choice wines . . .
The Lord God will wipe away
the tears from all faces.

The image of the universal banquet has a long history in the mythology and folklore traditions of the world. Eight centuries before Christ, Isaiah pictures for his Jewish hearers the richness of the Messianic banquet on the heavenly mountain of God, when Yahweh will remove the sorrow and humiliation of Israel.

READING 2: Philippians 4: 12-14, 19-20

In him who is the source of my strength I have strength for everything.

Imprisoned in Ephesus, Paul offers words of thanks to the Philippians for their gift of money sent through Epaphroditus. Paul assures his good friends and benefactors that he is able to cope with whatever hardship because of the strength he receives from God.

GOSPEL: Matthew 22: 1-14 (or 22: 1-10)

"The reign of God may be likened to a king who gave a wedding banquet for his son . . ."

Jesus' controversy with the Jews continues in today's Gospel, with the parable of the wedding feast. The parable (found in the "Q" source of sayings of Jesus which all three synoptics used as a principal source) is another illustration of Israel's rejection of God's promise. The invitation is therefore extended to everyone—Gentiles, foreigners and those who do not know God—to come to the Lord's table. (Matthew's readers would see the "destruction of those murderers" and the "burning of their city" as a reference to the destruction of Jerusalem by the Romans in 70 A.D.)

Jesus tells a second parable within the parable of the wedding feast. The wedding garment is the conversion of heart and mind required for entry into the kingdom. The Christian who does not wear this mantle of repentance and good deeds will suffer the same fate as those who reject outright the invitation to the wedding.

Themes:

• accepting God's invitation to the wedding

We can be so busy making a living that we fail to make a life; we can become so obsessed with organizing life that we forget the essence of life itself. God has invited each of us to his Son's wedding feast—the fullness of God's life in the resurrection. A major obstacle is our inability to hear his invitation amid the noisy activity that consumes us.

• the one wedding feast

All of us deeply admire the world's Mother Teresas, Father Damians, Albert Schweitzers, Dorothy Days and St. Francises. Yet the same God who called each of them to their work calls us to do the same.

We are all invited to the same wedding feast of joy. The question posed by today's readings is how we respond to the invitation: with excuses? with rationalizations? with refusals?

May we learn to stop and hear the voice of God calling us to the wedding feast of his heavenly kingdom.

• putting on the wedding garment

In accepting an invitation to a wedding, we dress accordingly. The wedding garment of today's Gospel is the garment of good works we provide ourselves for the Lord's banquet: the garment sewn of repentance, joyful expectation and humble service to others.

For Reflection:

• In what ways do today's Christians miss their invitation to the Lord's wedding feast?

• How should the images in today's readings of the banquet and wedding feast affect our understanding of Church?

• What elements of the wedding feast might be brought to your parish life and liturgy?

• How would the "perfect" wedding garment be pictured or designed for the Lord's wedding banquet?

Date: _____

HOMILY WORKSHEET for the 28th Sunday of the Year

1. SEEDS

What today's readings say *to me*: _____

_____

_____

PARABLES, STORIES and EXPERIENCES that speak to the themes of today's readings: _____

_____

_____

SPECIAL CONSIDERATIONS this week: Audience? Events in the community? Unique dimensions to this celebration?

_____

_____

_____

What RESPONSE do I seek from my listeners?
❏ to affirm/enlighten them in their faith?
❏ to teach/inform them about _____

_____

❏ to have them take a specific action _____

_____

2. PLANTING

The point I want to make in this homily (*ONE sentence*): _____

_____

_____

HOMILY OUTLINE

OPENING (*introductory STORY*): _____

_____

_____

_____

_____

_____

Point 1. APPLICATION of STORY to Scripture themes: _____

_____

_____

_____

_____

_____

Point 2. CONNECTION between Scriptural themes and the listeners' life experience: _____

_____
_____
_____
_____
_____
_____

Point 3. RESPONSE/CONSIDERATION sought from listeners: _____

_____
_____
_____
_____
_____
_____

CLOSING STATEMENT (*refers back to STORY*): _____

_____
_____
_____
_____
_____
_____

3. HARVEST—A Checklist:

❑ Does my completed homily make the point I articulated above (*under PLANTING*)?

❑ Am I excited about this homily. Am I readily able to convey my own enthusiasm, my sincere conviction of what I am going to say?

❑ Am I ready to preach this homily? Have I rehearsed this homily out loud until:

> ❑ I am comfortable with the *flow* of this homily: I can make the *transitions* from point to point, from idea to idea, smoothly and clearly;

> ❑ I am using *words* and *expressions* that my listeners can understand and appreciate: I am not speaking in theological jargon or "holy card" talk;

> ❑ my *delivery* (voice, gestures, speaking rate, pronunciation and enunciation, pauses, etc.) and

> ❑ my *inflection* and *emphasis* of key words and phrases are natural and effective?

❑ My homily lasts _____ minutes. Is it ❑ too long? ❑ too short? ❑ just about right?

4. GLEANINGS—Thoughts and notes AFTER the Homily

What worked, what didn't work in this homily; response and reactions from the community; ideas for next time; etc.

_____
_____
_____
_____
_____
_____
_____
_____
_____
_____
_____

29th Sunday of the Year

The Readings

READING 1: Isaiah 45: 1, 4-6

The Lord's anointed Cyrus,
*   whose hand I grasp,*
Subduing nations before him,
*   and making kings run in his service,*
Opening doors before him
*   and leaving the gates unbarred.*

The 50-year exile of the Jews under the Babylonians is about to end. King Cyrus of Persia has defeated the Babylonians and has announced the liberation of the Jews (538 B.C.). Isaiah sees Cyrus as the instrument by which Yahweh reasserts his presence in Israel's history. Just as a foreign nation served as the rod of his anger (Isaiah 10: 5), so, through the foreign King Cyrus, Yahweh liberates his people.

READING 2: 1 Thessalonians 1: 1-5

Our preaching of the Gospel proved not a mere matter of words for you but one of our power; it was carried on in the Holy Spirit and out of complete conviction.

Today's second reading is the beginning of Paul's first letter to the Christian community at Thessalonica in Northern Greece. Scholars believe that 1 Thessalonians is the first of the 27 books of the New Testament book to be written. On behalf of his co-workers Silvanus and Timothy, Paul greets the Thessalonians and offers a prayer of thanks for the Holy Spirit, which made the apostles' teaching effective and the community's acceptance possible.

GOSPEL: Matthew 22: 15-21

"Give to Ceasar what is Caesar's,
but to God what is God's."

Two opponents of Jesus, the Pharisees and Herodians (supporters of Herod's dynasty), join forces to trap Jesus. If Jesus affirms that taxes should be paid, he loses the esteem of the religious nationalists; if he denies that taxes should be paid, then he is subject to arrest as a political revolutionary. But the very fact that his inquisitors could produce the emperor's coin from one of their purses was to admit a Roman obligation—if one used the sovereign's coin then one automatically took on an obligation to the sovereign; in other words, the Pharisees and Herodians, in trying to trap Jesus, answered their own question. But Jesus takes the debate to an even higher level by challenging them to be just as observant in paying their debt to God.

Themes:

• our personal responsibility "to give God what is God's"

The confrontation over Caesar's coin is not a solution to any church-versus-state controversy; Jesus' response to the Pharisees confronts them—and us—with the demand for personal conviction and to take responsibility for our actions. Neither our faith nor our politics can be used to excuse or rationalize our failure to do what is right and just. Life is a constant series of choices, with God holding each one of us accountable for the choices we make.

• government: "to give to Caesar what is Caesar's"

The Pharisees who confront Jesus with Caesar's coin are trying to trap him into making a choice between one's country and God. But Jesus' response indicates that our sense of citizenship does not necessarily have to be at odds with our faith. When government seeks to provide for the just welfare of its citizens, it does the will of God.

The Preamble to our nation's Constitution reads more like a covenant we Americans have made with one another than a legal outline of how our government will operate. Although God is not mentioned at all, we can sense his Spirit in the Preamble: "We the people of the United States, in order to form a more perfect union, establish justice, insure domestic tranquility, provide for the common defense, promote the general welfare, and secure the blessings of liberty for ourselves and our posterity. . ."

To strike that balance between the things of "Caesar's" and the things of God demands that we participate in the affairs of government responsibly and intelligently, in order that our public policies reflect the ways of our God.

For Reflection:

• We hear a great deal from fundamentalist organizations about "Christian" candidates, "Christian" issues, the "Christian" way to vote. What does the Gospel demand of the authentic Christian in terms of his/her citizenship?

• Can patriotism ever be contrary to the Gospel?

• Are there times when you find yourself using social convention or common practice as an excuse for acting in a way you know is contrary to the Gospel?

Date: _____

HOMILY WORKSHEET for the 29th Sunday of the Year

1. SEEDS

What today's readings say *to me*: _____

_____

_____

PARABLES, STORIES and EXPERIENCES that speak to the themes of today's readings: _____

_____

_____

SPECIAL CONSIDERATIONS this week: Audience? Events in the community? Unique dimensions to this celebration?

_____

_____

_____

What RESPONSE do I seek from my listeners?
❑ to affirm/enlighten them in their faith?
❑ to teach/inform them about _____

_____

❑ to have them take a specific action _____

_____

2. PLANTING

The point I want to make in this homily (*ONE sentence*): _____

_____

_____

HOMILY OUTLINE

OPENING (*introductory STORY*): _____

_____

_____

_____

_____

_____

Point 1. APPLICATION of STORY to Scripture themes: _____

_____

_____

_____

_____

_____

Point 2. CONNECTION between Scriptural themes and the listeners' life experience: _____

_____

_____

_____

_____

_____

Point 3. RESPONSE/CONSIDERATION sought from listeners: _____

_____

_____

_____

_____

_____

CLOSING STATEMENT (*refers back to STORY*): _____

_____

_____

_____

_____

_____

3. HARVEST—A Checklist:

❑ Does my completed homily make the point I articulated above (*under PLANTING*)?

❑ Am I excited about this homily. Am I readily able to convey my own enthusiasm, my sincere conviction of what I am going to say?

❑ Am I ready to preach this homily? Have I rehearsed this homily out loud until:

❑ I am comfortable with the *flow* of this homily: I can make the *transitions* from point to point, from idea to idea, smoothly and clearly;

❑ I am using *words* and *expressions* that my listeners can understand and appreciate: I am not speaking in theological jargon or "holy card" talk;

❑ my *delivery* (voice, gestures, speaking rate, pronunciation and enunciation, pauses, etc.) and

❑ my *inflection* and *emphasis* of key words and phrases are natural and effective?

❑ My homily lasts _____ minutes. Is it ❑ too long? ❑ too short? ❑ just about right?

4. GLEANINGS—Thoughts and notes AFTER the Homily

What worked, what didn't work in this homily; response and reactions from the community; ideas for next time; etc.

_____

_____

_____

_____

_____

_____

_____

_____

_____

_____

_____

30th Sunday of the Year

The Readings:

READING 1: Exodus 22: 20-26

*"You shall not molest or oppress an alien, for you were once aliens yourselves in the land Egypt .
. .If you ever wrong them and they cry out to me, I will surely hear their cry.*

This section of the Book of Exodus is the "Code of the Covenant," a detailed explanation of the moral, civil and ritual legislation by which the Israelites were to become a holy people. Today's reading outlines the laws of charity toward the poor and foreigners and the promise of Yahweh's protection of the helpless and defenseless. The Lord will tolerate no inhumanity from the people he has chosen as his own.

READING 2: 1 Thessalonians 1: 5-10

The word of the Lord has echoed forth from you resoundingly.

Paul encourages the young Church at Thessalonica to be a model of faithful community for the new churches in the region.

GOSPEL: Matthew 22: 34-40

*"You shall love the Lord your God
with your whole heart,
with your whole soul,
and with all your mind . . .
You shall love your neighbor as yourself."*

In this week's Gospel, as in last week's, the Jewish leaders seek to "trip" Jesus. The question the lawyer poses was much discussed in rabbinical circles: Which is the greatest commandment? The Pharisees' intention in posing the question to Jesus was to pigeon-hole him into a single rabbinical school, thereby opening him up to criticism from all other sides. Jesus' answer, however, proves his fidelity to both the Jewish tradition and to a spirituality that transcends the legal interpretations of the commandments.

Themes:

• to love the "foreigner" and the "alien"

In today's first reading, Yahweh reminds Israel that they should not "oppress and abuse an alien, for you were once aliens yourself in the land of Egypt." In today's Gospel, Jesus' command to love our neighbor means seeing one another as we see ourselves: realizing that our hopes and dreams for ourselves and our families are the same dreams others have for themselves and their families. The fact is that all of us, at one time or another, are aliens, outsiders, foreigners and strangers. The commandment to "love your neighbor as yourself" is not confined to our "own" people or to a list of specific situations, but should impact every relationship we have and every decision we make.

• the risk of love

Consider one clergyman's perspective on love, marriage and divorce:

> "One of the things that concerns me about the divorce rate . . . is not the husbands and wives. They'll survive. They'll hurt, but they'll survive. I'm really afraid that we are raising a whole generation of children who will be afraid to love. Because it hurts so much when it doesn't work out, they will look for intimacy without commitment and for reward without risk."*

The words of today's Gospel are so well known that they've become one of the "slogans" of our faith. But the implication of loving as God "commands" is staggering. We are called to love God and one another totally: without limit, without condition, without counting the cost, in good times and in bad times, always and in all ways. May our prayer be that we have the courage, the perseverance, and the energy to love as God loves us.

For Reflection:

• When is loving someone as we love ourselves most difficult?

• How can we love God with our "whole" hearts, souls and minds?

• Have you ever been the "alien," "the foreigner," "the outsider?"

• Has your perspective of another person ever changed dramatically as a result of considering how you would cope in that person's situation?

*Rabbi Harold S. Kushner, *ARE YOU HAPPY? Some Answers to the Most Important Questions in Your Life,* edited by Dennis Wholey (Boston: Houghton Mifflin and Company, 1986), page 14.

Date: _____

HOMILY WORKSHEET for the 30th Sunday of the Year

1. SEEDS

What today's readings say *to me*: _____
_____
_____

PARABLES, STORIES and EXPERIENCES that speak to the themes of today's readings: _____
_____
_____

SPECIAL CONSIDERATIONS this week: Audience? Events in the community? Unique dimensions to this celebration?
_____
_____
_____

What RESPONSE do I seek from my listeners?
❑ to affirm/enlighten them in their faith?
❑ to teach/inform them about _____
_____

❑ to have them take a specific action _____
_____

2. PLANTING

The point I want to make in this homily (*ONE sentence*): _____
_____
_____

HOMILY OUTLINE

OPENING (*introductory STORY*): _____
_____
_____
_____
_____
_____

Point 1. APPLICATION of STORY to Scripture themes: _____
_____
_____
_____
_____
_____

Point 2. CONNECTION between Scriptural themes and the listeners' life experience: _____
_____
_____
_____
_____
_____
_____

Point 3. RESPONSE/CONSIDERATION sought from listeners: _____
_____
_____
_____
_____
_____
_____

CLOSING STATEMENT (*refers back to STORY*): _____
_____
_____
_____
_____
_____
_____

3. HARVEST—A Checklist:

❑ Does my completed homily make the point I articulated above (*under PLANTING*)?

❑ Am I excited about this homily. Am I readily able to convey my own enthusiasm, my sincere conviction of what I am going to say?

❑ Am I ready to preach this homily? Have I rehearsed this homily out loud until:

❑ I am comfortable with the *flow* of this homily: I can make the *transitions* from point to point, from idea to idea, smoothly and clearly;

❑ I am using *words* and *expressions* that my listeners can understand and appreciate: I am not speaking in theological jargon or "holy card" talk;

❑ my *delivery* (voice, gestures, speaking rate, pronunciation and enunciation, pauses, etc.) and

❑ my *inflection* and *emphasis* of key words and phrases are natural and effective?

❑ My homily lasts _____ minutes. Is it ❑ too long? ❑ too short? ❑ just about right?

4. GLEANINGS—Thoughts and notes AFTER the Homily

What worked, what didn't work in this homily; response and reactions from the community; ideas for next time; etc.

_____
_____
_____
_____
_____
_____
_____
_____
_____
_____
_____
_____

31st Sunday of the Year

The Readings:

READING 1: Malachi 1: 14 - 2: 2, 8-10

You have turned aside from the way,
and have caused many to falter
by your instruction;
I, therefore, have made you contemptible
and base before all people.

The Jews have returned to Jerusalem after the exile. The temple has been rebuilt. But things are not like they were before. Shaken by their experience, Israel has re-made God in image and likeness. Yahweh, the living God of the covenant, has become instead a symbol of Jewish nationalism. The prophet Malachi ("messenger of God"), the last of the minor prophets, sharply rebukes the priests of Israel for their poor and irresponsible leadership, their indifference, and their failure to correct the abuses in worship and the spiritual, moral and social problems Israel faces.

READING 2: 1 Thessalonians 2: 7-9, 13

While we were among you we were as gentle as any nursing mother fondling her little ones. So well disposed were we toward you, in fact, that we wanted to share with you not only God's tidings but our very lives, you had become so dear to us.

Paul fondly remembers the time he spent among the Thessalonians in Northern Greece, during his second missionary journey around 50 B.C. Though Paul and his companions are warmly received by many Gentile converts, the Jews of Thessalonica harassed Paul and accused the new Christians of treason before the Roman authorities. Paul is forced to leave the city. Timothy later returned to Thessalonica to keep the community together. Timothy's positive report to Paul is reflected in the apostle's loving and encouraging words. In today's reading, Paul says he loves his Thessalonian brothers and sisters like both a mother who cares for her children and a father who exhorts them to live lives worthy of the teaching they have received.

GOSPEL: Matthew 23: 1-12

"The greatest among you will be the one who serves the rest."

Today's Gospel is another powerful indictment of the scribes and Pharisees. The scribes were the religious intellectuals of the time, skilled in interpreting the Law and applying it to everyday life; the Pharisees belonged to a religious fraternity ("the separated brethren") who prided themselves on the exact, meticulous observance of the Law. Jesus condemns them for their failure to live up to their teachings. Religious ostentation and pretension are rejected in favor of the Christian ideal of leadership contained in loving service to the community.

In warning his disciples not to use the titles "Rabbi," "teacher" and "Father," Jesus condemns the spirit of pride and superiority such titles denote. Those who minister as teachers and leaders should be humbled by the fact that they are not teachers or leaders in their own right but by the inspiration and grace of God.

Themes:

• to lead by example

Today's readings exalt the leader who leads by example: the prophet Malachi criticizes those priests and leaders of Israel whose empty words ("you do not lay it to heart") have caused many to abandon their faith; Paul recalls his days preaching among the Thessalonians when "we wanted to share with you not only God's tidings but our very lives, you had become so dear to us"; and Jesus minces no words when he says "the greatest among you will be the one who serves the rest." In the Gospel perspective, the greatest leaders and teachers are those who share their vision of faith not in words alone but by the power and authority of their example.

• the joy of humble service

The great conductor Leonard Bernstein was asked once what instrument in a symphony orchestra was the most difficult to play. The maestro gave this surprising answer: "Second fiddle. I can get plenty of first violinists. But to find one who can play second fiddle with enthusiasm—that's a problem. Yet, if there is no one to play second fiddle, we have no harmony."

Jesus' whole life is a parable of humble and selfless service to others. For the person of faith, joy is found not in "star billing" or stature or recognition but in the ability and opportunity to contribute and give in the spirit of Christ.

For Reflection:

• Share stories of people you have known who have led others by the power and inspiration of their example and humility.

• In light of today's readings, how would you define the term "religious authority"?

• Our Church's tradition includes the use of many beautiful ornate symbols in worship: incense, music, bells, vestments, etc. How do we keep these things in perspective if we are to be faithful to Jesus' words in today's Gospel?

• Where in our Church do you hear the "harmony" played by those who take on the parts of "second violinists" in their humble service and prayer?

Date: _____

HOMILY WORKSHEET for the 31st Sunday of the Year

1. SEEDS

What today's readings say *to me*: _____

_____

_____

PARABLES, STORIES and EXPERIENCES that speak to the themes of today's readings: _____

_____

_____

SPECIAL CONSIDERATIONS this week: Audience? Events in the community? Unique dimensions to this celebration?

_____

_____

_____

What RESPONSE do I seek from my listeners?

❑ to affirm/enlighten them in their faith?

❑ to teach/inform them about _____

_____

❑ to have them take a specific action _____

_____

2. PLANTING

The point I want to make in this homily (*ONE sentence*): _____

_____

_____

HOMILY OUTLINE

OPENING (*introductory STORY*): _____

_____

_____

_____

_____

_____

Point 1. APPLICATION of STORY to Scripture themes: _____

_____

_____

_____

_____

_____

Point 2. CONNECTION between Scriptural themes and the listeners' life experience: _____

_____
_____
_____
_____
_____
_____

Point 3. RESPONSE/CONSIDERATION sought from listeners: _____

_____
_____
_____
_____
_____
_____

CLOSING STATEMENT (*refers back to STORY*): _____

_____
_____
_____
_____
_____
_____

3. HARVEST—A Checklist:

❑ Does my completed homily make the point I articulated above (*under PLANTING*)?

❑ Am I excited about this homily. Am I readily able to convey my own enthusiasm, my sincere conviction of what I am going to say?

❑ Am I ready to preach this homily? Have I rehearsed this homily out loud until:

   ❑ I am comfortable with the *flow* of this homily: I can make the *transitions* from point to point, from idea to idea, smoothly and clearly;

   ❑ I am using *words* and *expressions* that my listeners can understand and appreciate: I am not speaking in theological jargon or "holy card" talk;

   ❑ my *delivery* (voice, gestures, speaking rate, pronunciation and enunciation, pauses, etc.) and

   ❑ my *inflection* and *emphasis* of key words and phrases are natural and effective?

❑ My homily lasts _____ minutes. Is it ❑ too long? ❑ too short? ❑ just about right?

4. GLEANINGS—Thoughts and notes AFTER the Homily

What worked, what didn't work in this homily; response and reactions from the community; ideas for next time; etc.

_____
_____
_____
_____
_____
_____
_____
_____
_____
_____
_____

32nd Sunday of the Year

The Readings:

READING 1: Wisdom 6: 12-16

Resplendent and unfading is Wisdom,
and she is readily perceived by those who love her,
and found by those who seek her.

Today's first reading is a poetic vision of true wisdom as a paradox: to seek wisdom—God's word—is to discover her.

READING 2: 1 Thessalonians 4: 13-17 (or 4: 13-14)

If we believe that Jesus died and rose, God will bring forth with him from the dead those also who have fallen asleep believing in him.

The Thessalonians believed that the Second Coming was imminent. But what would happen to those Christians of the community who had already died? In this reading (which was read as the Epistle in the pre-Vatican II Funeral Mass) Paul assures them that they, too, will share in the Resurrection and be united with the Lord.

GOSPEL: Matthew 25: 1-13

"The reign of God can be likened to ten bridesmaids who took their torches and went out to welcome the groom . . ."

These last Sundays of the year focus on the Parousia, the Lord's return at the end of time. The parable of the bridesmaids, found only in Matthew's Gospel, is taken from Jesus' fifth and final discourse in Matthew, the great eschatological discourse.

According to the Palestinian custom, the bridegroom would go to the bride's house on their wedding day to finalize the marital agreement with his father-in-law. When the bridegroom would return to his own home with his bride, the bridesmaids would meet them as they approached, signalling the beginning of the wedding feast. The approaching wedding feast is used by Jesus to symbolize his coming at the end of history as we know it. Jesus' return will take many by complete surprise. What constitutes being "ready"? What does the "oil" symbolize in this allegory? Looking ahead in the Gospel to be read over the last three Sundays of the year (Matthew 25: 45), the love we have for others as evidenced in works of kindness and compassion is the "oil" we store in our lamps awaiting for Christ's return.

Themes:

• **Christ's return: the end of the world *we* have created**

The ultimate news story—the end of the world:

STOCK EXCHANGE HALTS TRADING AS WORLD ENDS
                    —The Wall Street Journal

WORLD ENDS; MAY AFFECT ELECTIONS SOURCES SAY
                    —The Washington Post

ANALYSIS: END OF WORLD HIT THIRD WORLD HARDEST
                    —The New York Times

WE'RE GONE...STATE BY STATE DEMISE ON 6A. . . FINAL, FINAL, FINAL SCORES ON 8C
                    —USA Today

Those are the headlines that one editor suggested would appear on the day of the Parousia. How would we write that headline? What will the end of *our* world—our deaths—mean? Our first thoughts may be of work never to be completed and dreams never to be realized. Today's readings remind us that the end of this life is the beginning of a new one—the eternal life of the "Bridegroom," the Risen Christ. He must be the axis around which our whole being and life turn.

• Christ's return: coming to know him in our lives

People often spend so much time and energy trying to be "in" that they actually become "out"—out of touch with the values that make us fully human. The compulsion to be in fashion and in step with the opinion makers and power brokers can remove us from the important things in life. The wisdom of God (Reading 1) invites us to seek Christ the Bridegroom in every moment we have been given in this life until the wedding feast of the life to come.

For Reflection:

• In November (the month of All Saints and All Souls), when the dark final days of autumn give way to the cold of winter, our thoughts naturally turn to the reality of death. Share stories of people you have known who have taught you important lessons about death and dying through their encounters with death.

• Is there anything reassuring in these last Scriptural readings of November?

• Ours is a society and culture that tend to deny the reality of death. Why?

Date: _____

HOMILY WORKSHEET for the 32nd Sunday of the Year

1. SEEDS

What today's readings say *to me*: _____

_____

_____

PARABLES, STORIES and EXPERIENCES that speak to the themes of today's readings: _____

_____

_____

SPECIAL CONSIDERATIONS this week: Audience? Events in the community? Unique dimensions to this celebration?

_____

_____

_____

What RESPONSE do I seek from my listeners?
❑ to affirm/enlighten them in their faith?
❑ to teach/inform them about _____

_____

❑ to have them take a specific action _____

_____

2. PLANTING

The point I want to make in this homily (*ONE sentence*): _____

_____

_____

HOMILY OUTLINE

OPENING (*introductory STORY*): _____

_____

_____

_____

_____

_____

Point 1. APPLICATION of STORY to Scripture themes: _____

_____

_____

_____

_____

_____

Point 2. CONNECTION between Scriptural themes and the listeners' life experience: _____

_____

_____

_____

_____

_____

Point 3. RESPONSE/CONSIDERATION sought from listeners: _____

_____

_____

_____

_____

_____

CLOSING STATEMENT (*refers back to STORY*): _____

_____

_____

_____

_____

_____

3. HARVEST—A Checklist:

❑ Does my completed homily make the point I articulated above (*under PLANTING*)?

❑ Am I excited about this homily. Am I readily able to convey my own enthusiasm, my sincere conviction of what I am going to say?

❑ Am I ready to preach this homily? Have I rehearsed this homily out loud until:

  ❑ I am comfortable with the *flow* of this homily: I can make the *transitions* from point to point, from idea to idea, smoothly and clearly;

  ❑ I am using *words* and *expressions* that my listeners can understand and appreciate: I am not speaking in theological jargon or "holy card" talk;

  ❑ my *delivery* (voice, gestures, speaking rate, pronunciation and enunciation, pauses, etc.) and

  ❑ my *inflection* and *emphasis* of key words and phrases are natural and effective?

❑ My homily lasts _____ minutes. Is it ❑ too long? ❑ too short? ❑ just about right?

4. GLEANINGS—Thoughts and notes AFTER the Homily

What worked, what didn't work in this homily; response and reactions from the community; ideas for next time; etc.

_____

_____

_____

_____

_____

_____

_____

_____

_____

_____

_____

33rd Sunday of the Year

The Readings:

READING 1: Proverbs 31: 10-13, 19-20, 30-31

When one finds a worthy wife,
her value is far beyond pearls.
She reaches out her hands to the poor,
and extends her arms to the needy.

The Old Testament Book of Proverbs is a collection of wise sayings, collected over a period of 500 years from sources throughout the world. Today's reading, from the final chapter of Proverbs, is part of a poem envisioning the ideal wife as wisdom in action: a woman of prayer, of loving service to her family and of charity to all. Read in the light of today's Gospel, it is a portrait of the faithful servant of God.

READING 2: 1 Thessalonians 5: 1-6

You are children of light and of day.

More important to Paul is not the exact time of the Lord's return in the future but the attitude of expectation we must adopt in the present. He exhorts the Christian community at Thessolonica to remember that they have been called, in baptism, to live in the daylight of knowledge and hope in the Risen Christ. We do not live in fear but in joyful expectation of his return at the end of time.

GOSPEL: Matthew 25: 14-30 (or 25: 14-15, 19-20)

The parable of the talents.

The Lord will judge us according to how we used the talents each of us has been given. The greater the gifts, the greater God's expectations.

Themes:

• the "stewardship" of talent and ability

Every one of us possesses some degree of talent, ability and skill. The "talents" we possess have been "entrusted" to us by the "Master." Jesus teaches in today's Gospel that our place in the kingdom of God will depend on our stewardship of those gifts from God. The "good wife" in today's reading from Proverbs and the two industrious servants of the Gospel are successes in God's eyes because their lives are of benefit to others. Their greatness will be exalted by God. But the servant who cannot see beyond himself, who squanders his talents, who uses them irresponsibly for personal profit or self-gratification, is useless and will have no place in the kingdom of God.

• the opportunities we have to serve

Everyone is given many opportunities to reap and gather. Some of us have the opportunity to influence public policy and defend the public good, while others among us are given less dramatic but no less important opportunities, perhaps having no discernible affect beyond our immediate families. Making the ethical and moral business decision, serving as an occasional volunteer in a soup kitchen, spending a few minutes to console a hurting child—all demand as much courage and commitment as acts of higher visibility. The Gospel challenge is to be ready and willing to respond to the opportunities we have to give joyfully and generously of ourselves for the sakes of others.

For Reflection:

• Share stories of individuals whose "investments" of their talents—abilities and skills the world considered relatively small and insignificant—yielded extraordinary returns.

• What "talents" do we possess that our world is crying out for? What talents do people possess that they tend to underestimate or ignore as valueless?

• What talents do you see in your parish community that are being buried in the ground? Why do you suppose that happens? What can be done to bring them out?

Date: _____

HOMILY WORKSHEET for the 33rd Sunday of the Year

1. SEEDS

What today's readings say *to me*: _____

_____

_____

PARABLES, STORIES and EXPERIENCES that speak to the themes of today's readings: _____

_____

_____

SPECIAL CONSIDERATIONS this week: Audience? Events in the community? Unique dimensions to this celebration?

_____

_____

_____

What RESPONSE do I seek from my listeners?
❏ to affirm/enlighten them in their faith?
❏ to teach/inform them about _____

_____

❏ to have them take a specific action _____

_____

2. PLANTING

The point I want to make in this homily (*ONE sentence*): _____

_____

_____

HOMILY OUTLINE

OPENING (*introductory STORY*): _____

_____

_____

_____

_____

_____

Point 1. APPLICATION of STORY to Scripture themes: _____

_____

_____

_____

_____

_____

Point 2. CONNECTION between Scriptural themes and the listeners' life experience: _____

_____

_____

_____

_____

_____

Point 3. RESPONSE/CONSIDERATION sought from listeners: _____

_____

_____

_____

_____

_____

CLOSING STATEMENT (*refers back to STORY*): _____

_____

_____

_____

_____

_____

3. HARVEST—A Checklist:

❑ Does my completed homily make the point I articulated above (*under PLANTING*)?

❑ Am I excited about this homily. Am I readily able to convey my own enthusiasm, my sincere conviction of what I am going to say?

❑ Am I ready to preach this homily? Have I rehearsed this homily out loud until:

    ❑ I am comfortable with the *flow* of this homily: I can make the *transitions* from point to point, from idea to idea, smoothly and clearly;

    ❑ I am using *words* and *expressions* that my listeners can understand and appreciate: I am not speaking in theological jargon or "holy card" talk;

    ❑ my *delivery* (voice, gestures, speaking rate, pronunciation and enunciation, pauses, etc.) and

    ❑ my *inflection* and *emphasis* of key words and phrases are natural and effective?

❑ My homily lasts _____ minutes. Is it ❑ too long? ❑ too short? ❑ just about right?

4. GLEANINGS—Thoughts and notes AFTER the Homily

What worked, what didn't work in this homily; response and reactions from the community; ideas for next time; etc.

_____

_____

_____

_____

_____

_____

_____

_____

_____

_____

_____

Christ the King

The Readings:

READING 1: Ezekiel 34: 11-12, 15-17

"I myself will look after and tend my sheep . . . I will judge between one sheep and another, between rams and goats."

The people of Israel, exiled from their homeland and living in servitude under the Babylonians, cry out for a king to lead them. Ezekiel offers this oracle of consolation and hope: God will no longer entrust his people to evil and incompetent leaders, but will himself look after and "tend" his chosen and faithful people. The theme of personal responsibility of one's life (a major teaching of Ezekiel) and the judgment between one sheep and another reflect today's Gospel description of the Last Judgment.

READING 2: 1 Corinthians 15: 20-26, 28

Christ has been raised from the dead, the first-fruits of those who have fallen asleep.

Some of the Corinthians are denying the resurrection of the dead, apparently because of their inability to imagine how any kind of bodily existence could be possible after death. Paul addresses this issue in chapter 15 of his first letter to the Corinthians. In the verses that make up today's second reading, Paul praises Christ as the "first fruits" of the Resurrection—Christ represents the promise that is the future of all the faithful. The Risen Christ who has vanquished death now reigns over all forever.

GOSPEL: Matthew 25: 31-46

"Come. You have my Father's blessing! Inherit the kingdom prepared for you from the creation of the world. For I was hungry and you gave me food, I was thristy and you gave me drink. I was a stranger and you welcomed me, naked and you clothed me. I was ill and you comforted me, in prison and you came to visit me."

Matthew's is the only description of the Last Judgment in any of the Gospels. It is Jesus' last discourse recorded by Matthew before the events of the Passion begin to unfold. In the vision he presents, Christ is the king who sits in judgment "as a shepherd separates sheep from goats." Mercy and charity will be the standards for determining one's entry into the future kingdom of God.

Themes:

• the Christ of the nameless poor

The old geezer in rags sleeping on the heating grate in a downtown alley . . .

The skeletal form of an African mother, hugging her hungry child, shielding her baby from the harsh sun and the flies, waiting for help that will never come . . .

The child looking for her family amid the rubble of wooden planks and tin sheeting that was their house before the earthquake struck . . .

The teenager fighting to survive in the jungle of the inner-city ghetto, and the mother of that teenager, struggling through a series of dead-end jobs so that, perhaps some day, her children might escape the poverty she has always known . . .

The nameless poor. We see their pictures in newspapers and magazines, we hear their stories on evening newscasts, we may have even met them ourselves at one time or another. But nobody who is poor or in need is nameless. They share a name that we know and recognize. Their name is Jesus. "Whatever you do for one of the least of my brothers and sisters, you have done for me. Whenever you neglect one of these least ones, you have neglected me." May we see in the face of the poor, the troubled and forgotten the face of Jesus Christ, the Savior God sent to redeem us, the Lord who will come in glory to judge the living and the dead.

• the "kingship" of Christ

We Americans don't take kindly to kings—just ask George III. So what are we to make of today's feast of Christ the *King*? Christ the "President" doesn't quite work, does it? The very title of today's celebration smacks of a certain "triumphalism" that many people no longer want anything to do with.

In nations ruled by a royal family, the concept of monarchy is based on two premises: that the king rules by "divine right," that is, by the authority of God; and that the character of the entire nation is vested in their king, sometimes expressed in the idea of the sovereign being the "father" of his children, the governed.

In this light, Christ is indeed King. Jesus is the anointed one of God, the *Christus*, the Messiah raised up by the Father. And he is the very essence of his people, the Church. His Gospel is the bond that unites us as Church; the Eucharist, his body, gives life to that Church.

We end the liturgical year honoring Christ, the sovereign Lord of our lives. Through our selfless charity and love for all humanity may we prepare for the coming of his kingdom, when he comes in glory to judge the living and dead.

For Reflection:

• Who are the people in whom we are *least* likely to recognize Christ?

• How can we make God's kingdom a reality in our own communities?

• What impact should our claim that Christ is our King have on our lives, we who people the earth 2,000 years after our "King"?

Date: _____

HOMILY WORKSHEET for the Solemnity of Christ the King

1. SEEDS

What today's readings say *to me*: _____

_____

_____

PARABLES, STORIES and EXPERIENCES that speak to the themes of today's readings: _____

_____

_____

SPECIAL CONSIDERATIONS this week: Audience? Events in the community? Unique dimensions to this celebration?

_____

_____

_____

What RESPONSE do I seek from my listeners?
❏ to affirm/enlighten them in their faith?
❏ to teach/inform them about _____

_____

❏ to have them take a specific action _____

_____

2. PLANTING

The point I want to make in this homily (*ONE sentence*): _____

_____

_____

HOMILY OUTLINE

OPENING (*introductory STORY*): _____

_____

_____

_____

_____

_____

Point 1. APPLICATION of STORY to Scripture themes: _____

_____

_____

_____

_____

_____

Point 2. CONNECTION between Scriptural themes and the listeners' life experience: _____

_____

_____

_____

_____

_____

Point 3. RESPONSE/CONSIDERATION sought from listeners: _____

_____

_____

_____

_____

_____

_____

CLOSING STATEMENT (*refers back to STORY*): _____

_____

_____

_____

_____

_____

3. HARVEST—A Checklist:

❑ Does my completed homily make the point I articulated above (*under PLANTING*)?

❑ Am I excited about this homily. Am I readily able to convey my own enthusiasm, my sincere conviction of what I am going to say?

❑ Am I ready to preach this homily? Have I rehearsed this homily out loud until:

❑ I am comfortable with the *flow* of this homily: I can make the *transitions* from point to point, from idea to idea, smoothly and clearly;

❑ I am using *words* and *expressions* that my listeners can understand and appreciate: I am not speaking in theological jargon or "holy card" talk;

❑ my *delivery* (voice, gestures, speaking rate, pronunciation and enunciation, pauses, etc.) and

❑ my *inflection* and *emphasis* of key words and phrases are natural and effective?

❑ My homily lasts _____ minutes.   Is it ❑ too long? ❑ too short? ❑ just about right?

4. GLEANINGS—Thoughts and notes AFTER the Homily

What worked, what didn't work in this homily; response and reactions from the community; ideas for next time; etc.

_____

_____

_____

_____

_____

_____

_____

_____

_____

_____

_____

Extra Homily Worksheets

Date: _____

HOMILY WORKSHEET for _____

1. SEEDS

What today's readings say *to me*: _____
_____
_____

PARABLES, STORIES and EXPERIENCES that speak to the themes of today's readings: _____
_____
_____

SPECIAL CONSIDERATIONS this week: Audience? Events in the community? Unique dimensions to this celebration?
_____
_____
_____

What RESPONSE do I seek from my listeners?
❏ to affirm/enlighten them in their faith?
❏ to teach/inform them about _____
_____

❏ to have them take a specific action _____
_____

2. PLANTING

The point I want to make in this homily (*ONE sentence*): _____
_____
_____

HOMILY OUTLINE

OPENING (*introductory STORY*): _____
_____
_____
_____
_____
_____

Point 1. APPLICATION of STORY to Scripture themes: _____
_____
_____
_____
_____
_____

Point 2. CONNECTION between Scriptural themes and the listeners' life experience: _____

_____
_____
_____
_____
_____

Point 3. RESPONSE/CONSIDERATION sought from listeners: _____

_____
_____
_____
_____
_____

CLOSING STATEMENT (*refers back to STORY*): _____

_____
_____
_____
_____
_____

3. HARVEST—A Checklist:

❑ Does my completed homily make the point I articulated above (*under PLANTING*)?

❑ Am I excited about this homily. Am I readily able to convey my own enthusiasm, my sincere conviction of what I am going to say?

❑ Am I ready to preach this homily? Have I rehearsed this homily out loud until:

    ❑ I am comfortable with the *flow* of this homily: I can make the *transitions* from point to point, from idea to idea, smoothly and clearly;

    ❑ I am using *words* and *expressions* that my listeners can understand and appreciate: I am not speaking in theological jargon or "holy card" talk;

    ❑ my *delivery* (voice, gestures, speaking rate, pronunciation and enunciation, pauses, etc.) and

    ❑ my *inflection* and *emphasis* of key words and phrases are natural and effective?

❑ My homily lasts _____ minutes. Is it ❑ too long? ❑ too short? ❑ just about right?

4. GLEANINGS—Thoughts and notes AFTER the Homily

What worked, what didn't work in this homily; response and reactions from the community; ideas for next time; etc.

_____
_____
_____
_____
_____
_____
_____
_____
_____
_____
_____